CUT YOUR
SPENDING
IN HALF

without settling for less

CUT YOUR SPENDING IN HALF

without settling for less

HOW TO PAY
THE LOWEST PRICE
FOR EVERYTHING

BY THE EDITORS OF RODALE PRESS

Rodale Press, Emmaus, Pennsylvania

The table in "Slash Your Spending with Store Brands" on page 19 copyright © 1993 by Consumers Union of U.S., Inc., Yonkers, NY 10703-1057. Reprinted by permission from *Consumer Reports,* September 1993, page 567.

The bar graph on page 30 copyright © 1993 by Consumers Union of U.S., Inc., Yonkers, NY 10703-1057. Reprinted by permission from *Consumer Reports,* September 1993, page 564.

"How to Shop for a Builder" on page 209 is courtesy of the National Association of Home Builders.

"Neighborhood Problems to Watch Out For" on page 223 is courtesy of the U.S. Department of Housing and Urban Development.

The recipe for sidewalk chalk on page 333 is adapted from *Mudworks* by MaryAnne F. Kohl. Copyright © 1989 by MaryAnne F. Kohl. Reprinted by permission of Bright Ring Publishing.

"How Much to Save?" on page 348 reprinted from *College Savings Times* newsletter, October 1992. Copyright © 1992 by the Massachusetts Association of Student Financial Aid Administrators. Reprinted by permission.

Library of Congress Cataloging-in-Publication Data

      Cut your spending in half without settling for less : how to pay the lowest price for everything / by the editors of Rodale Press.
          p.   cm.
      Includes index.
      ISBN 0–87596–188–6   hardcover
      ISBN 0–87596–313–7   paperback
      1. Consumer education—United States.   2. Shopping—United States.
I. Rodale Press.
TX335.c88 1994
6440'.73—dc20   94–1390
                                                       CIP

OUR MISSION

We publish books that empower people's lives.

RODALE ❦ BOOKS

CUT YOUR SPENDING IN HALF WITHOUT SETTLING FOR LESS
EDITORIAL AND DESIGN STAFF

Editors: Edward Claflin, Sid Kirchheimer

Contributing Writers: Hiyaguha Cohen, Anne Colby, Bob Fendell, Sandra Gordon, John Grabowski, Marian Haber, Carolyn Janik, Janice Kirkel, Ruth Rejnis, Elizabeth Seymour, Gary Stern, Judith Trotsky, David Wallace, Claire Walter, Nicholas S. Yost

Cover and Book Designer: Vic Mazurkiewicz

Illustrator: Carol Inouye

Research Staff: Hilton Caston, Cynthia Nickerson, Sandra Salera-Lloyd

Copy Editor: Susan G. Berg

Office Staff: Roberta Mulliner, Julie Kehs, Mary Lou Stephen

PREVENTION MAGAZINE HEALTH BOOKS

Editor-in-Chief, Rodale Books: Bill Gottlieb

Executive Editor: Debora A. Tkac

Art Director: Jane Colby Knutila

Research Chief: Ann Gossy Yermish

Copy Manager: Lisa D. Andruscavage

Notice

The information contained in this book is based upon information obtained from contributors, from interviews and from a wide range of authoritative sources. It is intended as an approach to deal with decisions about spending money and is not intended for investment purposes. Rodale Press, Inc., assumes no responsibility for any injuries suffered or damages or losses incurred during or as a result of following this information. All information should be carefully studied and clearly understood before taking any action based on the information and advice presented in this book.

CONTENTS

58
OUTLETS

Look for a Manufacturer's Label—Save 40% • Search the Big Bins—Save 60% • Ask for a Discount—Save 20% • Buy Sleepwear in May—Save 10%

61
FORMAL WEAR

Buy Used Tuxedos—Save $300 • Rent a Gown—Save $1,000 • Go to a Discount Bridal Shop—Save 50%

62
GETTING BARGAINS IN THE BIG APPLE

Call the Chamber of Commerce—Save 40% • Mail Your Purchases Home • Keep Your Eyes Peeled in the Big Apple

65
MAIL ORDER

Open the Catalog in the Middle—Save 40% • Get Answers before Ordering

66
SECONDHAND STORES

Head for the 'Burbs • Go to Goodwill for Summer Wear • Make Pals with the Boss • Choose Your Words • Keep Tabs on the Tailoring

69
CARE AND MAINTENANCE

Give Your Wardrobe a Day's Rest • Line Your Pants • Go Easy on Starch • Press instead of Clean

MEDICAL EXPENSES

74
TRIM COSTS IN SICKNESS AND IN HEALTH

74
DRUGS

Ask for the Generic—Save 50% • Seek Out Samples • Order by Mail—Save 40% • Buy the Big Bottle—Save 35% • Count Your Pills before Leaving • Ask about Age Discounts—Save 10% • Go with Store Brands—Save 20%

INTRODUCTION

HOW TO PINCH PENNIES WITHOUT CRAMPING YOUR LIFESTYLE

Cutting your spending, some say, is easy. What's difficult is enjoying your life while doing it.

That's because you're probably used to getting less when you spend less. After all, you get what you pay for, right?

Well, not always. Some people get much, much more.

For instance, did you ever think that you could cut your grocery spending by as much as half every week without sacrificing one item from your shopping cart? You can, if you're aware of the various supermarket gimmicks aimed to make you spend more—and the strategies that help you get around them.

What about buying furnishings, appliances, clothing and other retail goods—including jewelry, furs and other luxury items—for one-third to one-half less than what others pay simply because you know the "trade" secrets about how these items are marked up . . . and for whom?

Imagine slashing $20,000 off the price of building your dream home—without changing a thing in its design. Or cutting thousands off the price of a new car simply because you're wise to the "games" salespeople play. Or insuring your car for hundreds less than you're paying now without hurting your coverage. Or sending your child to college with Uncle Sam paying most of the tab. Or taking your family on a vacation for just a fraction of what others pay and not sacrificing a single moment of pleasure. Or seeing first-run movies, plays and concerts for a song.

It's all in these pages: nearly 1,000 tips and techniques to help you make the most of your money without having to settle for less. That means you can always pay the lowest price for everything, without the sacrifice of quality, comfort or fun that usually comes with a "bargain."

Cut Your Spending in Half without Settling for Less isn't just about spending less. It's about spending smart. You'll learn not only how to save money but also how to do it so that you don't have to settle for second best. And unlike other books that generically promise you how to cut your spending, we show exactly how much: Most tips give you a realistic percentage of your possible savings.

1

How did we do it? Well, it wasn't always easy.

You see, we figured the only way to get you the most practical, usable and workable tips and techniques for "smart spending" was to get it straight for the horse's mouth. So we did what no other book has managed to do successfully—we interviewed the people who get rich off your overspending.

For instance, we convinced car salespeople and mechanics to reveal the "tricks" they use to squeeze more money from car buyers. We got supermarket owners and food wholesalers to confess the "gimmicks" and pricing strategies used to get you to pay more for food. And we cajoled real estate agents and mortgage brokers into spilling the beans on the "hidden" ways they get buyers and sellers to spend more than they need to.

We also got what we were *really* looking for—the ways you can get around it all to save hundreds or thousands of dollars each year. Of course, such priceless guidance comes at a price—namely, the anonymity of the "experts." As we heard again and again: "If my customers found out what I'm telling you, I'd be out of business. . . ."

But our mission didn't end with getting their pearls of insider wisdom. We then practiced much of what they preached. We went shopping for goods and services, using their negotiating strategies to save money (and even learning a few of our own). We scoured warranties, sales brochures, even price lists—using their advice on how to read between the lines. We did price comparisons and quality checks to determine what was money well spent—and what was just going into some salesperson's pocket.

Now it's all in your hands: the one "smart spending" book that tells you how to cut corners without cutting into your lifestyle.

So stop pinching pennies that only cramp your lifestyle. Live well and prosper. You can!

Edward Claflin
Managing Editor

Sid Kirchheimer
Executive Writer

Cut Your Spending on

FOOD

- Supermarket Gimmicks
- Meat and Poultry
- Overpriced Items
- Coupons
- Saving Strategies That Work
- Dining Out
- Splurging for Less
- Cookware Bargains and Food Preparation
- Entertaining

MAKE THE MOST OF EVERY MEAL

The typical American family spends anywhere from $6,000 to $15,000 on food each year—more money than it cost to buy a new car just a few years ago or a new house a few generations ago.

And like payments for that car and house, your food bill may be considered a fixed expense (since you probably spend the same or a similar amount each month). But actually, feeding your family is more flexible than you may imagine.

Government statistics show that you can cut your current food spending by as much as half—without having to sacrifice good nutrition or make drastic lifestyle changes.

That means your family can save hundreds of dollars each month. Without having to live on bologna and beans. Without making restaurant meals just a treasured memory. Without giving up quality refreshments for parties in your home.

In other words, you can have your cake and eat it, too—only for less money than you're used to spending.

All it takes is a little extra time, effort and insight into the right ways to stretch your food dollar.

SUPERMARKET GIMMICKS

Most grocery stores—particularly large chains—are strategically designed and stocked with one purpose: to get you, the consumer, to spend as much money as possible whenever you go food shopping.

And it works.

The typical American family spends nearly $70 buying unplanned or "impulse" items each week—most of them a direct result of your grocer's strategic stocking or tempting displays. These unplanned items represent one-half of the total food bill for the average family.

Why? Because these supermarket gimmicks are effective! But here's how to get the last laugh on your grocer—and do it all the way to the bank.

List Those Unplanned Purchases
Save 50%

Just about everyone enters a store with a shopping list. But very few people leave the store having followed their lists the way they should.

Statistics show that most shoppers buy at least one unplanned or "unlisted" item in each supermarket aisle each time they go grocery shopping. Considering the average supermarket has between 12 and 14 aisles, that adds up to at least a dozen unplanned items every time you shop.

Granted, you'll always find a few items at the grocer's that you forgot to list. But spending that extra $70 a week (or over $3,500 a year) is usually the result of failing to keep track of unlisted items.

"People who stick to their lists and buy only the products they forgot to list rarely spend more than an extra $10 or $15 a week," says one

---

WHERE YOUR MONEY GOES

- Americans buy more Coke, Pepsi and other cola drinks than any other single food product. An average of $89 is spent every year by American households on cola, compared with ready-to-eat cereals ($87), ground beef ($86), cheese ($85) and milk ($81).
- In dining-out expenses, the typical household annually spends $600 on dinners, $460 on lunches and $99 on breakfasts. But people spend even more on snacks than they do on breakfasts: We buy about $124 worth of snacks and nonalcoholic drinks, purchased from convenience stores, coin-operated machines and other non-supermarket sources.
- Fast-food sales generate more than $60 billion a year in the United States.
- The average per-person food expenditure is $1,600 a year. Among upper-income Americans (those making more than $75,000), the average is $2,200.

How Much Do You Really Spend on Food?

Don't know how much you really spend on food each month? This amount could surprise you! To get an exact figure (the most eye-opening there is), designate an envelope for food receipts. Carry it with you or put it in a place where you'll look at it often.

For one month, each time you go to the grocery store, check over your food receipts and cross off the nonfood items such as soap and toothpaste. Then save all your food receipts, including receipts you gather from ready-to-eat foods such as soda, coffee and snack foods and from restaurant meals, vending machines, delis and convenience stores. Make your own receipt if one isn't provided for you.

Collect all the receipts in the envelope, and at the end of the month, total them up. This is the amount you spend on food in a month—your food budget starting point.

---

grocer. "It's those who come in here without lists, or who don't follow the ones they have, who spend twice as much as they planned."

One obvious answer is to stick to your grocery list. One less well known but even more effective tactic: Each time you place an unplanned purchase in your grocery cart, write it on your grocery list (in a different color ink than the items previously listed). This way, you'll see exactly how quickly those unplanned purchases add up—and you'll find out where you're spending too much.

Don't Get Caught by End Cap Traps

Retailers know that product displays at the ends of the store aisles are a consumer booby trap. Studies show that shoppers buy more products displayed at the ends of the aisles just because they believe the prices are slashed.

But beware: You can't assume that all products showcased at the end-of-the-aisle position are on sale just because they have fancy banners and special signs. More often than not, these "end cap" positions are filled with excess inventory being sold at regular price—only with more fanfare than usual.

Group Your List
Save 15%

It's no coincidence that bread, milk and other frequently purchased items are located on opposite ends of the store. Grocers know that it's an effective way to keep you in their stores longer, so you buy more.

They also know that most shoppers don't organize their shopping

---

PLAN YOUR LIST TO CUT YOUR AISLE TIME

The more you backtrack in the supermarket, the more food dollars you're likely to spend. To make your shopping more efficient—and to reduce the hazard of overspending—"group" your shopping list so that foods are listed by category or by aisle. Here's how it works.

Random Shopping List

Organized Shopping List

Items are jotted down in no special order. You'll spend more time hunting through the aisles for the items you want —and probably buy more.

Same items, but they're listed section by section, so you don't have to do any backtracking. The asterisk (*) indicates that you have a coupon for that item.

lists. The usual method is to jot down an item whenever it pops into mind. But if you do that, you're going to spend a lot more time in the store as you backtrack through aisles that you've already visited. This adds time *and* unplanned purchases.

One way to shorten your supermarket time (and cut unnecessary expenses) is to "group" items on your grocery list by categories. That is, all fruits and vegetables should be listed together, all paper products together, all baked goods together. That way, you're less likely to backtrack through the store aisles and make additional unplanned purchases.

We tried this strategy on two shopping trips: One used a standard random listing of 20 items, while the other grouped the same 20 items. Both trips were for a week's worth of groceries for a family of five.

Using the grouped list, shopping took 20 minutes (with only two unplanned purchases), and the bill was $89. Using the random list, shopping took 35 minutes, there were seven unplanned items, and the bill was $107. Total savings using the grouped list: $18.

Read the Unit Price
Save 75%

Another common supermarket gimmick is to boldly list the product's price (what you pay at the register for a bottle of juice or a box of rice) while virtually hiding its unit price (the cost per ounce or other unit of weight or volume). You'll find the unit price right below or beside the actual product price. It is usually shown, but less prominently. If you find that the unit price is not listed on the display shelf, simply divide the price of the food by its net weight or volume.

Crispy Better Bran Flakes	
Total Price	Amount You Get **18 ounces**
$1.63	Unit Price
You Pay	**$1.45** per pound

To get the best food buys, check the unit price on the label on the grocery shelf below the food. The unit price shows the cost for an ounce, pound, pint, quart or number in a package.

STAY OUT OF THE SUPERMARKET TRAPS

Supermarkets are expertly designed to slow you down and make you spend more than you planned. Here are some of the tempting and eye-catching displays that are meant to lure impulse buyers.

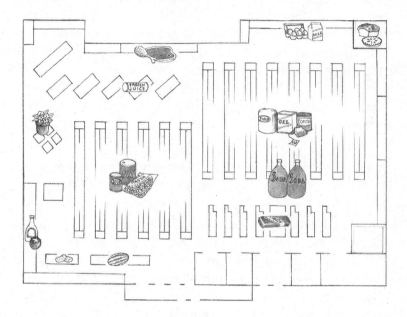

 Step inside, and you'll find seasonal supplies—such as watermelon in summer—placed near the front door.

 Higher-priced ready-made salad dressings are often placed near the lettuce and tomatoes, so you'll buy them on impulse rather than make your own or proceed to the lower-priced items on the grocery shelf.

 Those fresh flowers look beautiful—but are they really on your shopping list?

 Refrigerated cases block your path to make you slow down and look.

 The aroma of the bakery beckons you to walk across the store, which may persuade you to pick up a few more impulse items.

 Products displayed at the ends of aisles look like they're on sale—but they're usually not.

 The dairy products are way over in the far corner of the store so that you'll pick up some extra items . . . even if you need just a quart of milk.

 Waiting in line to check out, you'll be looking at a candy shelf where the goods are marked up as much as 400 percent.

Knowing the unit price is important because of the long-believed myth that buying in bulk always saves you money. Sometimes it does, and sometimes it doesn't: It all depends on the product.

Generally, you'll save when you buy heat-and-serve frozen dinners packaged in large quantities. And it usually pays to buy nonperishable items in bulk, especially rice, cornmeal, oats, sugar, bakery mixes, cereal, dried beans, peas, nuts and herbs. (And they're usually "no-name" brands, which are cheaper than name-brand counterparts.) The savings, which can be as high as 75 percent, result mainly because it's more expensive to package smaller quantities.

But we discovered that the newest ploy—offering "fresh" items such as fruits, vegetables, deli meats and cheeses in bulk—sometimes offers no savings at the supermarket. In fact, these items can cost as

---

SHOP SMART—NOTICE THE UNIT PRICE

It helps to have your calculator along for price comparisons. Shopping for frozen green beans, we discovered we could save over $1 per pound buying the store brand. On cornflakes, we saved $2.28 per pound on a name brand by buying a large, 18-ounce box instead of individual packs.

Use unit pricing to compare brands . . .

ITEM	PRICE ($)	UNIT PRICE ($)
Store-brand frozen green beans in a 10-ounce package	.68	1.09 per pound
Name-brand frozen green beans in a 9-ounce package	1.19	2.12 per pound

. . . and differing package sizes.

ITEM	PRICE ($)	UNIT PRICE ($)
Name-brand cornflakes in an 18-ounce box	1.49	1.32 per pound
Name-brand cornflakes in individual ¾-ounce packs (6 ounces total)	1.35	3.60 per pound

BLANCH AND FREEZE FOR ECONOMY

When you buy fresh produce in bulk, you'll get a lot more than you can eat in a week. But it doesn't take long to blanch vegetables that you want to store in the freezer.

Blanching is a process where you place vegetables in boiling water for a short time and then immediately "douse" them in cold water before sticking them in the freezer. It's done so that vegetables store better and stay fresher longer. Just blanch for the time shown, let cool, and store in freezer bags.

VEGETABLE	MINUTES TO BLANCH
Asparagus	3
Beets, small	Until tender
Broccoli, thin stalks	3–4½
Brussels sprouts	3–4½
Corn, cut from ears	3–7
Green or wax beans	2½
Kale	2½
Lima beans	1½
Okra, medium whole	3–4
Peas, green	1½–2½
Peppers	2
Spinach	2½
Turnip greens	2½

much as 10 percent more when purchased in bulk. So if you see a "family pack" containing more items, look carefully to determine the unit price. And remember, some of these fresh foods can spoil easily, wasting even more money.

Buy Produce by the Case
Save 50%

Aside from growing your own, the cheapest way to get quality fruits and vegetables is to buy them by the case at farmers' markets—

'TIS THE SEASON TO BE BUYING

It pays to freeze or can fruits and vegetables during seasons when the prices are at an all-year low. Here's a calendar of best produce buys.

January and February

Apples
Grapefruit
Oranges
Pears

March and April

Apples
Grapefruit
Oranges
Pears
Strawberries

May

Asparagus
Pineapple
Strawberries
Tomatoes

June

Asparagus
Cherries
Corn

Melon
Strawberries
Tomatoes

July

Berries
Cherries
Corn
Grapes
Lemons
Melon
Nectarines
Peaches
Plums
Strawberries
Tomatoes

August

Apples
Corn
Grapes
Melon
Nectarines
Peaches
Pears

Plums
Tomatoes

September

Apples
Broccoli
Cauliflower
Grapes
Green peppers
Peaches
Pears
Plums
Tomatoes
Winter squash

October

Apples
Broccoli
Brussels sprouts
Cauliflower
Cranberries
Grapes
Oranges
Pears
Pumpkin

Sweet potatoes
Winter squash

November

Apples
Broccoli
Brussels sprouts
Cauliflower
Cranberries
Grapefruit
Grapes
Oranges
Pears
Pumpkin
Sweet potatoes
Winter squash

December

Apples
Cranberries
Grapefruit
Grapes
Oranges
Pears
Sweet potatoes
Winter squash

not at the supermarket—during the peak growing season.

If all you want is fresh produce, buying a case isn't worthwhile, since much of it will spoil before you have a chance to use it. But if you plan to make preserves, jellies and sauces, you can save up to 50 percent buying by the case.

Farmers' markets offer some bargains in bulk, as long as you "wait for abundance," says Tony Mannetta, the assistant director for Greenmarket, the largest farmers' market in New York City.

To do that, call about one month before season's height and arrange to make purchases with the farmers themselves. To find out which are the best buying seasons in your area, contact your local Cooperative Extension Service officer or check out the chart on the opposite page.

MEAT AND POULTRY

Unless you're a vegetarian, the single biggest expense area of your food budget is for meat and poultry. The U.S. Department of Agriculture tells us that one of every three dollars spent on food goes to buy steaks, ground beef, chicken, roasts and other carnivore delights.

That amounts to nearly $2,500 a year for a family of four meat eaters. But you don't have to switch to a veggie diet to cut your food bills. In fact, you can beef up your savings by over $500 a year simply by practicing these buying strategies.

Buy against the Season
Save 15%

The seasons determine what kinds of meat consumers buy in quantity—a factor that drives up prices. In summer, for instance, porterhouse and New York strip steaks are more popular (and higher-priced) because of grilling season. Roasts, meanwhile, go down in price because they're considered a "winter" cut.

If you have a freezer, you can save on your meat bill if you buy your steak in bulk just before the season or right after it. If you buy in spring or fall, you'll save about 15 percent over buying the same cuts in season. April, for instance, is a good month to stockpile grilling meats such as steaks and lean ground beef that are popular fare in the summer.

Or save even more—as much as 20 percent—by stocking winter meats in late summer. August is a good time to stock your freezer with winter meats such as rump roast, eye of round and pork chops. Even if you don't have a freezer, you can save by buying out-of-season cuts when they're least expensive.

Look at the Cuts, Not the Price
Save 20%

You'll end up overspending on meat if you follow the all-too-common practice of paying more attention to the sticker price than to the actual cut.

In an effort to save, people look for the lowest sticker price they can find. What they also get is as much as one-third bone, gristle or fat—stuff that you don't eat.

Instead, butchers tell us that you're usually better off buying a more expensive cut that has little or no "waste." Even if the cost of the better cut is 10 percent higher on a per-pound basis, you'll save about 20 percent on a per-bite basis, since you're eating more and throwing away less.

Do Your Own Cutting
Save 35%

The more the butcher uses his knife, the more you pay. So do your own slicing, and you'll save about 35 percent.

"For example, I sell individual steaks at $6.98 per pound and whole strip loins at $4.59 per pound," a meat supplier in New York State tells us. "If you buy whole strips and cut them into individual loins, you get the same meat—at two-thirds of the cost."

Other cuts recommended for the do-it-yourself butcher include brisket, peeled rib-eye (also called Delmonico steak) and sirloin tip. And don't forget poultry, either: Buying a whole chicken and cutting it up is more economical than buying precut chicken parts.

"You can save an awful lot of money buying whole chickens and cutting them yourself," says chef and cookbook author Tom Ney. "You can buy a whole chicken for 59 to 79 cents a pound, compared with as much as $4 a pound for boneless and skinless breasts."

All you have to do is learn how to cut it. Your butcher can show you the proper technique. Also, many supermarkets offer meat-cutting classes to customers: Just call your local supermarket and ask for information. For do-it-yourself butchering, Ney advises that you buy two

CUT YOUR MEATS TO CUT COSTS

To save money, buy your beef in large cuts, then do the slicing at home. All you need is a sharp knife to cut your meat bills.

TENDERLOIN

With the fat side up, cut steaks that are 1 to 2 inches thick for broiling, 1 inch thick or less for pan broiling or pan frying.

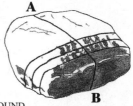

TOP ROUND

Turn the fat side up and split the top round in half. Cut from A to B (with the grain), then cut across the grain to make steaks 1 to 1½ inches thick.

CHUCK ROLL

Slice steaks about 1 inch thick, leaving the netting or strings intact during cutting and cooking.

TOP LOIN

Cut steaks across the grain—1 to 1½ inches thick for broiling, 1 inch thick or less for pan broiling or pan frying.

RIB-EYE

Cut as shown into steaks 1 to 1½ inches thick for broiling, 1 inch thick for pan broiling or pan frying.

TOP SIRLOIN

Fillets should be 1 to 2 inches thick for broiling and 1 inch thick or less for pan frying. Cut tender beef cubes from the tapered end for fondue or kabobs.

BRISKET

Separate the two muscle sections, removing the flat cut (A) from the muscle underneath (B) by cutting along the underside (see dotted line). After the flat cut has been removed, cut it into two roasts.

GET A DEAL—AND FREEZE IT

Fresh meat can be frozen for three months to a year without losing quality—but some types of meat keep better than others. You can use the chart below to figure out storage times. Be sure to store all meat in freezer wrapping—and clearly date all packages.

MEAT	STORAGE TIME (AT 0°F OR COLDER)
Fresh Meat	
Beef cuts	6–12 months
Ground beef, veal and lamb	3–4 months
Leftover cooked meats	2–3 months
Pork cuts	6 months
Veal and lamb cuts	6–9 months
Processed Meat	
Bacon	1 month
Frankfurters	1–2 months
Luncheon meats	1–2 months
Sausage	1–2 months
Smoked ham	1–2 months
Frozen Combination Foods	
Meat pies	2–3 months
Prepared dinners	2–3 months
Stews	3–4 months

knives, which cost about $15 each: a good stiff-bladed boning knife and a long slicing knife.

Buy Family Packs
Save 20%

Even if you're not doing your own cutting, you'll get a better deal buying meat in larger quantities—saving anywhere from 5 to 20 percent, depending on the cut. Butcher shops and supermarket meat departments offer discounts because large orders give them a more stable cash flow.

The biggest savings, of course, result from buying complete sides of beef, which typically yield 240 pounds of beef and can feed a family of four for six to eight months (assuming that they eat meat three times per week). A side of beef can cost 20 to 30 percent less than buying the same amount of meat over time.

But even buying family packs containing five or more pounds can result in discounts ranging from 10 to 50 cents per pound, yielding savings of up to 20 percent.

Before buying big, however, do some planning. Know exactly how

---

CONSIDER THE SERVINGS

When you're shopping for meat, be sure to consider how many servings you'll get from each kind of cut. Here's a guide to help you figure out the actual cost per serving.

Little Bone or Fat (three to four servings per pound)

Bone-in round steak	Flank steak
Boneless beef chuck roast	Ground meat
Boneless ham	Stew meat
Boneless round roast or steak	

Some Bone or Fat (two to three servings per pound)

Bone-in chuck roast	Bone-in pork steak
Bone-in chuck steak	Whole chicken
Bone-in ham	Whole turkey
Bone-in pork chops	

Much Bone or Fat (one to two servings per pound)

Beef short ribs	Spareribs
Lamb rib chops	T-bone steak
Picnic shoulder roast	Veal rib chops
Porterhouse steak	

you plan to use the meat—week by week. This will help determine how much and what kinds of meat to buy. Also, consider available freezer space and keep only what your family can consume within the recommended storage time.

Use a Little Tenderness
Save 30%

Marinating for as little as 20 minutes (to as long as 24 hours) will make less expensive and usually tougher cuts of meat more tender and delicious. These include cubes, flank steaks, stew meats and boneless roasts. You'll save anywhere from 10 to 30 percent compared with buying more "tender" cuts—and actually get a healthier piece of meat, because tougher meats have less fat (marbling).

OVERPRICED ITEMS

One way supermarkets reap even greater profits than usual is to create an illusion of better quality for certain items. Many consumers believe that paying top dollar means they're getting top quality. But that's not always so.

Sometimes you're paying for just a better-looking label, not a better-quality food.

Take Home the House Brand
Save 20%

The most common way to save is with house brands, also known as generics. Typically, these plainly packaged items that carry the store's name lack the fancy labels and name recognition of better-known national brands.

You get a much better deal on the house brands. On average, they cost 21 percent less than name brands. (Some of that higher price for name brands goes to cover the high cost of advertising.)

So why do most people still prefer the name brands?

Researchers say it's a common buying habit: People prefer the familiar—and name brands are more familiar because they are advertised more. Most consumers believe they are getting "better quality" with the name brands and are willing to pay more for them.

(continued on page 22)

SLASH YOUR SPENDING WITH STORE BRANDS

How much can you really save by choosing store brands? Here's a report on a shopping trip for 24 items—comparing prices of name-brand and store-brand products.
The savings? Over 40 percent!

PRODUCT	SIZE	NAME-BRAND PRICE ($)	STORE-BRAND PRICE ($)
Aluminum foil	200 feet	4.39	3.69
Bacon	1 pound	3.49	2.09
Baked beans	1 pound	1.39	.39
Black olives	5¾ ounces	1.99	1.19
Butter	1 pound	2.39	1.69
Carrots	1 pound	2.58	.59
Cat litter	10 pounds	2.45	1.87
Celery	1 bunch	1.89	.99
Coffee, French roast	12 ounces	2.79	1.59
Dog food	5 pounds	3.69	1.29
Flounder, frozen fillets	1 pound	9.00	4.19
Ham, boiled	1 pound	5.69	3.99
Ice cream	½ gallon	3.99	2.39
Ketchup	2 pounds	1.69	.79
Lemonade, frozen concentrate	12 ounces	1.29	.79
Mayonnaise	1 quart	2.79	1.19
Paper towels	90 sheets	1.39	.50
Peanut butter, creamy	28 ounces	3.29	2.89
Popcorn, microwave	10½ ounces	2.29	.99
Tea	100 bags	2.79	1.39
Tuna, solid white	6⅛ ounces	1.59	1.19
Vanilla extract	2 ounces	4.09	2.27
Vegetable oil	1 quart	2.19	1.69
White rice	5 pounds	3.99	1.59
Totals		**73.12**	**41.23**

UPGRADE YOUR DIET—AND SAVE WHILE YOU'RE AT IT

Some of the healthiest foods are among the cheapest. So there's no reason why you can't eat healthy—and still save!

Take oatmeal, for instance. It is filling and nutritious, yet one serving costs only about 28 cents per bowl. And it gives you a wide variety of minerals that help your blood, nerves and muscles—along with high fiber to help control cholesterol and improve digestion.

Here are some other low-cost foods that are good deals in both cost and nutrition. Nearly all are low in fat and calories as long as you use very little oil or butter in cooking.

FOOD	COMMON SERVING SIZE	PRICE PER SERVING ($)	IMPORTANT NUTRIENT
Apples	1 (5–8 ounces)	.50	Vitamin C
Bananas	1 (4 ounces)	.12	Vitamin B_6
Barley	½ cup cooked	.19	Iron
Beans, green (snap)	½ cup boiled	.20	Vitamin C
Beets	½ cup sliced	.50	Folate
Bran, oat	2 tablespoons	.06	Thiamine
Bread, whole wheat	1 slice	.07	Iron
Broccoli	½ cup chopped	.22	Vitamin C
Cabbage	½ cup shredded	.04	Vitamin C
Carrots	1 (2½ ounces)	.11	Beta-carotene
Celery	½ cup	.12	Folate
Chicken	3 ounces	.55	Niacin
Corn			
fresh	1 ear	.17	Folate
frozen	½ cup	.47	Folate
Cottage cheese, low-fat (1%)	½ cup	.23	Vitamin B_{12}
Eggplant	½ cup cubed	.19	Potassium
Grapefruit	½ (4 ounces)	.11	Vitamin C

FOOD	COMMON SERVING SIZE	PRICE PER SERVING ($)	IMPORTANT NUTRIENT
Grapes	1 cup	.70	Vitamin C
Kale	½ cup	.09	Vitamin C
Kiwifruit	1 (2½ ounces)	.25	Vitamin C
Lettuce, romaine	1 cup shredded, raw	.20	Folate
Milk, low-fat (2%)	8 fluid ounces	.08	Vitamin B_{12}
Oatmeal	¾ cup cooked	.28	Thiamine
Onions	½ cup chopped	.08	Vitamin C
Oranges	1 (4½ ounces)	.17	Vitamin C
Pears	1 (6–8 ounces)	.50	Vitamin C
Peas	½ cup boiled	.44	Folate
Peppers, green	½ cup chopped	.12	Vitamin C
Pineapple	1 cup cubed	.25	Vitamin C
Popcorn	1 cup popped (¼ cup dry)	.04	Fiber
Potatoes, white	1 (7 ounces)	.17	Vitamin C
Prunes	5 (1½ ounces)	.28	Iron
Pumpkin	½ cup canned	.29	Beta-carotene
Raisins	½ cup	.21	Iron
Rice	½ cup cooked	.06	Iron
Spaghetti, enriched	1 cup	.12	Iron
Spinach	½ cup boiled	.70	Vitamin A
Squash, zucchini	½ cup sliced	.12	Folate
Strawberries	1 cup	.65	Vitamin C
Sweet potatoes	1 (4 ounces)	.10	Vitamin A
Turkey	3 ounces	.40	B vitamins
Turnips	½ cup cubed	.15	Vitamin C
Wheat germ	¼ cup (1 ounce)	.20	Vitamin E
Yogurt, low-fat fruit-flavored	1 cup	.75	Vitamin B_{12}

Guess again, folks. The majority of house brands are manufactured by the same name-brand competitors and just sold to the store in different packages. The only difference between the products, believe it or not, is the label.

Pass on Gourmet Offerings
Save 30%

Flavored seltzer water is about one-third of the price of a similar-size bottle of Perrier. "Gourmet" bean dips and salsa cost 30 to 40 percent more than their "standard" counterparts. "Specialty" salad dressings can cost 60 percent more than regular types.

But pull back the fancy packaging and highbrow advertising, and what do you have? Usually, the very same ingredients as the less expensive varieties. In most cases, our experts tell us that the extra cost is only for image—and nothing else. Most notorious are items stocked in the gourmet foods aisle, where these specialty foods and sauces can be twice as expensive on a per-serving basis as similar items on other aisles.

Make Salads at Home
Save 50%

Another huge moneymaker for your grocer: in-store make-your-own salad bars. You'll pay twice as much, pound for pound, for a salad you make in the store compared with one that you make at home using ingredients that you've purchased in the produce section. Of course, these salad bars are more convenient for single people or for those who don't plan on using an entire head of lettuce or an entire bag of carrots within a few days.

Buy Generic Spices
Save 60%

Whenever you buy spices, go with the cheapest brand. Like many other generics, house-brand spices are usually manufactured by big-name national companies, so there's no difference in the actual product. And since name-brand spices are notoriously expensive, you could be paying as much as 60 percent more—and getting only a different label.

Add Your Own Extras
Save 60%

Generally, you'll pay anywhere from 15 to 60 percent more for products with added sugar, seasonings and other "extras" that you can easily mix in yourself.

Presweetened cereals are probably the best-known example. You'll typically pay about 50 percent more for a box of frosted cornflakes compared with regular cornflakes. And the only difference in quality is the additional sugar coating.

Beware of frozen vegetables, too. A bag that includes its own sauce will cost you as much as 60 percent more than the same-size bag of vegetables without the sauce. Besides, plain versions tend to have less fat.

COUPONS

Everybody knows that coupons save, right? All those hours spent clipping and sorting and filing are worth the couple of extra quarters saved here and there, right?

SKIP THE SAUCE AND SAVE THE CENTS

We wanted to find out how much extra you pay for specially prepared frozen vegetables—and here's the result of our comparison shopping. On chopped spinach, mixed vegetables and frozen corn, you'll pay at least 15 percent less if you buy frozen vegetables without extra butter or sauces.

FOOD	COST PER SERVING ($)	SAVINGS
Birds Eye creamed spinach	.86	
Birds Eye chopped spinach	.35	59%
Green Giant mixed vegetables in butter sauce	.63	
Green Giant mixed vegetables, no sauce	.53	15%
Green Giant niblets corn in butter sauce	.63	
Green Giant Fresh Harvest niblets corn, no sauce	.53	15%

Not necessarily. Coupons can cut your food spending, or they can add to it—depending how you use them.

For instance, how many times have you bought an item that you normally wouldn't have simply because you had a coupon? While you may have saved 25 cents or so off the item's usual price, you spent an extra $1.75 or so that you wouldn't have.

Like anything else, coupons are marketing gimmicks that are aimed at peeking consumer interest and boosting sales. But by using them wisely, you can save at least twice as much as the average $25 per month that the average family saves with coupons. Here's how you can do it.

Use Coupons during Sales
Save 50%

Perhaps the biggest mistake you can make is to redeem coupons too quickly. Let's say you just clipped a batch of them from your newspaper's weekly food section or Sunday supplement. Of course, you're tempted to redeem those coupons the very next time you go food shopping.

But wait! If you really want to save money, you should hold on to your coupons until the items you want to buy are on sale.

Manufacturers often "encourage" retailers to put products on sale about four times a year, or once a season. (Your grocer may place the item on sale more frequently, however, because of inventory, product popularity or other reasons.)

But the product sales are not always timed to coincide with publication of the coupons. In fact, you may have noticed that some retailers actually increase prices the week their coupons show up in newspapers or fliers.

The best strategy is to wait for a sale, which frequently occurs a month or two after the coupons are published. "Typically, if the coupon is worth 25 percent of the value of the item and that product is on sale, you can save about one-half of its normal cost," says Martin Sloane, a consumer specialist who writes a nationally syndicated newspaper column called "The Supermarket Shopper."

Sometimes you can save even more.

Example: A name-brand cereal company offered a 75-cent coupon on one of its products. When one retailer marked the cereal down from $3.69 to $1.49, we used the coupon to purchase the cereal for just 74 cents—nearly $3 less than the original price. Compare: If we had redeemed the coupon the week it was published, when the cereal was at its regular price, we would have paid $2.94 for the same item—just 20 percent off the original price.

While this example may not seem typical of the savings you may see, with careful shopping you will notice vast price differences—and spot times when it's best to use coupons.

Stockpile Coupons
Save 25%

If you can save big buying an item on sale with a coupon, then why not save really big by loading up on coupons and then buying the item in quantity when it goes on sale?

To maximize your buying power, trade some of the coupons you don't want for the ones that are most valuable to you.

There are probably pages of coupons you throw away because you don't need those products—but your friends, neighbors and co-workers can use them. By trading, you can collect numerous coupons for items that are on your shopping list while donating coupons that others need for their households. Once you get multiple coupons for the same item, you can "go to town" stockpiling—buying as many of that item as feasible when it's on sale.

Example: We shopped for boxed fruit snacks for the kids' lunch boxes when the items were regularly priced at $1.99, without a coupon. One Sunday, we found a sheet offering two 20-cent coupons for our favorite brand, so we began trading and stockpiling. By the end of the week, we had one two-coupon sheet from a neighbor, another two-coupon sheet from the in-laws and a third two-coupon sheet from a co-worker. All told, we collected eight coupons. That included our own two-coupon sheet.

(Meanwhile, our neighbors got our dog food and baby food coupons, Mom and Dad got coffee and toiletry coupons, and the co-worker got our heartfelt thanks.)

Within three weeks, the supermarket had our kids' favorite fruit snacks on sale for $1.69 a box, and we bought eight boxes, using one coupon for each. With the coupon, the price came to $1.49 each, or $11.92. If we had purchased them on a weekly basis at the usual price, the total would have amounted to $15.92—so we saved 25 percent and got enough snacks to last two months.

Buy the Small Size
Save 15%

All your shopping life, you've been told that you save more by buying the large "economy" size. But when using coupons, you're usually better off buying the smallest size—especially if you shop at a supermarket that offers double-coupon savings.

Using your highest-value coupons on the smallest-size products gets you the greatest savings—even though it may not always appear that way on an item-by-item basis.

PROFIT FROM COUPONS WITH GOOD ORGANIZATION

You can cut your grocery spending by nearly $1,000 a year if you use coupons. But good organization is the key to those savings. Here are some ways to keep your coupons in order and to use them before they expire.

Get a large accordion file. Forget those punky little recipe boxes. The best coupon holder is a large accordion file with at least 12 "sections." Label each section of the file with one category of grocery-store purchase—canned foods, paper products, toiletries, snacks, breakfast foods and so on.

Highlight the expiration date. To prevent stockpiling coupons you can't use, get two fluorescent felt-tip pens. Before filing the coupons, use one color to highlight those with a short life span (within six weeks) and another color for those giving you a year or more to use them. This way, you know which coupons you need to use first.

Highlight "couponed" items on your list. Unless you do the shopping yourself and/or have incredible recall, always highlight every item on your shopping list that has a coupon. This ensures that you (or your spouse) take all necessary coupons with you to the grocery store.

Think before you buy. Just because you have a coupon doesn't mean you should use it. Unless it's an item you regularly buy, or one that you think your family would enjoy, don't buy a $2 item simply because you can save 25 cents.

Example: A 14-ounce jar of Ragu slow-cooked homestyle spaghetti sauce went on sale for $1.50. The 28-ounce version, exactly double the size, sold for $2.14—which made it a better buy. But the supermarket offered double-coupon savings on a 50-cent coupon—which meant you could get $1 off. Using double coupons, then, the smaller jar (the 14-ouncer) sold for 50 cents, and the larger jar (28 ounces) for $1.14, making the smaller jar a better buy.

Use Coupons with Rebates

You can occasionally get some products for free—or even make a profit from buying them—if you use coupons in conjunction with a manufacturer's rebate (usually a check mailed to you after you send in proof of purchase).

This usually results from a big promotional effort on the part of the producer. The rebate and the coupon may not be advertised at the same time, but keep your eyes peeled for a big promotion. You'll notice increased advertising and maybe some price reductions within a few weeks. If you take advantage of all the promotional incentives, you can snatch some free items.

Example: A name-brand deodorant manufacturer issued a coupon for $1 off its regular price of $1.79, bringing the cost down to 79 cents. So we bought the item—but saved the receipt. A few weeks later, we found a rebate slip on a supermarket bulletin board for the cost of the product—$1.79. All we had to do was mail in the rebate form along with the receipt for the deodorant we had already purchased. All told, we got the item for free and even made a profit of 71 cents—$1 minus the cost of a stamp to mail the rebate form.

The only drawback to this strategy is that you have to save your receipts. If you don't mind that, be sure to check the rebate board near the exit of your supermarket each time you shop. Whenever there's an advertising blitz for some product, you'll be more likely to see rebate slips.

Saving Strategies That Work

So you may be wondering, how do you recognize a good deal? How can you determine the exact moment when you should pull out that sacred $1-off Yummy Applesauce coupon for maximum savings? How can you prevent bogus "bargains"?

FOOD BUDGETS THAT WORK

Common sense tells you that one way to cut your food spending is to follow a budget. Your food budget depends on many factors: income, family size, your economic goals, even the amount of time you want to invest in shopping. (Generally, the more time you're willing to invest, the less you'll spend on food.)

Unfortunately, most people overlook some crucial factors in the way they budget themselves. But you can cut your spending by avoiding these common budgeting mistakes.

Record everything. Most people spend a lot more than they think they do because they don't keep a written record of every purchase, says Paul Andreassen, resident scholar at the Jerome Levy Institute of Economics at Bard College in Annandale-on-Hudson, New York. Without keeping a written record, it's easy to forget the "little" purchases made throughout the week, such as bread, milk and eggs.

And since the average consumer shops for food nearly three times a week, these "small" items can add anywhere from 10 to 20 percent to your budget.

Include all food. Most people overlook restaurant and take-out food in their budgets—but you need to include eating-out and fast-food expenses as well as regular groceries. When you're adding up what you spend at the supermarket, be sure to keep tabs on these extras as well.

Budget for splurges. Without a "splurge factor," you set yourself up to blow your budget completely once you buy an item that's more than your budget allows. Besides, "you must allow yourself a psychological holiday from your budget if you are taking your budget seriously and plan on sticking with it," says Andreassen. So set aside a small reserve—maybe 5 percent—and allow yourself to splurge once a week or as often as your budget allows.

Keep a Price Book
Save 50%

Amy Dacyczyn, publisher of the *Tightwad Gazette,* a monthly newsletter on pinching your pennies until they bleed (and author of a book with the same name), says she saves big with the help of a price book—a binder or some other "holder" that allows you to keep records of prices for the same item in various neighborhood stores.

By keeping track of prices in the notebook, you'll find out the best places to shop each week. The notebook also reminds you when to redeem coupons or to buy in bulk for maximum savings.

"I get a three-ring notebook small enough to fit into a coat pocket or a pocketbook, and I devote one page to each particular food item," Dacyczyn tells us. "For example, I take peanut butter and list its prices in the stores in my area—warehouse stores, health food stores and regular supermarkets. Then I list the sale prices. After a couple of months, you'll notice that certain items always go on sale—and there's a 'bottom-line' sale price for everything."

Although a price book requires an initial time investment in compar-

THOSE LAST-MINUTE ITEMS CAN COST A LOT

Forget an item or two on your shopping list? Before you stop by the local convenience store or grocery, consider that you may have to pay a premium price for any "extra" that you buy.

On one comparison-shopping trip, we priced exactly the same items at different types of stores. Here are the results.

ITEM	TYPE OF STORE			
	Convenience Store ($)	Upscale Market ($)	National Chain Store ($)	Warehouse Market ($)
Cottage cheese, 12 ounces	1.49	1.15	1.15	1.05
Dessert topping, 16 ounces	2.19	1.59	1.29	1.33
Margarine, 1 pound	1.29	.95	.59	.47
Tuna in water, 6½-ounce can	1.15	.99	.54	.37
Whole milk, 1 gallon	2.45	2.57	2.72	2.47

JOIN THE CLUB TO SAVE BIG

By joining a membership merchandise club (for a $25 to $35 annual fee), you can get great savings on many items that you buy in large quantities. Here's a list of 13 different items, comparing unit prices at a national supermarket chain and a membership merchandise club store. Buying in bulk was the only difference; otherwise, the products were exactly the same. Just look at the savings!

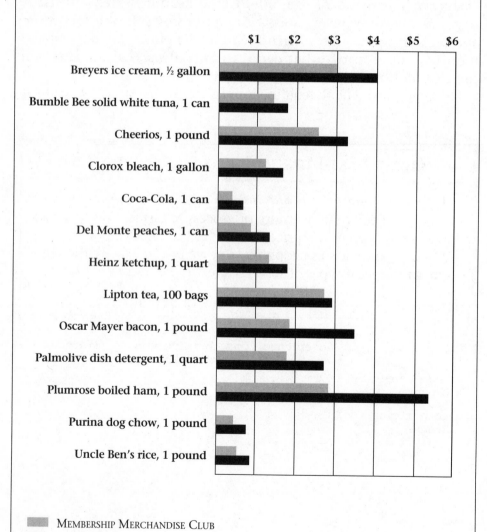

STOCK UP ANYTIME—AND SAVE

The following items have a good, long shelf life. So be sure to pick them up when you see them marked at the best price.

Baking powder	Italian seasoning
Baking soda	Ketchup
Balsamic vinegar	Nutmeg
Bay leaves	Paprika
Beef bouillon	Pepper
Bread crumbs, unseasoned	Poultry seasoning
Cayenne pepper, ground	Rice
Chicken bouillon	Rosemary
Chili powder	Salt
Chili sauce	Sesame oil
Cinnamon	Soy sauce
Cocoa, unsweetened	Tabasco sauce
Cornmeal	Tomato paste
Cornstarch	Turmeric
Cumin, ground	Vanilla extract
Dark brown sugar	Vegetable oil
Dijon mustard	Worcestershire sauce
Flour	White vinegar
Granulated sugar	Wine vinegar
Honey	

ison shopping and traveling from store to store, it allows you to track deals for years on end. Since Dacyczyn started her price book, she has managed to feed her family of eight for only $160 a month. Although your savings may vary, we're told that some families have managed to halve their total food bills within a few months by following this tactic.

Plan All Meals around Sales
Save 35%

Most people know enough to buy food on sale. If ground beef is on sale, you probably buy a package and have hamburgers for dinner one night. But buy enough for several meals, and you can trim as much as 35 percent off your food bill.

"I've been spending $30 or less a week on groceries for most of my married life," says Donna McKenna, a mother of four children in Casco, Maine, who became so proficient at saving money on food that she wrote a 60-page booklet called *The $30 a Week Grocery Budget.* "I check out signs in store windows and read the fliers sent in my mail for what's on sale where—and then plan a menu for a week's worth of meals around that."

If ground beef is on sale, for example, she buys enough to make hamburgers, meat loaf and a casserole—three meals. Or when yogurt's a good buy, she buys enough for several breakfasts and lunches. When using this strategy, pay special attention to meat and produce sales; together, these generally account for one-half of the total amount that you spend on food.

Brown-Bag Lunches
Save 60%

Probably the easiest way to cut your food spending is to brown-bag your lunch. The average adult eats out about 200 times a year—roughly four times a week. If you work outside the home, most of those meals are for lunch.

By making your own lunch at home (instead of buying it), you'll cut lunchtime expenses by at least 60 percent. You can usually make your own hearty lunch for well under $2, compared with buying out or ordering out (which usually costs about $5).

Don't believe it? Sandwiches made from tuna, turkey, egg salad or peanut butter and jelly can be made for less than 35 cents apiece. A cup of soup in a thermos costs between 10 and 15 cents. Rewarmed chili or casseroles cost less than 25 cents per serving. Have some popcorn or vegetable sticks for about a dime per serving. And for less than 20 cents per serving, you can have desserts such as homemade Jell-O, cookies or fresh fruit. Take along some juice in a thermos, and you're just over the $1 mark.

You'll save even more if you brown-bag for school-age children as well as yourself. Considering that most school lunches cost at least $1.50—and most kid-size brown-bag lunches are under $1—you can easily save nearly $100 a year in school cafeteria costs by packing Junior's lunches.

Dining Out

The average meal in a restaurant costs twice as much as the same meal prepared at home—without the tip. The average person eats 4 meals (out of 21) outside the home each week, but nearly one-half of the total food spending goes for restaurant and take-out fare.

Eating at home is the biggest cost saver, but we all like to dine out sometimes. When you do, here's how to make the most of your dining-out dollar.

Order Complete Meals
Save 35%

Bite for bite, you always get better value for your money by ordering an all-inclusive full dinner—main dish, soup, salad, vegetable and dessert—instead of ordering each dish à la carte. Even though the entrée is cheaper when you buy à la carte, you'll usually end up paying premium prices if you add any side dishes. Generally, you can save as much as 35 percent (or more) by ordering the complete dinner—so always look for it on the menu.

Frequent Franchises
Save 20%

The food may not be as specialized as you'd find in a private restaurant, but chains and franchises stress value—and deliver it. Often you can spend 20 percent less dining in a chain restaurant or franchise than you'd spend for the same meal at an "independent."

And chains have a special attraction for families: Besides offering more liberal children's menus, many chains and franchises now offer special deals—where kids eat free or at greatly reduced rates.

Get a Dining Card
Save 25%

If you like to dine out and you do a lot of traveling, then getting a restaurant discount card is one way to eat at hundreds of member restaurants across the country for less.

These cards, issued by Transmedia or Executive IGT (In Good Taste), act like credit cards: If you use them to pay for your bill at

AN APPETIZING IDEA FOR DINING-OUT SAVINGS

Here's a price-dodging idea: The next time you dine at a restaurant, make up your own meal. Order an appetizer and a salad in lieu of an entrée. "Many appetizers are as complex as entrées in terms of flavor and ingredients," says Clark Wolf, a New York City–based food and restaurant consultant.

With a combination of appetizer and salad, you'll be filled up without feeling like you've been cheated. Order an enhanced salad with your appetizer, such as a Caesar. Whereas "house" salads typically include lettuce, tomatoes and a few croutons, enhanced salads offer interesting ingredients, crunch and a "high chew factor," says Wolf. When you order a Caesar or similar salad, you're getting a satisfying meal without paying a premium price.

any of the participating restaurants, you get 25 percent taken off your bill—excluding tax, tip and liquor. It costs about $50 a year for either card. And with the card comes a list of member restaurants. (Phone numbers for both companies can be obtained from 800 directory assistance, if you want more information.)

Use Dining Coupons
Save 50%

No matter where you live, there are plenty of two-for-one meals—thanks to those regionally oriented coupon books available through Entertainment Publications. The company publishes about 150 versions of these books, which are often sold through the Lions Club, Kiwanis or similar groups and contain hundreds of deals on entertainment, leisure, lodging and especially dining opportunities.

Many of these coupons are flat discounts—usually in the 15 to 30 percent range. But the best deals are the dozens of "buy one, get one free" coupons that come in every book. With these coupons, you can get everything from hoagies to elegant meals. It's a cost-effective way to enjoy a night out with your spouse or friend, especially if you like trying new restaurants.

The coupon books cost between $25 and $45 (depending on your area), but that is quickly recouped if you use just one or two coupons.

For more information on where to buy these coupon books in your area, contact Entertainment Publications by calling 1-800-477-3234 or writing to P.O. Box 1068, Trumbull, CT 06611.

Head for the Outskirts of Town
Save 40%

If you live in a city, head for the 'burbs. The best buys in restaurant food tend to be away from the tourist center of town. In New York City, for instance, there are hundreds of restaurants in Brooklyn and Queens where you can get a great meal for under $15 that would cost $25 or more in Manhattan.

To find these meals on the outskirts of town, pick up a restaurant guide such as *Zagat Survey,* which evaluates restaurants in 36 cities (and their outskirts). These books are available at most bookstores.

Stop By a Cafeteria
Save 25%

In the South, hungry penny-pinchers know the portions are big but the bill is small at cafeterias such as Morrison's and Piccadilly. The midwestern equivalent—know to most Hoosiers—is Laughner's, which is located in the greater Indianapolis area.

But those aren't the only ones. Many other areas have cafeterias that serve full dinners for under $10. Because these chains tend to attract older persons on fixed incomes, most of them stress value. But no matter which cafeteria you choose, you'll receive a generous portion à la carte for about 10 percent less than you'd pay for a similar meal elsewhere. Add to that the fact that you don't have to tip a server, and you can knock at least 25 percent off your bill.

Eat during Off-Hours
Save 10%

You save two ways with this strategy. For one thing, many restaurants offer dinner specials before 6:00 P.M. (frequently known as early bird specials) or after 9:00 P.M. If you go during off-hours, you'll get the same menu but pay at least 10 percent less.

Also, you generally get more for your money during off-hours. Service is better, and portions tend to be more generous.

ORDER WINE BY THE BOTTLE AND SAVE

If you are dining out and want wine with your meal, consider ordering it by the bottle. For two or more drinkers, it's a much better deal than buying it by the glass.

A bottle typically fills five glasses, so some quick multiplication will tell you how much you can save. If wine costs $4 a glass, you can order a $15 bottle and save $1 per glass. In restaurants with moderately priced wine lists, you can save at least that much—or more.

Beware of half bottles. They are just slightly cheaper than regular-size bottles yet contain half as much (only 2½ glasses' worth).

Remember the Two E's
Save 15%

You can usually cut about 15 percent off your restaurant bill by remembering these two E's when ordering.

- *Ethnic:* The cheapest dining can usually be found at ethnic restaurants. That's because ethnic eats such as Asian, Mexican and Indian foods use a greater ratio of vegetables to meat. An added bonus about these foods is that they can be shared more easily than traditional fare.
- *Easy:* If you're an all-American eater, stick with simple choices, and you'll save. Entrées without fancy sauces or expensive garnishes cost less because they require less preparation effort in the kitchen.

Take the Family Home for Dessert
Save 20%

In many restaurants, dessert has the highest markup of any item. A slice of homemade cheesecake, for instance, costs about 70 cents. Have it at a restaurant, and you'll pay in the neighborhood of $3.50—about 500 percent more!

That's not to say you should pinch pennies on a romantic dinner for two by refusing dessert to cap off a great meal. But when you're taking the entire family out for dinner, don't routinely end the brood's feast with a round of desserts. A family of four can shave about one-fifth off its bill simply by passing on dessert at the restaurant.

SPLURGING FOR LESS

Don't let the fancy prices of gourmet fare frighten you. You can have your caviar and eat it, too—if you practice these cost-saving strategies.

Buy Off-Season
Save 20%

You can save at least 20 percent by buying imported olive oil, caviar, smoked salmon, real maple syrup and other high-priced items and delicacies when they're marked down—traditionally, when consumer demand is lowest. For instance, gourmet foods might be marked down at Christmas when stores are competing with each other. (But remember, even during the "bargain" season, you're still probably going to pay at least four times as much for gourmet foods as for "regular" eats.)

Be Alert to New Products
Save 20%

Be a "guinea pig" for new tastes, and you can trim another 20 percent off your luxury foods budget. That's because when gourmet food companies introduce new products, they typically trim one-fifth off the price of these items, whether you're buying retail or through mail order.

"This occurs about five times a year, when there are new product introductions," says Jenny Super, product manager at Wolferman's, a specialty bread company based in Kansas City, Missouri. Watch for specials at gourmet stores that specialize in one particular food item, such as cookies or ice cream.

Buy Wine by the Case
Save 15%

If the high price of wine has made you consider drinking from a brown paper bag, here's good news from the penny-pinching

CODDLE YOUR BOTTLES

You're throwing away good money—and missing out on your favorite vintage—if you store wine the wrong way. It can "turn" unless you store it properly.

To make sure your wine is properly stored, so it lasts longer, place bottles on their side, preferably in a wine rack. Wine should also be kept in a dark area (light changes the color of wine) and maintained at 55° to 65°F if you plan on keeping it longer than one year. Wine that you expect to drink within one year can be stored at temperatures as high as 78°. In either case, pick an appropriate temperature and stick with it—the temperature should be consistent.

front: Buy by the case, and you can easily cut your wine spending by 15 percent or more.

Most wine merchants want to move their merchandise and are willing to offer nice discounts when you buy a case—12 bottles. Often those dozen bottles don't have to be the same brand, so you can vary a little (although you usually can't choose 12 different wines), says wine merchant Ken Meier, owner of Meier's Cork and Bottle in Lincoln, Nebraska.

The trick is to know your tastes in wine. Know what you like—such as Pinot Noir or full-bodied Chardonnay. Then ask the wine merchant what the best value is in that category. "This puts the burden on the wine merchant to scope his inventory," says Meier.

COOKWARE BARGAINS AND FOOD PREPARATION

How you cook has a lot to do with how much you spend. A well-stocked kitchen saves money as well as time, preventing unnecessary trips to the grocery store and allowing you to experiment in low-cost meals.

Here's how to lower your food preparation costs.

Keep Recipes Simple
Save 10%

The less complicated a recipe, the less it costs to make. Generally, recipes with no more than six ingredients and five preparation steps cost about 10 percent less to make than similar dishes that are more involved.

Negotiate for Cookware
Save 15%

When shopping for new cookware, do it as though you were buying a new car or home—with a lot of negotiating. "Never pay full price for cookware," says Deborah Jensen, a cooking instructor at the New School for Social Research in New York City and owner of the Boatyard Cafe in Stonington, Connecticut. Although it's not well publicized, cookware retailers will accept less than the sticker price, and intense competition forces them to bargain with customers—especially with top-of-the-line merchandise. "Most retailers have the exact same items and put them on sale several times per year," says Jensen.

Buy at Discount Stores
Save 20%

While you may dream of owning copper pots or imported German cutlery, the reality is that you really don't need it. "You can buy perfectly good cookware and cutlery at stores like Best Products or K Mart," says chef and cookbook author Tom Ney. "Maybe it's not heirloom quality, but it is durable and a good value for the money and will cost about one-fourth of the price of the better merchandise."

For the best deals in cookware, Ney suggests that you head for these discount stores, as opposed to buying at kitchen specialty stores. Because they buy in volume, discount chains can sell the same (or similar) items that you'd find in specialty shops for about 20 percent less.

If you can't wait for a sale, check out the nearest Salvation Army or Goodwill store. With a little shopping (and it usually takes only a little, since cookware is a popular item), you can pick up quality cookware at thrift shops for just a fraction of retail prices—usually around 70 percent less. Garage sales are also good, although selection tends to be more limited.

When shopping in thrift stores, look for cast-iron cookware with absolutely no rust, suggests Jensen. "The heavier the pan, the more effective it is," she says. If it's rusted, though, don't buy it.

ENTERTAINING

Whether you're hosting a wedding to rival that of Charles and Diana or just having some friends over for a Sunday barbecue, there are plenty of ways to cut your entertaining costs without skimping on style.

Do Some Legwork Yourself
Save 20%

If you've hired a caterer for your affair, understand one thing: Everything the caterer does will be charged to you. "If you ask me to get a bottle of ginger ale that costs $1, I'll get it—and charge you $1.25," reveals one caterer.

So if you're really interested in saving money, do some legwork and save about 20 percent off your bill. Although all food chores should be left to the caterer, there are plenty of things you can do: Order and pick up the liquor and soda, and handle nonfood chores such as getting rental china, linens, chairs and other items.

Get Help from a Nearby College
Save 60%

If you have your caterer hire the service help, be prepared to pay servers about $25 per hour. But if you call a local college, you can get students—many with experience as servers—to work your affair for about $10 an hour.

You can find willing students by calling the college's fraternity or sorority council, the student council or the dean of students.

Eliminate a Course
Save 25%

The reality of weddings, bar mitzvahs and other fancy affairs is that few people eat salad after dinner or the grapefruit sorbet between courses. After all, who needs a separate almond cookie dessert when there's wedding cake?

These unnecessary frills may sound impressive when the caterer is taking your order, but they can add as much as 25 percent to your total bill. Eliminate these excesses, and no one will miss them. You can save yourself hundreds or thousands (depending on your event).

Use Plastic Cups
Save 90%

For at-home barbecues and other informal gatherings, use plastic cups, and you'll cut your expenses dramatically. Renting glasses will cost you at least 50 cents per glass (and caterers recommend three glasses per person); by comparison, you can buy 20 plastic cups for about $1—or about 5 cents each. Many recycling centers now accept plastic cups, so you can recycle them when you're done rather than throw them away.

Choose Recipes around the Seasons
Save 20%

In choosing a dish, let the calendar be your guide, and you can trim your cooking expenses by about 20 percent. That's because certain foods—fruits, vegetables and other fresh items—are much cheaper when you buy them in season rather than out of season.

"Start by asking what's fresh and in season, and then choose a recipe," says Beverly Gruber, owner of the Everyday Gourmet School of Cooking in Seattle. "Most people, unfortunately, do it the other way around: They choose a recipe and then find the ingredients."

Make Cheap Substitutions
Save 25%

You don't have to use the highest-priced ingredients to make a meal that tastes great. Many recipes are just as good with moderately priced substitutes.

For instance, you can substitute turkey in any recipe that calls for chicken—and save anywhere from 10 to 20 percent. Use catfish in recipes that call for swordfish, shark or other high-priced fish, and you can save 25 percent or more. Orange roughy is another low-cost fish that can be substituted for pricey varieties when you're doing a seafood special.

Cut Your Spending on

CLOTHING

- Retail
- Off-Price Stores
- Outlets
- Formal Wear
- Getting Bargains in the Big Apple
- Mail Order
- Secondhand Stores
- Care and Maintenance

Dress to Kill without Murdering Your Pocketbook

Hemlines may rise and fall, but when it comes to what we spend on them, there seems to be only one direction—upward.

Americans plunk down more than $112 billion each year buying clothes at shopping malls and department stores—about $500 for every man, woman and child living in the United States. And the bill is going up all the time. Each year we spend about $2 billion more than the year before. And that figure doesn't even include the billions more spent in off-price stores, outlets and mail-order houses, the newest haberdasheries for the cost-conscious and time-consumed.

It's no wonder, since clothing has some of the highest markup of all consumer goods. Retail prices are at least 200 percent of wholesale. And they can be as much as 500 percent in some stores. (Or in other words, that designer suit or pair of fancy sneakers can cost you five times as much money as it cost the retailer or wholesaler to buy from the manufacturer.)

But there are ways to look like a million without spending anywhere near that much. By discovering the secrets of when, where and even what to buy, you can get quality clothing for one-third to one-half less.

Retail

The local mall or department store may not seem like a penny-pincher's paradise, but it can be. Sure, the merchandise in these stores is usually sold at premium prices to help pay for the high overhead and expensive real estate. And yes, the much-ballyhooed "holiday sales" are often little more than lip service. After all, even with 20 percent off, you're still paying more than you would at an outlet.

But the reality is, most people still do most of their shopping at large department stores and other retail outlets. So if you're among the mall-going masses, here's how to cut your spending on clothes when buying retail.

44

WHERE YOUR MONEY GOES

- Women spend nearly twice as much on clothes as men—an average of $607 a year compared with $345. When it comes to buying children's clothing, $105 is spent for girls compared with $80 for boys.
- The median amount that women spend on shoes is $120 a year—which is more than men or women spend on any other single article of clothing. Dresses rank a close second, with an annual median expenditure of $118; and jewelry is third ($117). Women spend about $108 a year on tops (blouses, sweaters and the like), and men spend $81 on shirts. The least amount of money is spent on pajamas and socks: For these items, the average is about $5 a year.
- Nearly $4 billion a year is spent buying men's suits. But even more money is spent on T-shirts for babies—about $5 billion annually.
- The typical household spends approximately $70 a year on dry-cleaning costs.

Get a Store Credit Card
Save 25%

One easy way to cut your clothing costs is to get a credit card at your favorite store. Even if you never use them (and you shouldn't if you want to cut your spending, because of the added finance charges), store credit cards can be a cost cutter because cardholders get advance notice of "private" sales for "select" customers.

During these sales, department stores typically cut prices anywhere from 15 to 25 percent. What's more, because they're private sales (often held during slow shopping periods, such as on weekdays or during certain hours), you can get first crack at new inventory when it arrives.

National chains such as J. C. Penney, Sears and Macy's notify credit card customers of these special sales by mail and sometimes offer discount coupons; you don't even have to use your credit card to make the purchases.

LEARNING THE LINGO

The first step to keeping more of your riches is to understand the language of the "rag" business. And a big part of that business is knowing who sells what to whom—and at what markup. Every store has some markup, of course—otherwise, how would they make a profit? But the store you should be looking for is the one with the best-quality goods at the lowest possible prices. Therefore, the markup is minimal. Here's the lowdown on the rag trade.

Department stores typically buy goods directly from a manufacturer and have the highest markup. This means you pay twice as much as the store's cost. Sale items are then "reduced" from that markup. You pay more because department stores advertise most frequently and have high rents in malls and other prime locations. Department stores have a great selection and are good places to purchase items that are the current fashion trend. But don't forget, you're subsidizing some of their high rent and advertising costs every time you pay for an item.

Discount stores traditionally carry clothing that's similar to what's found in department stores. But the clothing sold in discount stores is 10 to 30 percent cheaper because it's not as well constructed or the materials are cheaper. (For instance, a discount store might sell exactly the same style sold in a department store, but the garment is made from polyester instead of cotton.)

However, discount store chains such as K Mart, Wal-Mart and Bradlees have been working to improve the quality of clothing they offer in order to be competitive with other stores. Some now offer exactly the same items that are sold in department stores. These clothes still cost less, however, because the discount store buys in volume and has less overhead. (Usually, these stores are located in less prestigious locations such as the local shopping

Buy in January
Save 50%

You've probably noticed that the best deals in toys, gift wrapping and holiday cards begin on December 26, the day after Christmas.

center instead of the high-rent mall.) Underwear and casual clothes are your best bets here.

Off-price stores get merchandise from department stores and directly from manufacturers. This is merchandise that has gone unsold, so the manufacturer or department store is eager to unload it. Because the off-price store gets a "deal" on a whole shipment of clothes, the garments are priced somewhere between the wholesale cost and the original department store prices.

Among the prominent off-price stores are TJ Maxx, Filene's Basement, Marshalls and Burlington Coat Factory. They keep their prices low by locating at distant, less expensive sites and advertising only occasionally. The selection may suffer, or it may be great! It's hit or miss because these stores buy only what they can get. But you can usually find a selection of all types of clothing.

Manufacturer outlets are stores run by a clothing manufacturer or by a company that acts as the "middleman." Outlets often buy overruns (when the factory makes too many of a particular item), factory samples and irregular or second-quality goods. Many well-known clothing producers such as Liz Claiborne and Alexander Julian have their own outlet stores, where they sell their own clothing at prices that are 20 to 70 percent less than the usual retail prices.

Liquidators buy any items that have been "unloaded" in large quantities by other stores. Liquidators such as Job Lot, Pic N' Save and Value City began doing big business in the late 1980s as department stores merged or failed, dumping huge amounts of merchandise on the open market. Since liquidators spend only pennies on the dollar, they can offer some very expensive clothing for only a fraction of its original price. Of course, they also carry merchandise that nobody else wants. But if you have a discerning eye and the patience to explore acres of racks and bins, you can put together your whole wardrobe at just a fraction of department store prices.

Well, wait another week, and you can reap some equally excellent savings in clothing.

That's because retailers want to unload goods that weren't sold during the Christmas shopping spree, which occurs from Thanksgiving to December 24. And why? Because they need to make room for the new spring clothing line, which usually starts arriving at the end of January or in early February.

If you look for sales in that post-Christmas season, you'll find prices slashed by as much as 50 percent. You can get some of the year's best deals on clothing during the entire month of January—and still get a good two months of wear out of newly purchased winter clothes.

Hint: If you want to reap these savings for Christmas, try what many cost-conscious gift givers are now doing—presenting loved ones with Christmas gifts of IOUs or gift certificates for their favorite stores, so they can buy more for their money after the holiday rush. (It's an especially good idea if you have fickle teenagers who prefer to choose their own duds.)

GET THE GOODS THAT SANTA DIDN'T—IN JANUARY

Prices take a nosedive after Rudolph leads the big delivery van through the sky—but how much can you really save by shopping in January instead of December? To find out, we compared pre-Christmas and post-Christmas prices in a department store, discount store and off-price store. And here's what we discovered.

ITEM	PRE-CHRISTMAS PRICE ($)	JANUARY PRICE ($)	SAVINGS
For Women			
Coat (department store)	430.00	249.99	42%
Suit (department store)	169.00	79.00	53%
Jeans (discount store)	34.99	19.99	43%
Sweater (discount store)	34.00	24.99	27%
Blouse (off-price store)	16.95	9.90	42%
For Men			
Suit (department store)	395.00	299.90	24%
Sport coat (department store)	150.00	74.99	50%
Tie (off-price store)	12.95	10.65	18%

Buy Summer Clothes in July
Save 40%

January isn't the only time to reap great deals on clothes while they're still in season. You can also buy summer clothes in mid-summer—and cut spending as much as 40 percent (about the same levels as after the season).

Sure, you may have heard that the best deals are in September—when you no longer need summer garb. In reality, the deals start in July and August. With vacations and the dog days of summer, this is a slow time for department stores—and prices significantly drop as retailers try to spark store traffic and make room for the new fall line.

Get Overcoats in October
Save 35%

It may pale in comparison to finding the New World, but Christopher Columbus made at least one contribution to clothes buying: Most department stores advertise Columbus Day sales. But many shoppers don't realize that one of the best values is women's overcoats.

During the Columbus Day weekend, you can save anywhere from 15 to 35 percent off regular prices. So if you miss buying in the spring (when prices are even lower), the second weekend in October is the best time to buy women's raincoats and winter coats—giving you a full season's use of your new purchase.

Check Out Army-Navy Stores
Save 50%

One of the most underrated retail clothing stores is the local Army-Navy store. Granted, inventory may be somewhat limited, but there are deals aplenty.

Case in point: A popular casual look (originally inspired by Don Johnson of "Miami Vice") is a jacket or sweater over a brightly colored cotton T-shirt. Sure, you can go to Banana Republic or another popular store and spend $12 or more for the T-shirt. But head to the nearest Army-Navy store for its colored T's, and you'll pay $6 or less for the same item.

Army-Navy stores also have jeans, slacks and sportswear at prices anywhere from 10 to 40 percent below regular retail prices.

Purchase Last Year's Sneakers
Save 30%

Each year, athletic shoe manufacturers update their models by making small changes. And we do mean small. Sometimes it's nothing more significant than altering the color of the trademark stripe! These minor details are what set new models apart from old and establish "trends" among the most powerful sneaker consumers: teens.

These slight changes usually result in a price increase—typically between 5 and 15 percent. But as soon as the new models come in, you can buy yesterday's "must-have" sneaks at closeout prices, saving as much as 30 percent compared with the new styles.

Although different manufacturers introduce their new lines at different times, you're most likely to get good sneaker buys in late fall or early winter. (Introducing summer gear at that time gives retailers several months to see what's "hot" and to discount the older models.) Keep your eyes peeled from January to March for closeout specials. Or visit shoe stores during this season and ask the clerks to show you last year's models.

Mix and Match Your Work Clothes
Save 40%

One of the best things about buying in department stores and specialty retail stores (such as Talbot's and Anne Klein) is they're more likely to sell timeless classics rather than passing fads. That's important to know if you're a career woman with limited cash flow.

If you need to wear suits for work, you don't have to buy six complete two-piece suit outfits. Instead, buy one "matching" suit and complete the rest of your wardrobe with separates—skirts, slacks and blazers that can be mixed and matched on different days of the week. And since retail stores specialize in providing "coordinating" possibilities with their inventory, it will save you a lot of shopping time—as well as cut about 40 percent off the cost of your business wardrobe.

A gray business suit is the classic for the modern professional woman. Then complete your work wardrobe by adding three skirts (in blue, beige and plaid) along with coordinating blazers. Using this mix-and-match method, you'll get the equivalent of six business suits.

THE BUSINESS OF WOMEN'S SUITS— WHAT DOES IT ADD UP TO?

Looking your best is just part of doing business—and for most women, that means at least six great-looking professional ensembles to complete your work wardrobe.

But even if you buy good quality at department store prices, you can save hundreds of dollars buying clothes that go well together rather than six complete suits. Here's how things stacked up on a shopping trip when we compared buying suits with buying separates.

First we shopped for six women's suits, which ranged from $119.99 to $184. Adding their prices together, the total cost for all six suits was $988.99.

Then during a second shopping spree, we found four blazers and four skirts that were equivalent in quality to the suits that we had priced earlier. Least expensive was a plain beige skirt, which cost $25. At the high end of the price scale was a charcoal wool skirt for $53. We also purchased a blue skirt for $44 and a plaid skirt (with a beige and blue pattern) for $49. Total cost for the skirts: $171.

The four blazers ranged in price from $99 to $138. Total cost for the blazers: $455.90.

Adding together the costs of the skirts and the blazers, the total tab for buying separates was $626.90, compared with $988.99 for the six suits. *Conclusion:* Buying separates instead of suits, we saved $362.09, or 37 percent.

Buy a Blazer

Don't fret, guys. You, too, can slash hundreds off your wardrobe. Mix-and-match attire isn't acceptable if you're in the white-collar crowd—but you can get a lot of mileage out of a navy blue blazer. In fact, it's the one piece of clothing that no professional, male or female, should be without.

It can be formal or casual, depending what it's paired with. The color is always right, no matter what the season. Navy blue blazers are available in various weights suitable for various times of year—hopsack for summer, cashmere or camel hair for winter or a wool blend for year-round wear.

Because of its versatility, a navy blue blazer can be mixed and matched with most business wear, eliminating the need for other outfits and saving you hundreds of dollars.

Off-Price Stores

Off-price stores such as TJ Maxx, Filene's Basement, Marshalls and Burlington Coat Factory offer the best of both worlds: the low prices of outlets, and the selection and convenience of department stores.

The low prices result from locating in strip shopping malls and other areas near major malls (so the stores escape the high mall rents yet don't require the long drives to out-of-the-way outlets). And since off-price stores buy clothes in volume directly from the manufacturer or leftovers from department stores, they get a large inventory and can afford to pass on the savings to consumers.

It's not always easy to tell an off-price store (since a store doesn't refer to itself by that name). The best way, perhaps, is to look at the price tag. Off-price stores often compare their prices with retail prices. Another tip is the selection: Off-price stores tend to carry inventory from a lot of designers, while outlets and department stores tend to be more limited.

You may not always find what you expect when you walk into an off-price store, but you may find something unexpected that you do need. Off-price stores get a wide variety of items at below-retail prices, but they may be overstocked on some items—size 46 Italian suits, for instance—and understocked on others. So your best policy is to stop by now and then to see if the store has what you want in your size and preferred color.

Head to the Men's Department
Save 50%

Women's clothing traditionally is more expensive than men's—even for similar items. You may notice that if a woman's silk blouse costs $60, a similar man's shirt will retail in the neighborhood of $30.

HATE SHOPPING?
HERE'S WHAT YOU SHOULD KNOW

Maybe you're not the sort of person who likes to shop 'til you drop. That being the case, here's how to cut both your time and your expenses when shopping for clothing.

Think dark. Unless dark colors are unflattering to you, try to build your wardrobe around deeper shades such as navy blues, hunter greens, rusts, maroons and grays. They are more versatile and can make your wardrobe seem more expanded than it actually is. Besides, they hide dirt better, so they don't require cleaning as often.

To spend the minimum of time and money shopping for business clothing, try to develop a stable of outfits around three or four dark colors that complement neutral solids and patterns in all hues. Bright colors draw attention, so people will notice if you wear a garment often.

Try before you buy. Manufacturers' sizes vary greatly. One manufacturer might make a size 8 or size 12 that fits a woman whose "true" size is 10. In fact, the same manufacturer may vary sizes from year to year. (They tend to err on the generous side, so people don't feel as if they're squeezing out of their "real" sizes if they put on weight.)

The bottom line: Try on clothes whenever possible—even if they carry a familiar label. You'll save time, mileage and aggravation if you can buy the right size the first time and avoid return trips to the store for exchanges.

When money is an object, think blue or gray. Most clothing experts suggest that men (as well as women) own at least four suits for work. But if you want to save money and not buy the suggested four, stick to colors such as gray and blue. They're more versatile, and you can wear a greater variety of ties, shirts and shoes with those colors.

While you can buy both for less at off-price stores, tradition still holds: Several items of women's clothing tend to be twice as expensive as the same items designed for men. Silk blouses/shirts are an ex-

LOOK FOR BARGAINS IN BOYS' WEAR

If you're a woman shopping for clothing between size 5 and size 12, there may be a great deal waiting for you in the boys' department of your nearest department store. Even clothes with designer labels are 20 to 50 percent less in the boys' department than similar items in the women's department. Look for great bargains on shirts, sweaters, pants, jackets, robes and belts.

As for sizes, it may take a few visits to the dressing room to figure out how to translate boys' sizes into women's sizes. To save you a few steps, here are the general guidelines.

WOMEN'S SIZE	BOYS' SIZE
5/6	14 top, 29/30 pants
7/8	16 top, 30/31 pants
9/10	18 top, 31/32 pants
11/12	20 top, 32/33 pants

cellent example. You can get great deals on men's shirts at off-price stores. The only real difference between men's and women's styles is a slightly different cut—which doesn't count for much in these days of "baggy" looks. Also, a man's shirt buttons are on the opposite side, but this is unnoticeable when the shirt is buttoned.

The same holds true for casual jackets and athletic wear. So if you head to the men's department, you may be able to spend half as much on already reduced clothing.

Buy Next Year's Winter Clothes
Save 80%

Department stores offer substantial savings during January on winter clothes, but off-price stores are even better. You can make out like a bandit if you get winter clothes at off-price stores after you need them: Coats, gloves, hats and other winter accessories may be marked down drastically.

Sure, all stores offer savings after the season, but off-price stores sometimes practically give away their stock—with markups up to 80 percent off regular prices. (Maybe it's because off-price stores pride themselves on providing value in clothing for the entire family, and outfitting the kids in new winter coats can put a significant dent in your spending.)

So when your brood outgrows this year's winter coats, check out the nearest off-price store in late February or March for great values on next year's outfits. By buying winter gear for next season, you can outfit your family for just a fraction of what you'd spend in the fall. Just remember to buy slightly larger than usual for the kids.

WHAT DO YOU SAVE AT AN OFF-PRICE STORE?

To answer that question, we chose a number of name-brand items in department stores, then priced exactly the same items in off-price stores. Here's how the prices compare.

ITEM	DEPARTMENT STORE ($)	OFF-PRICE STORE ($)	SAVINGS
For Women			
Sweater (cotton)	42.00	19.90	53%
Cotton blouse (The Limited)	48.00	16.95	65%
Wool skirt (Liz Claiborne)	74.95	64.90	13%
Linen dress pants (Liz Claiborne)	70.00	40.00	43%
Black leather high heels (9 West)	50.00	29.99	40%
Terry-cloth robe (Bill Blass)	49.00	27.99	43%
For Men			
100% cotton dress shirt (Perry Ellis)	39.50	22.95	42%
Silk necktie (Evan-Picone)	26.00	12.95	50%
Wool trousers (Christian Dior)	75.00	49.95	33%
Leather oxford shoes (Dexter)	69.00	39.99	42%

ARE YOU BUYING QUALITY?

Pity the poor souls who check only the label to decide if their clothing is quality. Instead of being a sucker for the designer label, check these details—no matter what you're buying.

Is there extra fabric at the seams? Cheaper manufacturers cut corners by not leaving any room to let seams in or out at the waist, seat or sides.

Do patterns match? With good-quality merchandise, patterns match uniformly, especially on the back and around all pockets.

Are the hem seams visible? Skirts, pants and jackets should all have invisible hem seams. Garments of real quality have silk threads, which won't fade after years of dry cleaning.

Is the color darker or lighter in any areas? Check for uniform color. Fabric shouldn't be faded in certain parts of the garment—particularly the areas exposed to light.

Is the stitching straight? Stitches should lie in a straight line with no loose threads. Single-needle tailoring on shirts and blouses means stitches won't unravel. Most popularly priced sport coats and suit jackets are assembled by "fusing" the outside fabric and inside lining to a center piece of fabric using glue. In a better-quality suit, you should be able to pull apart those two pieces and feel a third, separate piece in between that has been sewn instead of fused.

Does the fabric have "backing" and quality lining? Make sure there's a felt backing underneath the collar of a sport coat or better-quality jacket. Most good-quality suits have lining throughout the entire inside—not just in portions of the jacket.

Is the waistband reinforced? Look for a single-piece waistband in pants. It should be reinforced to prevent rolling or bunching.

Are lapels properly shaped? Lapels should be gently rounded and drop into place smartly when you tug on them.

Are shoulder pads secure? If the shoulder pads bunch up or fall out of place, it's a sign of cheap merchandise.

Where's the double stitching? All jeans should have double rows of stitching. Look for the same feature on tailored shirts: You don't want rips at stress points such as the armholes.

Seek Out Private Labels
Save 40%

One thing you'll notice in off-price stores is a lot of different labels—many with names you've never heard of. Here's a secret: About one-fourth of all the clothing sold in the United States is private label, meaning it's designed and manufactured by a big-name company under a less established name. And off-price stores specialize in selling these private labels.

Because of complex licensing agreements, manufacturers can't always sell their wares under their most established names. (Doing so risks upsetting the department stores that pay top dollar for these goods.) For instance, Ralph Lauren has several lines of clothing and accessories that come from various licensees. It's these lesser-known private labels that usually find their way to off-price stores, while the Ralph Lauren line goes to big department stores.

Because many private labels don't have the same name recognition as other labels by the same manufacturer, off-price stores can purchase these lines at substantial discounts—and sell them to consumers for about 40 percent below retail. True, you may not be getting the "right" label, but you're getting the same fine quality.

Thomas David, for instance, is a label you'll find at many off-price stores and outlets (and a few department stores) in suit jackets and sportswear. If you notice this green label in a $140 navy blue blazer, it means you're getting the same designer navy blue blazer that retails for $250 at the so-called finer stores.

Since private labels change constantly, it's best to ask knowledgeable clerks at off-price stores for the private-label brands of your favorite manufacturers. But don't be alarmed when you don't recognize the names: It just explains why you're probably getting designer clothing for much less money.

Head for Upscale Neighborhoods

Off-price stores tend to be very regional—tailoring their merchandise to the area that they serve. Just as you wouldn't expect to find a Rolls-Royce dealer in Appalachia, don't expect a store located in a middle-class, family-filled suburban area to stock high-fashion designer clothing aimed at rich socialites. And if you're shopping for back-to-school clothes, don't expect to find them in off-price stores located in a neighborhood of apartment and condominium dwellers.

To find what you're looking for, it's best to travel to off-price stores in neighborhoods that cater to those who would buy the same type of clothing. This may mean a little more driving, but it won't be a wasted trip.

OUTLETS

Outlet stores don't make shopping easy: They're usually located in out-of-the-way places; they rarely advertise (except by distributing handouts or putting up billboard ads near their locations); and since their inventory is usually limited to their manufacturers' whims, shopping can be a hit-or-miss adventure.

But when you "hit" at an outlet, it's usually a jackpot. In a typical year, Americans spend more than $8 billion on clothing while shopping at outlet stores. But they would have paid more than $12 billion if they had bought the same items at full retail prices, according to Dawn Frankfort, consumer marketing director for the *Joy of Outlet Shopping*, a magazine that lists outlet stores throughout the United States and Canada.

Some outlets have clothing that's priced up to 70 percent lower than what you'd find in retail stores. Unfortunately, some people have discovered that with outlet shopping, you often get what you pay for. The real key in many outlets isn't finding great bargains; it's finding great value.

So here's how to make the most of your time and money when shopping in outlets—so you can truly cut your spending without settling for less.

Look for
a Manufacturer's Label
Save 40%

Just because a store calls itself an outlet doesn't mean it is one. A true outlet is a store where manufacturers sell their own quality merchandise direct to the public, usually for about 40 percent less than retail prices. For instance, at London Fog outlets, you can find London Fog–label trench coats, normally retailing for $195, at prices under $115.

WHAT ARE THE SAVINGS AT AN OUTLET STORE?

If there's an outlet store anywhere near you, it's probably worth getting to if you want a particular high-priced item. To demonstrate why, we compared prices at outlet stores with prices at department stores for the same article of clothing. Savings can be 50 percent or more, as this comparison shows.

ITEM	DEPARTMENT STORE ($)	OUTLET STORE ($)	SAVINGS
For Women			
Linen 2-piece suit (Jones New York)	184.00	129.00	30%
Wool blazer (Liz Claiborne)	180.00	108.00	40%
Rayon dress (Liz Claiborne)	150.00	80.00	47%
Leather handbag (Coach)	166.00	125.00	25%
Hosiery (Evan-Picone)	4.75	3.50	26%
For Men			
Raincoat (London Fog)	289.00	135.00	53%
Wool overcoat (Ralph Lauren)	395.00	199.00	50%
Wool 2-piece suit (Ralph Lauren)	900.00	449.99	50%
Tweed sport coat (Evan-Picone)	188.00	132.00	30%

Beware, however, of so-called outlets that sell goods from various manufacturers. They are the equivalent of liquidators rather than outlets. Often they buy seconds and other "unwanted" merchandise that's not easily sold through other channels.

To find the nearest outlet stores, you can order a copy of the *Joy of Outlet Shopping*, which lists nearly 9,000 true outlets in North America. Write to the *Joy of Outlet Shopping*, P.O. Box 17129, Depart-

LABEL LANGUAGE

Need to know what the labels on outlet-sold items really mean? Here's a guide to ensure that you're really buying what you think you're buying.

Closeout. The last items from a particular season, line or style of merchandise. Usually, when you buy closeout goods, you're getting last year's merchandise.

First quality. These are the same goods found at full-price retailers, usually direct from the factory.

Irregulars or imperfects. Items with small flaws. Because the imperfections are slight—often unnoticeable—the items are sold at a cut-rate price rather than discarded.

Overstocks. These goods may be first quality or closeouts. They were left over at the factory after all the orders were shipped.

Seconds. These items have more noticeable flaws, such as mismatched patterns, tears or stains. But they're still usable as long as the buyer isn't too finicky about appearance.

---

ment CS, Clearwater, FL 34622-0129. (The cost is about $6 plus $1.50 shipping and handling.)

Search the Big Bins
Save 60%

Outlets stress savings, not service. And one way you can really save is by going through those huge bins containing mounds and mounds of new clothes.

True, it's a hassle to rummage through these bins to find the right size and style, but it's time well spent. "Back-room bargains" are often as much as 60 percent less than prices in other areas of the outlet store. The merchandise being sold is often overstocked or returned items, so it's good quality, but beware: These bins can also hide irregulars. So once you've picked out the item you want—and you like the price you see on the tag—be sure to look at it carefully to make sure it's an item you will really wear.

Ask for a Discount
Save 20%

Whenever you're buying at discount prices, you may be able to get even more knocked off the price if you know how to negotiate.

When clothes are in good condition, they're usually marked "first quality." But if you detect any flaws, you can often negotiate for even more savings! Since clerks especially want to move the "second string" of goods, ask for an additional 10 to 20 percent off for items with pulled threads, loose buttons, spots or stains, mismatched patterns, frayed hemlines or similar defects—if you don't mind making the repairs yourself.

Buy Sleepwear in May
Save 10%

Even at outlets, some items are discounted more than usual during certain times of the year. For sleepwear, the big discount time is late spring, when prices in outlets drop an additional 10 percent or so. May is the time to march into outlet stores for pajamas and nightgowns.

FORMAL WEAR

You may put on your pants one leg at a time, but you put on a lot more than pants. There are special duds such as gowns, wedding dresses and tuxedos that you wear only occasionally, for special occasions. Here's how to buy them all for less.

Buy Used Tuxedos
Save $300

When you consider that it costs over $90 to rent a quality tuxedo package—suit, shirt, tie, cummerbund and studs—you may decide to buy the whole package after all. True, a new designer tux can cost more than $400. But you can get a good used tuxedo for about $100—and sometimes the store will give you a new shirt and a tie/cummerbund set at no extra charge.

As a rule, if you wear a tuxedo more than three times a year, you're better off buying than renting. But even if you need a tux only once or twice every few years, you'll still save hundreds in rental fees over the years if you buy a used tux that you end up wearing a half-dozen times.

Spring is the best time to buy a used tux because that's when many stores receive new outfits for the prom and wedding season. Since tuxedos are cleaned and pressed after each rental, the used inventory often looks brand-new.

Rent a Gown
Save $1,000

For the woman who has everything—except a formal dress—buying that designer gown for one-time use represents a major investment. But here's good news: You don't have to spend $1,200 or more to buy a designer gown. There are stores that will rent one to you for $150 to $350. That's the price range for three days' use. And along with the gown, you can get handbags, wraps and costume jewelry. One Night Stand is one such establishment, with stores in New York City and London. Similar stores may be listed in your local Yellow Pages under "Formal Wear Rental."

Go to a Discount Bridal Shop
Save 50%

Everyone loves a June bride—but no one loves the cost of wedding garments. A typical wedding gown costs $800 or more—pretty pricey for an item that will spend many decades in the closet. And all the bridesmaids' dresses are sold at premium prices as well. But here's good news for the whole wedding party: The bride and her attendants can save hundreds of dollars if they buy from a wedding gown discounter.

Stores such as David's Bridal Warehouse, which operates in a number of East Coast cities and Florida, have cut the cost of getting married by offering discounted bridal gowns and bridesmaid dresses at savings of 50 percent or more off retail. So if you or your kin are planning a big wedding, look in your Yellow Pages under "Bridal Shops" or "Formal Wear" for a store near you.

GETTING BARGAINS IN THE BIG APPLE

Most native New Yorkers know all the ropes when it comes to getting bargains in clothing. But if you're visiting from out of town—for business or pleasure—here are some tips on how to find the best deals in the fashion capital of the nation.

Call the Chamber of Commerce
Save 40%

No matter where you travel, it's a good idea to call the local chamber of commerce for advice on bargain basements and outlets. This is particularly advisable in New York City, since new stores are opening all the time.

The call is usually worth the effort. The chamber of commerce can bring you up to date on bargain stores that have recently opened, where you can usually buy quality items for 40 percent or more below retail.

Mail Your Purchases Home

New York City offers some terrific bargains, but they come at a price—namely, the city's sales tax on clothing.

You can skip the local sales tax by asking to have your purchases shipped to your home. Of course, then you have to pay postage. But for high-priced purchases, the postage is usually a lot less than sales tax would be.

SHOPPING IN NEW YORK CITY

Travel across America, and you'll find many clothing stores that are local favorites and also "flagship" stores for the national chains. Chicago has Chernin's for shoes. Boston is the home of Filene's Basement, and neighboring towns around Boston manufacture both Saucony and New Balance running shoes. Seattle has Nordstrom Rack, which is the upscale department store's outlet center.

But no city has better shopping opportunities than New York City. If you're planning a trip to the Big Apple, you can take a nice bite out of your clothing spending by checking out the "Sales and Bargains" section of *New York* magazine each week. It lists local merchants and manufacturers' outlets that sell goods at notable prices.

Keep Your Eyes Peeled in the Big Apple

While in New York City, put on your best walking shoes and hit the streets. Different neighborhoods are known for their deals, so be prepared to do some traveling. Besides the Garment District (see the map below), here are some other great shopping locales.

- For women's clothing, visit showrooms lining Seventh Avenue and Avenue of the Americas between 34th Street and 40th Street. Some of the best known include Simply Samples at 150 West 36th Street, off Broadway; Ben Farber at 462 Seventh Avenue, between 34th Street and 35th Street; and Showroom 7 at 241 West 37th Street, 12th Floor.
- For men's clothing, explore the area between Fifth Avenue and Broadway, from 15th Street to 23rd Street. Also try Saint Laurie at 899 Broadway; Moe Ginsburg at 162 Fifth Avenue; and Rothmans at 200 Park Avenue South.

THE GARMENT DISTRICT

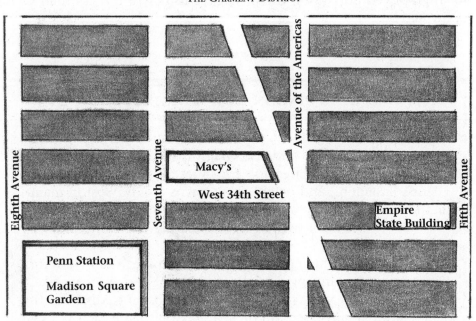

There are deals aplenty to be found in many parts of New York City, but the most famous area is the Garment District in lower midtown Manhattan. It's a mecca of bargains for savvy shoppers.

- For underwear, lingerie and scarves, go to Lismore Hosiery at 334 Grand Street; Mayfield at 303 Grand Street; and D and A Merchandise Company at 22 Orchard Street—all on the Lower East Side.

In general, another good area to explore for all kinds of discounted clothing is lower Fifth Avenue and Orchard Street.

Mail Order

As free time dwindles, people are looking for more ways to save time. One way is mail-order shopping. The main advantage to mail order is that you get quality merchandise with excellent order-by-phone or order-by-mail service. For the easiest shopping, all you do is pick up the phone and place an order.

There are two disadvantages, however: Usually, people put the order on their credit cards—and unless you pay off the charge immediately, you'll end up paying high interest. Also, mail-order items don't necessarily come cheap, so you need to be discriminating about what you order.

Leading mail-order houses including Eddie Bauer, Land's End and L. L. Bean do offer merchandise at competitive prices, but usually not bargain-basement price tags. But here's how to save when ordering through the mail or by phone.

Open the Catalog in the Middle
Save 40%

Like their retail counterparts, more mail-order companies now offer special clearance sales, with reductions up to 40 percent off the usual prices. Typically, the items offered for clearance are winter clothes sold at the end of the winter season or summer clothes on sale at summer's end. But apart from the seasonal sales, you might find some great bargains on mail-order items that are offered at discount prices because of over-ordering.

Get Answers before Ordering

The convenience of ordering through the mail quickly turns to inconvenience if you end up returning your order. Since it's you who pays the postage, the key to shopping by catalog or from TV is to get answers to your questions up front—before you order. Ask about shrinkage, colors, true-to-size measurements, washing details and other questions that could prompt you to return the item.

Although most mail-order houses have very liberal exchange and refund policies—most back up the items unconditionally—it's in your best interest to get specifics about return/exchange policies and shipping costs. But if you change your mind after ordering, you can simply refuse delivery. That tactic ensures that you won't have to pay return postage.

SECONDHAND STORES

If you don't object to secondhand clothing, you can get first-rate savings. Thrift stores and consignment shops sell plenty of fashionable, quality clothing at just a fraction of what you'd pay in retail, discount or even outlet stores. The only catch is that you have to be willing to put some time into this method of shopping, since the best merchandise goes the quickest.

Secondhand stores generally fall into two categories.

Thrift stores are usually run by not-for-profit organizations such as Goodwill or the Salvation Army and have the biggest selection. Since their inventory is donated, they have a lot of discarded merchandise that nobody would want.

Consignment shops are private businesses that sell used clothing. Though most focus on good-quality designer women's wear, a growing number of consignment shops are also offering children's clothing. These stores are more trend-sensitive than thrift stores, so they tend to have less junk. But they're also more expensive, since they're run for profit. As their name implies, their merchandise is sold on consignment—meaning the "donor" gets a cut when an item is sold.

Head for the 'Burbs

People tend to donate to local charities, which is exactly why thrift stores are a shopper's gold mine: A growing number of these shops are located in affluent areas. The richer the neighborhood, the more likely you'll find top-quality designer clothing—no doubt donated by residents of that area. But no matter how good the clothing, you'll still pay only pennies on the dollar compared with buying retail.

WHERE BLUE BLOODS SAVE GREEN

Palm Beach is probably the last place you'd expect to find a thrift shop. But then perhaps it's by buying fancy threads at a fraction of their retail worth that the Old Money residents of "the island" manage to keep their money for so long.

At the Church Mouse (which calls itself a resale boutique rather than a thrift shop), the high-society locals buy designer gowns and other formal wear for anywhere from $25 to $500. Keep in mind that these clothes sell for thousands or even tens of thousands of dollars when new.

"Like a thrift shop, everything we sell is donated," says Church Mouse board member Janet Ware. "But it's not the type of clothing you'd find in your typical thrift shop. We get beautiful upscale merchandise donated from all over, not just from people who live on Palm Beach."

Of course, it's not Palm Beach style to drop names, but plenty of locals—who consist of some of America's richest families—shop secondhand at the Church Mouse, which is run by a local Episcopal church (and the money generated from clothing sales benefits local charities).

Just to see what was available, we did some test shopping at a few suburban thrift shops. Here's what we found: a $65 Liz Claiborne two-piece outfit priced at $7; several Perry Ellis shirts (men's and women's), originally $30 to $50, for $3.49 each; Calvin Klein lingerie, normally priced at $20, for $3.49; Dockers shorts that retail for $25 for $6.97. Average savings—80 to 90 percent! Furthermore, most of these items were in superb condition and looked as though they'd scarcely been worn.

Go to Goodwill for Summer Wear

A thrift store is a great place to buy the kids' clothing. Usually, the clothing is in very good condition because the kids outgrow it long before it wears out. As many parents know, a thrift store is the perfect place to buy summer wear.

For T-shirts, shorts and other casual summer clothes, you can't go wrong. On a good day, you might spend about $30 to outfit a child with five pairs of shorts and five T-shirts. *Compare:* Shopping retail, you'd get one pair of shorts and, if you're lucky, two T-shirts for the same money. Items like these tend to be the most often donated, so thrift stores have a large inventory. You not only get your choice of price but also get to choose style and color—assuming the inventory is large enough.

Make Pals with the Boss

Whether you're shopping at thrift stores or consignment shops, it pays to make pals with those running the business. By developing a friendly relationship with the owner or manager, you can convince him to give you a call when new items come in. Besides getting first crack at new inventory, "pals" are more likely to get an additional slight price break of between 5 and 10 percent for the asking.

Choose Your Words

Even if consignment-shop goods are very cheap, you can still ask for a special break. But ask gracefully, and you'll be more likely to get the deal you want.

Like this: Say you've found a suit that you're interested in buying, but it's too expensive. Instead of announcing "That's too much" or "It's not worth that price," tell the salesperson "It's more than I had planned to spend." That gives the clerk the option of suggesting a lower price or maybe offering a comparable item that's more within your budget.

Keep Tabs on the Tailoring

When you scour the secondhand clothing stores, keep in mind that a bit of tailoring can transform your old find into an almost-new garment. Sleeves and hems are the easiest to fix, so don't pass up a great buy because of minor tailoring hassles.

On the other hand, you should avoid buying clothes that you have to let out in the waist or legs. Older clothes that are slightly faded or have permanent creases will be virtually unwearable if they're let out in these areas.

CARE AND MAINTENANCE

No matter how much you spend on clothing, you'll spend less replacing those items if they are cleaned and maintained properly. With the right kind of care, you can add years of life to most garments. And here's how.

Give Your Wardrobe a Day's Rest

Clothes and shoes shouldn't be worn every day—even if they're the most comfortable, high-quality items you have in your closet. You'll extend the life of your wardrobe if you can give each outfit at least one day's rest after each wearing to allow it to regain its shape and maintain its fit.

Suits, dresses and other garments should be hung on shaped wooden hangers. And always put shoe trees in your leather footwear before putting it away.

TO BUY OR NOT TO BUY

Some low-cost new clothing is worth buying even if it needs alterations. But how do you tell whether alterations are feasible? Here are some clues.

Yes

- Seam allowances are big enough: You can let the garment out.
- Buttons need to be changed or moved.
- Waist or back seams must be taken in.
- There's at least a two-inch hem for lengthening.

No

- Garment is more than one size too large or too small.
- Shoulders need to be narrowed or widened.
- Lining has to be replaced.
- Garment is made from silk, velvet, leather or sheer fabric.

SEASONAL STORAGE THAT SAVES YOUR CLOTHING

You don't have to shop for expensive new clothes every season if you store good-quality garments carefully. Here are four suggestions from experts.

Make sure the garment is clean and dry. Hang it in a cloth garment bag that will allow the clothing to breathe.

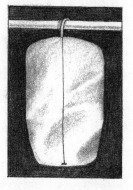

Store in a cool, dark, dry place. (Avoid storing in the attic, where excessive heat may cause old stains to reappear.)

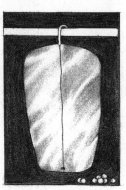

Use moth balls or bay leaves to repel insects.

Use molded hangers for coats and blazers. Avoid metal hangers, which can stain material (especially silk).

Line Your Pants

For about $5, in-store tailors can line the seat of a man's suit pants with the same lining material that's in the jacket. It's money well spent because the lining will extend the life of your suit by several years. Unlined pants are usually the first thing to go in a suit. With this seat lining, you'll prevent pants from prematurely wearing out.

Another tactic—encouraged by many clothing experts—is to buy a second pair of pants. Stores ranging from J. C. Penney to Brooks Brothers offer suit "separates" that allow you to buy a matching coat and pants together or separately. Usually, the extra pair of pants will run an additional $35 to $50 on the price of your suit. But you can probably wear the suit twice as long—because pants wear out about twice as fast as a jacket does.

Go Easy on Starch

Summer is the season for looking crisp and fresh, but don't rely on starch to help you. Spraying starch on your clothes can prematurely wear out your garments. Besides, starch can make wrinkles more visible—an important fact when you consider that wrinkles are more evident in cotton and other summer fabrics.

If you must use starch, use it sparingly—otherwise, you may find yourself replacing your clothing years before you should.

Press instead of Clean

Dry cleaning men's and women's suits is expensive and often unnecessary. In fact, dry cleaning more than twice a year can fade colors and make the fabric brittle because such harsh chemicals are used.

So unless there's a specific stain, experts recommend pressing instead of cleaning. A pressing costs about one-third less than dry cleaning—and removes wrinkles without ironing. Suits end up looking crisp and clean, but without the wear and tear of chemical cleaning.

Cut Your Spending on

MEDICAL
EXPENSES

- Drugs
- Hospitals
- Doctors
- Insurance
- Children's Health Expenses

TRIM COSTS IN SICKNESS AND IN HEALTH

The cost of staying healthy is enough to make you sick . . . but you probably already know that. After all, how can you not hear about the rising costs of health care? Once an issue discussed mostly by doctors, it's now a hotly debated platform (and a golden goose) for politicians, insurance companies, lawyers and consumer activists—as well as for Little League coaches and members of the Tuesday afternoon bridge club.

It's easy to see why: The cost of health care is skyrocketing. If the early 1990s are any indication, medical costs will continue to soar at a rate of about 10 percent per year. Even if costs level out, we'll still be spending about $900 billion each year—which is more than twice the amount we spend on our national defense, or about one of every seven dollars spent on the gross national product.

More bad news: This is an area where there's little room for bargains, since you're not likely to get a $500 price break on a hernia operation because it's the off-season. So you can't always cut your medical costs as easily as in other areas of spending.

But it's not impossible, either. In fact, most people can slash hundreds or even thousands of dollars off what they spend each year trying to stay healthy—without settling for second-rate medical care or health products. Here's how.

DRUGS

During the 1980s, the increase in drug prices was three times the rate of inflation. If this trend continues, economists predict the same prescription that cost $20 in 1980 will be more than $120 by the year 2000.

That's a bitter pill to swallow, especially when you consider that in the 1990s, the typical pharmaceutical company has enjoyed profits more than three times those of other Fortune 500 corporations. But here's how to keep some of that money for yourself.

> **WHERE YOUR MONEY GOES**
>
> • More than $2 billion is spent each year on products to treat side effects of prescription drugs. Of that $2 billion, most of the money goes toward other prescription drugs that prevent the first drug from adversely affecting you. The balance is spent on drugs that cure the side effects of the original prescription.
> • The typical job holder's contribution for employer-provided health insurance is $1,200 a year—or about $23 a week. That includes $550 spent each year on fees for doctors, dentists and laboratory tests that are not covered by insurance. Another $350 is spent on medications and on non-medication items such as eyeglasses and contact lenses.
> • The average American household spends $400 a year on personal care and hygiene products such as shampoo, soap and cosmetics. (For comparison: The same household spends an average of about $450 a year on education.)

Ask for the Generic
Save 50%

Most "name" drugs have a generic counterpart that contains the very same active ingredient and works just as effectively. Yet depending on the drug, generics can cost anywhere from 20 to 800 percent less than name brands—although most are about one-half of the cost.

Why the difference in price? Drug companies spend millions researching, developing and then promoting the name drugs to doctors and pharmacists, and they must recoup that money—so they charge a premium price. But generics use the technology developed for the name drugs and copycat the recipes to produce the same drugs for less. (Sometimes generics have different, lower-cost binders and fillers, which do not affect the drugs' healing effectiveness.)

Generics don't get to market unless the Food and Drug Administration feels that they get absorbed into the bloodstream as quickly and in the same quantity as the name brands. Yet even though there isn't one documented case of generic drugs causing a medical problem, doctors still routinely prescribe the name brands.

GENERIC DRUGS OFFER SAVINGS

How much can you save with generic drugs? A lot! Here's a comparison of the prices of some commonly prescribed pharmaceuticals and their generic counterparts. All figures are for the same dosage.

CONDITION	BRAND NAME	COST ($)	GENERIC NAME	COST ($)
Anxiety	Valium	21.79	Diazepam	7.99
Bacterial infection	Keflex	46.79	Cephalexin	21.79
Hypertension	Inderal	18.49	Propranolol	4.99
Muscle pain	Flexeril	25.79	Cyclobenzaprine	20.49

But there's a way around this, so you don't have to pay more. When your doctor takes out a prescription pad, simply ask "Is there a generic drug available for my condition? If so, I'd prefer it."

If you've already received a prescription, ask your pharmacist about generics. Unless the doctor writes "Dispense as written" on the prescription, most states allow pharmacists to provide generics instead of name brands to any customer requesting them.

Seek Out Samples

Doctors are given free samples of antibiotics and other prescription medications by drug company representatives. These are meant to be given to patients. So if your doctor says you need a particular drug, ask if you can be provided with enough samples to treat your condition. If the doctor has the medication in his office, it hasn't cost him anything—so he'll probably be happy to let you have it for free.

Order by Mail
Save 40%

If you have a chronic condition, you can order your medication in bulk through mail-order houses—and save anywhere from 5 to 40 percent off pharmacy prices.

Your doctor can supply you with names of private mail-order houses. They include Action Mail Order (1-800-452-1976), Medi-Mail (1-800-331-1458) and the American Association of Retired Persons (AARP) Pharmacy Service, run by the AARP and open to anyone over age 50 for an $8 annual membership. For a medication price quote, call 1-800-456-2226.

A word of caution, however. Don't just assume that you'll always get the cheapest price on every drug by ordering through the mail. If you frequently refill the same prescription, compare the prices at different mail-order houses—and also compare with prices at "chain" pharmacies.

Buy the Big Bottle
Save 35%

As with other products, buying over-the-counter medications in bulk can save you money. So for those products you use frequently—such as pain relievers and over-the-counter cold remedies—you'll save up to one-third buying the larger size.

For instance, a bottle of 100 aspirin that costs $8.99 amounts to 9 cents per tablet. A bottle of 50 tablets for $5.99 amounts to 12 cents per tablet—a 25 percent markup. While the savings vary from product to product, you'll generally save anywhere from 20 to 35 percent buying the larger size.

But make sure you check the expiration date. The bigger bottle is no bargain if you can't finish it before it expires.

Count Your Pills before Leaving

Whenever possible, count the pills in the bottle you receive and check the total against the prescription before leaving the pharmacy. Discrepancies between the number of pills prescribed by the doctor and what patients receive from pharmacists are common.

Ask about Age Discounts
Save 10%

Many pharmacies offer discounts to senior citizens, and some also give price breaks on medications for infants, children or students—so ask if you qualify.

IT PAYS TO SHOP AROUND

According to one study, the price of a particular drug can vary as much as 600 percent from one pharmacy to another. Much of that difference depends on factors such as special promotions, overhead costs such as rent and advertising and even the volume of pharmaceuticals purchased.

Experts agree that from a health standpoint, you should carefully choose a pharmacist and stick with that person. Generally, you get the best one-on-one service at smaller, independently run pharmacies—usually in your neighborhood. In these establishments, pharmacists are more likely to keep careful records of customers, which is one way to help avoid any possible side effects from new drugs that have been prescribed.

But from a financial standpoint, you usually get the best deals at larger "chain" pharmacies and those connected to larger supermarkets. Here's a cost comparison of what we found when shopping for different drugs at three different types of stores: a pharmacy located within a large food supermarket; a large "drug emporium" chain (a supermarket-size store that sells drugs and related products); and a privately owned independent neighborhood drugstore.

DRUG	SUPERMARKET ($)	EMPORIUM ($)	INDEPENDENT ($)
Cephalexin	6.75	9.50	16.99
Cyclobenzaprine	14.83	15.60	17.45
Diazepam	5.66	5.10	10.90
Flexeril	20.53	20.40	23.10
Keflex	40.98	38.45	45.17
Valium	16.98	16.05	29.84

Also, see if the pharmacy runs any specials on medications you need. Many frequently used prescription drugs periodically go on sale, just like other products. Either way, you may be able to save 10 percent or more off the price of the drugs.

Go with Store Brands
Save 20%

Most store-brand over-the-counter medications and products have ingredients that are identical to those found in name brands. (In fact, you'll notice they often have similar packaging.) The only real difference is the price—anywhere from 20 to 30 percent less for the store brands than for the more frequently advertised name brands.

For instance, you could pay $11.99 for a box of Sudafed nasal decongestant. But the store brand with the identical ingredients costs about $5.49—a savings of 46 percent.

So unless you feel that advertising improves a product's effectiveness, go with the store brand and save.

HOSPITALS

One night in a hospital bed usually costs about $800—more than ten times the amount just two decades ago. And that doesn't include the "extras"—such as surgery, medical checkups, medications and even tissues—that swell the costs to more than $1,000.

That means that a "minor" procedure can wind up costing tens of thousands of dollars. A major operation such as bypass surgery can cost as much as a house.

For most folks, insurance pays 80 percent or even less on certain items, meaning that you'll probably have to dip into your own pocket for a couple of thousand. So whenever possible, it pays to avoid lengthy hospital stays and unnecessary expenses. Here's how.

Take Your Own Pillow

Before you even set foot into a hospital, you could be on your way to savings hundreds of your own money—by telling the billing office that you'll use your own pillow.

Standard services such as pillows, towels and nightgowns are extremely expensive in hospitals, costing hundreds of dollars a day. So any charge you can avoid will mean a lower bill—as long as the billing office knows this beforehand.

For instance, some hospitals charge $300 or more each day for pillows, linens, nightgowns and slippers. But if you call the billing office before you go to the hospital and make arrangements to provide these items yourself, you can knock this charge off your bill.

Brown-Bag Your Three Squares

Same goes with meals: Since hospitals have clinical dietitians who prepare menus based on patients' needs, meals are notoriously expensive. Unless you need a special diet, it's cheaper (and probably tastier) to have friends and family bring your meals.

Check In on Tuesday

If you need to go to the hospital for tests, don't check in on a Friday. It's the most expensive day, because labs usually close for the weekend and you may waste 2½ days—and hundreds of dollars—just waiting for the labs to reopen Monday morning.

Since that waiting around will add at least $2,000 to your bill (based on the $800-per-night bed rate, although there will be extras), and most insurance pays 80 percent, you're looking at paying $400 out of pocket.

If you can, try to wait until Tuesday to check in. That way, the staff has time to catch up on the Monday rush, and your tests can be processed quickly.

Go Outpatient When You Can

Many procedures that have traditionally required a hospital stay can now be done on an outpatient basis, eliminating the need for a hospital bed (and a significantly higher bill). Same-day surgery is now common for hemorrhoid and hernia operations, cancer biopsies, cataract removal and dozens of other procedures—including childbirth without expected complications.

So before checking into a hospital, ask your doctor if your condition can be handled on an outpatient basis. If it can, you could cut $1,000 or more off your hospital bill.

Say No to Unnecessaries

In a hospital, you're charged for everything you use—and maybe even then some. For instance, if you need a tissue, you're charged for the box.

The best way to get around these extras is to take what you think you need (such as tissues) and refuse anything you feel you don't need (such as sleeping pills after you've had surgery).

If you do need some nonmedical supplies from a hospital, understand that you're charged for the entire unit—not just what you use. So instead of asking the nurse for a tissue, ask for the entire box. You'll be charged for it anyway.

Of course, you can get into some real money by agreeing to "routine" blood and urine tests that aren't related to your condition. If the doctor asks for the tests, no one will question it because the hospital and the lab make money from them. But all that lab work translates into a way of upping your bill. It's your right to refuse any tests unless your doctor gives you a good reason for needing them.

Demand an Itemized Bill

One study found that 97 percent of hospital bills in this country contain errors. Another study put that figure at 95 percent. Not a single study found that these bills are usually in the patient's favor.

The only way to spot excess charges is to demand an itemized bill and to go over it line by line. Most hospitals won't provide you with an itemized bill unless you request it—and you always should. Even if your insurance company is picking up the tab, higher hospital bills mean higher premium payments, so you wind up paying either way.

Take Your Loved One Home

More than one-half of medical costs are incurred in the last five days of life. Usually, this is a time when we say "We'll spend whatever we have to . . . money doesn't matter." But your loved one may prefer to be at home rather than kept in a hospital. Those last few days in the hospital may be a time when no amount of money can make a difference—yet people are tempted to spend tens of thousands of dollars on professional care.

So unless the doctor has strong objections, consider having your loved one spend those precious last few days at home. The surroundings are much more comfortable (since most people would rather be at home than in a hospital room), and the time you can spend with your loved one will be more personal.

Consider a Birthing Center
Save 65%

If you're a mother-to-be and your doctor approves, you can save up to two-thirds off the usual cost of hospital childbirth by having your child delivered at a birthing center rather than at a hospital. (There are approximately 125 birthing centers across the country.) Deliveries are usually done by a midwife, under the supervision of an obstetrician.

For more information on birthing centers near you, write to the National Association of Childbearing Centers, 3123 Gottschall Road, Perkiomenville, PA 18074-9546 (send $1 for shipping and handling).

Shop Around
Save 50%

Studies show that there's a wide gap in what area hospitals charge for the same room and what they charge to treat the same conditions. In fact, some hospitals charge as much as 100 percent more than others, according to one finding. Among nearly two dozen hospitals in and around Columbus, Ohio, for instance, the same gallbladder removal procedure varied from around $3,000 to nearly $7,600.

Most doctors are affiliated with more than one hospital, so you can pick and choose hospitals. And most hospitals can give you an accurate estimate of your bottom-line bill before you need to check in.

DOCTORS

Doctors control every aspect of your health. They not only diagnose your illnesses but also serve as gatekeepers to pharmacies, hospitals and other medical facilities. Besides the quality of care you receive, doctors also determine the amount you pay, since they set up their own fees and usually have at least some idea of how much drugs and certain procedures cost.

While you should always choose the doctor who gives you the best care, here's how to get top-notch doctoring at bargain-basement prices.

Get Advice by Phone

If you belong to a health maintenance organization, the doctor gets a set amount per patient from the insurance company. That means the doctor will always be paid the same, no matter how often he sees you.

Because of this—as well as the fact that some doctors see 100 or more patients per day—many physicians are happy to provide advice over the phone rather than have you come in for an office visit.

These free consultations (doctors rarely charge for these calls) are a good way to avoid the expense that results from trying to get answers you already know. If you're due for a follow-up visit, for instance, but you know your condition has obviously improved, you can usually substitute a quick phone call for an office visit. Similarly, if you need to get prescriptions filled, the doctor can call the pharmacy directly, saving you the time and expense of going to the office. So before making an appointment, ask the doctor's receptionist if your questions can be answered by phone.

Avoid Insurance Hassles
Save 50%

You can negotiate a doctor's fee—and you'll usually succeed if you offer an incentive. Many doctors are willing to cut their rates by as much as half for patients willing to pay up front rather than putting staff through the time and hassle of processing insurance claims.

If you carry regular health insurance and rarely go to the doctor, you may not meet your initial deductible—so you won't be reimbursed by the insurance company for money spent. If that's the situation, paying up front is a good way to cut a significant amount for a one-time office visit.

When you arrive at the office, ask the receptionist if the doctor offers discounts to patients who pay cash.

Help Science—And Get Medicine for Free

Universities and medical schools are constantly researching diseases and their cures. If you have a chronic condition or need special

HOME REMEDIES OFFER HEALING FOR LESS

Instead of running to the drugstore for some expensive relief, you might want to turn to your kitchen cabinet—and ease your pain for just pennies. Here are some medically approved, doctor-recommended home remedies for common health problems.

Age spots. Rub a slice of raw red onion or a cotton ball soaked with fresh lemon juice on the spot (but be careful not to get the surrounding skin). With this treatment, you can "bleach" out these harmless dark spots that result from years of sun exposure. The onion or lemon treatment works just as well as commercial over-the-counter products—and costs a lot less.

Athlete's foot. Soak your feet in a mixture of two teaspoons of salt per pint of warm water. This will help zap excess perspiration and hamper the fungus growth that causes athlete's foot. If you have excessively sweaty feet, use a hair dryer on your feet to dry them after bathing.

Bee stings and insect bites. Take the ouch out of stings and bites by making a paste of meat tenderizer and water. Apply it directly on the affected area. This works because most insect venom is protein-based, and the meat tenderizer breaks down protein. But be sure the meat tenderizer contains papain, the active sting-cooling ingredient. (Just read the label to find out.)

Corns. A brisk walk on the beach or another sandy surface acts as a natural pumice stone and helps "file down" foot corns—without the strong acids of commercial products.

Diaper rash. Save your money on baby powder. Store-bought types do little to treat diaper rash. A cheaper and more effective remedy: Spread a thin layer of cornstarch in a baking pan and

medical care, participating in these studies can benefit you in two ways.

- It will help you identify leading researchers in that field, so you know where to get information "straight from the horse's mouth."

warm it in an oven at 150°F for about ten minutes. Let the cornstarch cool completely, then dust it on baby's bottom.

Foot odor. Instead of shoe inserts and other products, try soaking your feet in a solution made from tea. You simply take two tea bags and boil them in a pint of water for 15 minutes. Add two quarts of cool water. Test the water to make sure it's cool enough and then soak your feet for up to 30 minutes. The harmless tannic acid in the tea helps feet and eliminates odors.

Hay fever. Although it's no substitute for medications prescribed by your doctor, avoid melon during the sneezing season if you're prone to hay fever. Experts say that watermelon, cantaloupe and honeydew can cause an itchy throat and swelling of the lips and tongue if you're allergic to ragweed. If birch tree allergies are your Achilles' heel, try avoiding cherries, pears, apples and peaches, which produce similar problems in some people.

Hemorrhoids. For $2 or so, you can pick up a jar of petroleum jelly (which is the "medication" applied to some expensive creams). For external hemorrhoids, a dab applied to the rectum with a cotton ball helps reduce pain and swelling.

Poison ivy. Calamine and other itch-fighting lotions cost several dollars. But there's a low-cost salve that works just as well: When a rash is blistering, apply a paste of baking soda mixed with water. Or apply a piece of gauze soaked in ice-cold milk, which helps dry poison ivy and soothe the itch.

Stuffy nose. You can buy expensive decongestants—but do you really need them? Eating spicy foods that contain hot peppers, Tabasco and other mouth burners helps relieve congestion by triggering the "running" reflex of your nose. Sniffing an onion or other strong smell also works.

• It could save you hundreds of dollars in medical costs. By participating in these studies, you usually get free (and frequent) exams and medicine provided by some top specialists.

Even if you suffer from just an occasional cold or the flu, you can still cut your health care spending by participating in one of these studies.

See a Jack-of-All-Trades
Save 40%

Although there are certain circumstances when a specialist is necessary, you're usually better off seeing a general practitioner. A general practitioner (also called a primary care physician) is able to treat the vast majority of illnesses and conditions just as effectively as a specialist—for about 40 percent less.

Studies show that the typical office visit to a general practitioner is $46, compared with $80 for a specialist—one reason why specialists earn so much more money. And while a specialist is the best person to treat an uncommon or complicated disease affecting a certain body part, most experts recommend that you see a general practitioner for the "run-of-the-mill" problems.

Avoid Emergency Rooms
Save 50%

Unless a life-threatening or very serious illness or injury is involved, try to avoid an emergency room. Many people without regular doctors go to emergency rooms for treatment—only to have near heart attacks when they get their bills.

An emergency room visit is usually twice the cost of a visit in a doctor's office—or more. And most conditions can just as easily be handled as an "emergency" in your doctor's office. (In fact, going to an emergency room is no guarantee that you'll get faster treatment. Unless it's truly a life-threatening condition, you may wait for hours in a busy hospital emergency room.)

So if you don't have a regular doctor, find one. Or if you need a doctor when your regular physician can't be reached, ask for an on-call replacement.

Get Your Own Second Opinion

When your doctor suggests you need a second opinion, he will usually give a name and even provide you with a phone number. More often than not, the doctor's referrals are being made for friendship's sake—and you're just paying twice to hear the same view.

If you're paying for a second opinion, it only makes sense to get what you pay for—a truly objective view. And you should get a second opinion for major procedures such as surgery. So find your own doctor for a second opinion rather than accept another doctor's referral.

INSURANCE

There are only two developed countries in the world that fail to provide their citizens with national health insurance—the United States and South Africa. Which is exactly why so many Americans regard medical insurance as one of their most essential job benefits.

Still, more than 37 million Americans go without employer-paid health benefits. Many either pray to stay healthy or pay an average of $600 a month to get on a family medical insurance plan.

Even if your employer pays for most or all of your health benefits, you still need to use them wisely in order to keep your premiums low and make the most of your (and/or your employer's) money.

Become a Groupie
Save 40%

Loners lose when buying insurance, since individual policies typically cost anywhere from 15 to 40 percent more than group policies. They also tend to offer fewer benefits.

You can get into a group policy, even if you have no job or no friends with whom to "group." All you have to do is join an association, club or professional organization and tap into its policy. For instance, you can get group health insurance by joining the American Association of Retired Persons, auto clubs, trade unions, college alumni groups, local small business organizations and other groups.

Most group policies have lower monthly premiums and lower deductibles. Also, the group plan is more likely to accept people with pre-existing medical conditions (which rarely happens if you apply for an individual policy). But be sure to shop around when looking for a group plan, since premiums can vary widely.

Buy Direct from the Carrier
Save 10%

If you're buying your own medical insurance, bypassing an insurance agent or broker can shave 10 percent or more off the price of your policy. (An agent works for one company, while a broker represents dif-

WHAT INSURANCE TERMS MEAN

You can have a better idea of where your money goes by learning how to decipher the murky text in your policy.

Co-insurance. This is another term for the percentage of medical expenses you pay after you meet the deductible. Usually, the insurance company pays 80 percent of your expenses, and your co-insurance pays the remaining 20 percent.

Co-insurance stop-loss limit. Many policies set a stop-loss limit on the total amount of co-insurance you must pay in a calendar year. For instance, if your policy has a $2,500 stop-loss limit, the insurance company will pay 100 percent of your medical costs after you pay the deductible and the first $2,500. Beware of policies with no stop-loss limit. Otherwise, if you have 20 percent co-insurance and you run up $100,000 of bills—which you can easily do if you have a serious accident or illness—you'll end up paying $20,000 out of pocket.

Deductible. This is the amount of money that you must pay out of pocket to cover medical costs before the insurance company pays anything. Deductibles typically range from $100 to $500 per person and can go as high as $2,000, meaning you must spend that much money on medical fees and expenses before the insurance company pays its share. Typically, the higher

ferent companies; both get comissions for selling insurance policies.)

It may seem that acting as your own broker is time-consuming, but it's really not: After all, it takes a lot of time and effort to find a good broker—plus you really have to review all the policies that are presented to you.

Call insurance companies directly to find out how to review policies, but make it clear that you want to save money by not using an agent or broker.

Check into HMOs
Save 35%

If you're looking for the best price in health insurance, most experts suggest going with a health maintenance organization (HMO).

the deductible, the lower your monthly premium.

Exclusions. These are the things that your insurance may not cover. Typical exclusions include things such as outpatient mental health treatment, cosmetic surgery, maternity benefits and long-term care. Exclusions may also cover pre-existing conditions (those you had before getting your insurance), such as hernia, asthma and cancer.

Reasonable costs. This is the amount the policy will reimburse you for specific medical costs, based on what the insurance company considers to be the "going rate." The problem is that some companies set reasonable cost limits far below what doctors and hospitals in your area actually charge.

For instance, if your policy pays 80 percent of your costs and sets the reasonable cost for a day in the hospital at $500 when the going rate of local hospitals is $630, you may have to pay $230 a day (since $400 is 80 percent of your insurer's estimate of $500).

If you're shopping for health insurance, ask the company for a list of their reasonable cost limits. Many companies are hesitant to reveal this information, but it can be the deciding factor on whether you enroll with that company. So be persistent!

Renewal policy. Be certain that the insurer you choose guarantees renewal. Otherwise, it can refuse to renew your policy if you get sick.

An HMO tends to offer better coverage, and you pay very little in out-of-pocket expenses. Typically, the only direct charge is a $5 co-payment each time you visit the doctor or have any prescription filled. There is usually no deductible.

Since HMOs emphasize preventive care, they sometimes offer extras such as discounts for fitness club memberships, weight loss and nutrition classes and annual physicals. The main drawback, however, is that an HMO limits your choice of physicians. You can visit only a "participating" doctor—and since HMOs require the doctor to do a lot of paperwork, some doctors don't like to treat HMO patients.

While you may have to pay a higher weekly "contribution" for employer-offered HMOs, the extra up-front money pays off—especially if you have children. You should compare an HMO with Blue Cross/Blue Shield and similar insurance plans. Typically, these insurers require you to pay significant out-of-pocket expenses—a $250 or $500 deductible plus 20 percent of doctors' fees. Also, with a regular health insurer, you'll pay more for prescriptions. All told, the typical family spends anywhere from one-third to one-half less with an HMO than it would spend for regular health insurance.

Pay Premiums Annually

If you have hearty cash reserves and pay for your own health insurance, you can save a lot of money by paying your premium semiannually or annually rather than in monthly installments.

For instance, one insurance company charges a 25-year-old male living in California $223.20 if he pays monthly. But if he pays every six months instead of monthly, his cost is $1,294.64. The bottom line: By paying semiannually, he saves $44.56. And if he pays the entire year's premium in one lump sum, he doubles his savings. Most insurance companies offer similar discounts for paying in lump sums.

CHILDREN'S HEALTH EXPENSES

It's ironic how such tiny bodies can run up such large medical expenses. That's because when adults get sick, they tend to "gut it out." But when Junior has a sniffle or sneeze, Mom and Dad quickly call the doctor.

True, no one wants to deprive a child of health care. But there are a few ways to lower your expenses while you still give your child all the attention he needs.

Let the County Immunize Your Child

Immunization against certain diseases is required by law for all children. These mandatory shots total anywhere from $300 to $400 throughout childhood, yet some insurance plans don't cover the cost of getting them.

If that's the case with you, realize this: Every state in the United States provides free or low-cost immunization through state or county health services. Many of these agencies will pick up the cost (or sometimes split the difference with your insurance company), even if you're not considered low income. To find out about these programs in your area, contact your county or city board of health or state health department.

The Centers for Disease Control and Prevention (CDC), based in Atlanta, funds 63 immunization programs scattered across the United States. If you get your child in a CDC program, you can get shots for $5 or less, depending on your income. In some cases, these shots may be free.

Get Free Care for Your Kid

If your child is eligible for a medical study, you may be able to get top-notch care for little or no cost.

For instance, more than 10,000 children from Massachusetts were asked through their doctors to participate in the Boston University Fever Study. Among other things, the study investigated whether ibuprofen (Advil) was as effective in treating children's fevers as the more commonly suggested acetaminophen (Tylenol). As part of this study, pediatricians asked parents if they wanted to get free medicine (as well as a thermometer) in exchange for filling out a two-page questionnaire on how the medicine affected their child's fever. It took about ten minutes to fill out the questionnaire, and the parents received $20 worth of medical supplies.

While these studies are few and far between, it's worth asking your doctor if he knows of any. Because scientists try to verify what's already known, your children aren't being used as guinea pigs. Instead, researchers are trying to get more positive evidence to back up their initial finding. Usually, these studies require little input on your behalf and can help offset your medical bills.

Let the School Play Doctor

Each September, many schools sponsor area doctors to come in and give students free eye, hearing and dental exams. While these freebies aren't meant to replace a child's visits to his regular physician, they can be a cost saver—considering that the typical medical exam costs $50 or more.

Ask your school administration or Parent-Teacher Association about the medical programs at your child's school. Besides the examinations, there are programs such as administering fluoride tablets (in areas without fluoridated drinking water) and free flu shots that can help cut health care costs.

Cut Your Spending on

HOME MAINTENANCE
AND
ENERGY COSTS

- Lawn and Garden
- Windows and Doors
- Kitchen and Bath
- Painting
- Hot Water Heaters
- Roofing
- Pest Control
- Heating and Cooling

SAVE MONEY
ALL OVER YOUR PLACE

It's no wonder they say a man's home is his castle. You usually need a king's ransom to keep it properly maintained and comfortable.

There are all those leaks and squeaks. There's trying to keep up with the Joneses *and* those soaring energy bills. Attempting to have a beautiful and efficient abode is enough to send you to the poorhouse.

But it doesn't have to be that way. In fact, there are dozens of things you can do to make your home more attractive and less expensive to operate.

What's more, many of these jobs are inexpensive and take little time and even less talent. So whether you're an accomplished handyperson or just all thumbs, you can cut your maintenance costs and increase your home's energy efficiency. Keeping your home well maintained also makes you money in the long run—since it will be more desirable to buyers when you're ready to sell.

LAWN AND GARDEN

Take landscaping. It's cheap, with ornamental bushes and trees starting around $10. It's easy, requiring only the ability to dig a hole. And you profit in more ways than just having a beautiful yard.

WHERE YOUR MONEY GOES

- The typical household spends nearly $2,000 a year for utilities such as electricity, heating fuel, water, garbage collection and telephone service. These costs actually decreased slightly after the mid-1980s, mostly because homeowners improved energy efficiency.
- Homeowners spend nearly $600 a year on maintenance and repairs. Renters spend about $25.
- Almost $450 a year is spent on housekeeping supplies. About one-fourth of this money goes for cleaning products.

PLANTING DOES PAY—EVEN WITH WATERING

If you haven't planted shade trees around your home because you think it'll cost too much to water them, you're all wet.

Even if you figure in the cost of watering trees, the savings on lower heating and air-conditioning bills are five times the amount you'd save in water costs by not planting them, according to a study by researchers at the University of Arizona in Tuscon.

In other words, if it costs you $5 a month to water your trees, you'll typically save $25 a month in energy bills. To make the most of watering, do it at night or in the early morning, before 8:00 A.M. That's when there's the least evaporation, so more water has a chance to get down to the tree roots.

Studies show that for every dollar spent on landscaping, you recover $2 in increased house value when it's time to sell. In other words, a $500 landscaping job increases the worth of your home by about $1,000. Here's how to make the most of your lawn and garden for less.

Plant Some Trees
Save 30%

Leave it to Mother Nature to provide us with yet another financial windfall from her bounty: a significant savings in energy costs.

You can lower your heating and air-conditioning costs between 10 and 30 percent simply by planting deciduous trees—that is, the kind that shed their leaves in fall—on the south and west sides of your house. They'll shade those sides of the house in summer, but in winter, after their leaves fall, they let the sunlight through, which warms up the house. In fact, the shade from most trees can reduce or even eliminate the need for air-conditioning in summer.

If you plant evergreens on the side of the house that gets prevailing winter winds (usually the north side), they'll serve as a windbreak. The boughs of a full-grown pine or hemlock provide a shield against cold air, keeping your home warmer, so you need less heat.

But make sure you choose trees and shrubs that grow well in your

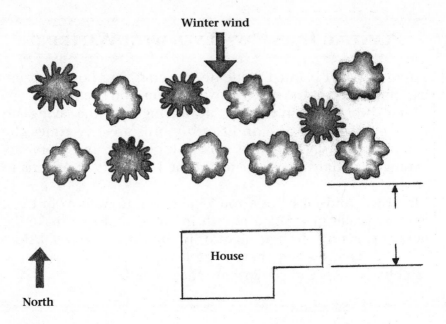

Winter wind

North

House

Evergreen trees on the north side of the house will block the winter wind.
Result: **a snug house and lower heating bills.**

area. Your state Cooperative Extension Service has lists of low-cost plants that do well in particular regions. (For the number of your state's Cooperative Extension Service, you can check the Blue Pages of the phone book or call your state government's information number.) Or look at plant lists in gardening books at the public library. The plants that grow fastest—and therefore give you the best value—are the ones best suited to your climate.

Buy in Bulk
Save 30%

Any time you're buying more than two trees, ask for a discount. Since nurseries and tree farms deal with a "live" inventory, they need to move merchandise quickly and are usually willing to give price breaks to customers who buy in bulk.

Our experts suggest that you ask for a 30 percent discount on each additional tree after you buy the first two at regular price. Or you can ask for one free tree for every three you purchase.

Plant in the Fall
Save 25%

Popular wisdom says that you should do your planting either in the spring (before it's too hot) or in the fall (before it gets too cold). But

---

SPEND LESS AROUND YOUR YARD

You can have a rich, beautiful lawn and well-kept garden beds without having to go broke. Here are some ways to care for everything that grows in your yard without spending a fortune.

Save on mulch. Instead of buying mulch at $3 a bag, call your municipality's streets department. Often your town or city government has road crews that remove fallen trees and grind them into mulch. This mulch is free for the asking. Also, tree care companies will often dump a load of mulch for free—especially if they've been pruning a tree in your yard or on your street.

You can also use old newspapers and brown paper bags as mulch—and they're very effective for weed control. Lay them in the same areas you'd use mulch, and wet them thoroughly (so they decompose). You'll also need to cover them with one layer of wood chips, so they don't blow away.

Save water. Most automatic sprinkler systems are set to a timer, and they'll begin spraying water on schedule, even if it's right after a huge thunderstorm. You can eliminate that problem by buying a Rain Check gauge, a device that makes sure the system won't water an already wet lawn. The gauge is easily connected to the sprinkler system, costs about $12 and is available at most garden shops and home centers.

Make free fertilizer. You don't need high-priced fertilizer when your lawn and kitchen produce organic materials to make your own. Start a compost pile—tossing in leaves, vegetable parings and nonmeat kitchen leftovers. Within a year, you'll have enough rich compost soil for a good-size vegetable garden.

Don't overspend on sod. If you're planting a lawn, use seeds or plugs. They're at least half as expensive as ready-made sod.

CUT COSTS—PLANT TREES

Landscaping can be expensive, but not if you're willing to do some digging. You can save hundreds of dollars if you buy trees in the fall and plant them yourself. Here's how.

To plant a balled-and-burlapped tree: Make a hole bigger than the root ball and line the bottom with a few inches of peat moss or other organic matter. Set the tree at the same level it grew before. (Don't bury the trunk—and make sure none of the roots is exposed.)

When the hole is partially filled, tamp the soil and open the top of the burlap as shown. Fill the rest of the hole, covering the burlap. Water thoroughly.

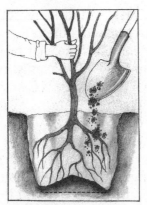

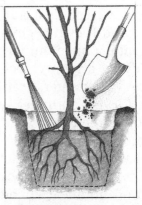

To plant a bare-root tree, allow plenty of room for the roots to spread out. Position the tree so that the base of the trunk is even with the soil line.

Fill the hole to slightly less than ground level with loose soil, working it around the roots. Then water to settle the soil.

even though fall is a good time to plant, most people wait for spring fever to hit before they visit the nursery. This year, don't wait for April or May: You're losing out on a bargain.

By buying and planting in the fall, you can get some fantastic bargains on trees and large ornamental plants because nurseries are trying to unload their stock before winter. Prices are typically between 25 and 50 percent lower in October and November compared with spring, as nurseries frantically try to move inventory.

What's more, many gardeners recommend planting in the fall. Trees are just going into their dormant period, so they're less likely to be set back by transplanting. And when the weather turns warmer and they begin putting on spring growth, they'll have a good head start.

Enlist Some Student Aid

If you're all thumbs rather than a green thumb when it comes to gardening work, there's a way to get a professional landscaping job for much less money: Call your local university.

Students studying landscape architecture or horticulture should be able to propose a new design for your property. And sometimes they can even do the planting themselves. Occasionally, they can even get you the trees and bushes for free. (And if you do have to pay, it's usually wholesale prices.)

The best way to get this "student aid" is to contact the department head at a local university. Then negotiate with the students who are recommended. If you pay the students an hourly wage, you should be able to get the same service for several hundred dollars less than a professional landscaper would charge.

WINDOWS AND DOORS

Many of the newly manufactured doors and windows are better insulated and sealed than those found in older homes. In fact, installing new windows, though expensive up front, will cut your spending because of their energy efficiency—if you live in the house long enough to earn back the initial costs. But there are other ways to save without any major investment. Here's how to pocket more money even if you have old doors and windows.

Pass the Candle Test
Save 10%

This winter, when the weather turns cold and the heat goes on, give your doors and windows the "candle test." Very carefully (you don't want anything to catch fire!) move a lighted candle slowly around the frame of each door and window. If the flame dances around, you know there's a draft, which means heat is escaping. If a lot of windows need sealing, you could be paying 10 percent too much every month in heating costs. And if you use air-conditioning during the summer, you're also overspending on your cooling costs.

A dancing flame means you need to caulk and weather-strip around the frames of doors and windows. You can do this to a complete house—about 12 windows and two doors—for less than $25 in materials.

Using a tube of caulk and a caulking gun, apply the caulk to the outside of the door and window frames. Smooth it out with a wet Popsicle stick or finger. After it sets, if you like, you can paint over the caulk. An entire house can be done in a few hours.

Many kinds of indoor weather stripping are available, both metal and plastic. If you use plastic weather stripping—which has its own

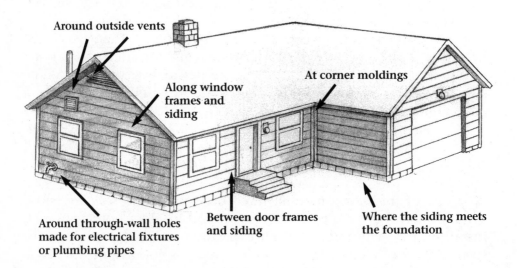

Around outside vents

Along window frames and siding

At corner moldings

Around through-wall holes made for electrical fixtures or plumbing pipes

Between door frames and siding

Where the siding meets the foundation

Caulk all exterior seams, cracks and joints to keep out water and pests that could damage your house. Here are the places to caulk.

CAULK IS CHEAP

Energy bills can skyrocket if heat leaks out through the cracks and crannies of your home. But it's easy to caulk the exterior. Here are four simple steps.

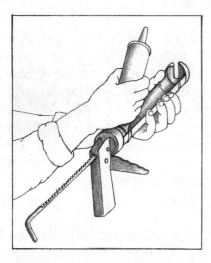

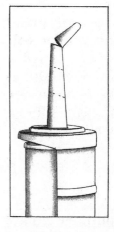

All standard caulking packages fit in a caulking gun. To load the gun, pull back the plunger rod (teeth side up) and fit the cartridge into the gun.

Trim the tip of the cartridge at a 45-degree angle—cutting it near the tip to make a thin bead or near the base to make a heavier bead. Using a long nail, puncture the seal inside.

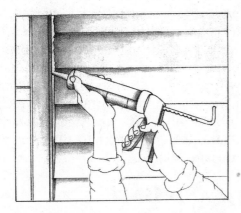

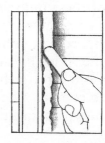

Hold the caulking gun at an angle to the joint and apply steady pressure on the trigger, filling the crack with sealant.

To shape the caulk into a smooth, concave seal, slide a wet Popsicle stick along the joint.

adhesive—be sure the door or window frame is clean and dry before attaching the adhesive. (Otherwise, it's likely to peel off.) Tacked-on metal stripping is more permanent and durable.

Draw (or Open) Those Shades
Save 10%

During warm weather, keeping shades or curtains closed—especially on windows that face south and west—can keep your home cool enough to reduce air-conditioning costs by about 10 percent. And vice versa during cold weather: When Old Man Winter is in peak form, keep the shades or blinds up—or curtains open all the way—to let in sunlight. Our experts estimate that you can reduce heating and cooling bills by about 10 percent by following this seasonal cycle.

Reflect Some Light
Save 15%

In southern climes, it's definitely more energy-efficient to have windows that reflect the sun's rays—but only some are designed to do this. Even without those windows, however, you can still figure out some low-price ways to keep out the heat.

You can buy awnings or solar reflective film for windows and glass doors. Awnings help block out the sun's rays, while the film reflects about 75 percent of these rays: Either measure keeps your home cooler and results in lowering air-conditioning costs by about 15 percent.

A few power companies (particularly in the South) will even help pay for these improvements. For a typical three-bedroom house, the power company's contribution may be about one-third to one-half of the total cost of either window treatment. Also, some power companies offer price breaks if you have a heat pump installed—to recirculate warm air and heat your home more efficiently. Contact your electric company's customer relations department to find out what company-paid incentive programs are offered.

KITCHEN AND BATH

Renovations in the kitchen and bathroom are probably the most cost-effective you can make in your home. With some well-placed investments in these areas, you can save in day-to-day living expenses—and you'll make money on these improvements when it's time to sell your home in a few years. Since so much of your time is spent in the kitchen and bathroom, improvements in these areas definitely improve your lifestyle as well. Here's how to invest a little in these areas for a lot of savings.

Repaint Your Bathtub

A bathtub may begin to look dingy after years of use—but do you need a new one? Probably not. Most tubs will last indefinitely, and they can be repainted for a fraction of the cost of a new tub.

Whether you're renovating your bathroom or just sprucing up the tub, compare the price of repainting with the price of a new one. And instead of spending the $800 to $1,500 it costs to purchase and install a new bathtub, have your current tub repainted instead. Professionally done, the job costs about $300.

Go with Flow Restrictors
Save 30%

For less than $10, you can install water flow restrictors in faucets or "low-flow" shower heads that can cut water consumption by up to 70 percent. Once they're installed, you'll hardly notice the difference in

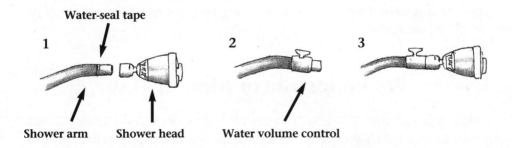

To install a water control device on the shower head: (1) remove the shower head from the shower arm and wrap the threads with a water-seal tape; (2) screw the volume control onto the shower arm and tighten until snug; (3) wrap water-seal tape around the threads of the volume control, replace the shower head, and tighten.

PROJECTS WITH THE BEST PAYBACKS

What are the best home renovations? According to *Remodeling* magazine, the following remodeling jobs are most likely to give you some payback when it's time to sell your home. They increase your home's value and appeal the most. The table shows how much each improvement increases your home's resale value, as compared with the original cost of the project.

JOB	AVERAGE COST ($)	RESALE VALUE ($)	RECOUP
Bath addition	9,500	9,000	94%
Family room addition	29,000	24,200	83%
New master bedroom suite	22,000	17,500	80%
Bath remodeling	7,300	5,700	78%
Deck addition	6,800	4,800	71%
Sunroom addition	18,900	13,500	71%

water flow—but you will notice the difference in your bills. The savings in water usage translates to cutting your hot water costs by about 30 percent. Besides being inexpensive, these devices are easy to install, since they fit right into existing fixtures and shower arms in about ten minutes.

Fix Up instead of Ripping Out

Kitchen cabinets get a lot of use, and they do show their age. But that doesn't mean you need to rip them out and replace them—at a cost of $5,000 to $10,000. Instead, dress up your existing cabinets for a new look. You can save 95 percent of that money if you buy new knobs and hardware to replace the old. Or spend well under $100 on materials to strip, sand and refinish the cabinets. Or for about 10 percent of the price of cabinets, you can put on new "fronts"—doors that look like brand-new cabinets. At a minimum, you should be able to save 80 percent of the cost of installation—and end up with cabinets that look as good as brand-new.

PAINTING

The first four letters of *painting* say it all. But it's not painting that causes most of the pain—it's the scraping and sanding that go beforehand. Nevertheless, doing your own painting is one of the best ways to cut your home maintenance costs and up the value of your home sweet home. Labor accounts for a whopping 80 to 85 percent of the cost of a paint job, according to our experts, even though fewer special skills are needed than for other repairs.

To Save—Spend in the Right Places

Don't settle for less than the best when you go out to buy paint and materials. A low-quality paint won't last more than a couple of years, meaning you'll have to repaint quickly and pay more money (and waste more time) than if you had coughed up a few extra bucks

---

BRUSH UP ON SAVINGS—PAINT LIKE A PRO

For a professional-looking paint job at a fraction of the cost, do it yourself. Here's how to use a roller so that the paint goes on smoothly.

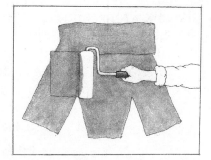

When using a roller on large areas, begin by making an M shape, starting with an upward motion of the roller.

Fill in the M by rolling back and forth horizontally.

up front. Don't skimp on quality brushes or rollers, either. Cheap bristles will fall out and get into the paint, and poor-quality rollers won't cover evenly. Once you've decided you can do the job, you've already saved hundreds—even thousands. So quality paint products are really an investment rather than a cost.

Stick with Similar Monochromes
Save 50%

Even if the label of a paint can promises one-coat application, you may need two coats if your new color varies greatly from the one you're painting over. This is especially obvious when you're covering a dark color with a lighter one. But it can be noticeable with all paints, no matter what their shade.

By sticking with similar tones, you can use about 50 percent less paint and get the job done a lot faster.

Buy Markdowns
Save 70%

If you need only a gallon or two and don't have your heart set on Auburn Sunset or Appalachian Rose, why not settle for another shade that's almost the same color? Just visit your nearest paint supply store and ask whether any custom colors are left over.

Custom colors are mixed specifically at a customer's request. But they often find their way back to the paint store because the customer bought too much or simply changed his mind. Or the clerk gets the mix wrong, and the custom color doesn't match the custom sample. Either way, the store is then stuck with a custom color, which is usually discounted at 40 to 70 percent off list price. If you ask the clerk to show you the custom color "rejects," you may end up paying as little as $2 per gallon, even for the best-quality paint.

Spray-Clean the Exterior
Save 50%

Some exterior painting jobs don't need paint at all. If the exterior siding of your home is just dirty, all it needs is a good cleaning to make it look "freshly painted."

Wand

Pressure washer

A pressure washing may restore the brand-new appearance of wood and aluminum siding—and at much less cost than a new paint job. When using a pressure washer to clean exterior siding, wear rubber boots, gloves and safety goggles—and don't point the high-pressure spray at doors or windows.

For about $75 a day, you can rent a pressure washer from most tool rental shops. That's about one-half of the cost of buying the paint needed to cover the exterior of a typical three-bedroom home.

Another benefit: You can pressure-wash the entire house in just a few hours, while it can take days to repaint it.

Don't Hire until Winter
Save 30%

If you want to hire someone to do painting for you, wait until the winter. Spring and summer are the big seasons for painters—and are no time to get bargains. But from late September to February, painters have less work. You can usually get a better bid during those months—often 20 to 30 percent less than "summer" prices. Snow season is no time to have the exterior painted, of course—but it's a perfect time to have someone do the interior work for less.

Don't Spend Twice—Get a Guarantee

When getting bids, be sure to ask the painter whether the work is guaranteed. A good paint job will last five years, and the contractor should be willing to correct any chipping, blistering or peeling problems at no cost to you during that time.

Be sure to check the painter's liability insurance coverage with the company that covers him. Painting can be dangerous work, and you don't want to be held liable for injuries any contractor sustains while on your property. Also, you should check to see if your state or community requires contractors to be licensed—and if so, ask for the painter's license.

HOT WATER HEATERS

A single load of wash uses 40 gallons of heated water. A bath needs about 20 gallons. A dishwasher consumes 14, while a shower takes 10. Add it all up, and the typical American family probably uses about 600 gallons a week—which may explain why your hot water heater consumes anywhere from 19 to 30 cents of every dollar spent on electricity.

But here's how to cut your hot water bills without having to resort to cold showers.

Get a Timer
Save 35%

Your hot water heater is heating water all the time—while you're at work, on vacation or even asleep. Every few minutes, the heater

EASY STEPS TO SAVE WATER

The surest way to cut your water bill is to cut water consumption. By practicing these six easy steps, you can slash your monthly water bill by as much as 20 percent.

WHAT TO DO	HOW MUCH IT SAVES
Take a shallow-water bath rather than a shower.	15–20 gallons/day
Run only full loads in the washer and dishwasher.	75–200 gallons/week
Keep a bottle of drinking water in the refrigerator.	200–300 gallons/month
Rinse vegetables in a filled sink rather than under running water.	15–250 gallons/month
Water the lawn in the evening instead of at midday.	300 gallons/month
Use native or drought-resistant plants.	750–1,500 gallons/month

"boils" water to the set temperature, and each boiling uses energy.

By installing a water heater timer, you can make your hot water heater work only during the off-peak hours—during the night, when rates are cheapest. Even though the heater shuts off in the morning, there's usually enough hot water to last through the rest of the day. If you keep the timer set for off-peak hours, you can cut your hot water costs by as much as 35 percent. Water heater timers cost about $30 at home improvement centers and can be installed by the do-it-yourselfer in about 45 minutes.

Choose the Right Temperature
Save 10%

Most hot water heaters are set to heat water to between 140° and 145°F. The thermostat is set at the time of installation, and most people don't bother changing it. But by lowering the setting to 120°, you'll have water that's hot enough for most household chores, and you can reduce your hot water energy costs. In fact, you can reduce

WHEN SHOULD YOU HIRE A CONTRACTOR?

By doing regular maintenance and renovations yourself, you can save up to 60 percent off the price of having a professional do the job. But by tackling jobs exceeding your ability, you may wind up paying 20 percent more through goof-ups and emergency service calls.

So how do you know when to call a pro? If you're an accomplished do-it-yourselfer, you probably already know what jobs are within your abilities (and when you should a call a pro). Unfortunately, it's usually those folks who only *think* they're handy who bite off—and pay—more than they can chew.

While you're the best judge of your abilities, here are some guidelines from experts to help determine when you should hire a professional. Those categories marked "DIY" are for the typical homeowner with some knowledge of home repairs, a proven track record of minor fix-ups and adequate to good proficiency with tools.

When you do hire a contractor (after calling references and checking licensing), insist on a written contract that spells out the payment schedule. You should never pay everything up front: Instead, give 25 percent to start the job and the rest upon completion. Or schedule payments in thirds.

The contract should also specify cancellation penalties and provide a complete description of the work to be done. Also, any change in the orders should be agreed to, in writing, by you and the contractor.

Beware of "formula" contracts purchased at office supply stores. They favor the contractor. Besides, why doesn't the outfit have its own letterhead?

water heating costs 2 to 10 percent by lowering the thermostat setting, according to studies by Florida Power and Light Company.

What's more, a 120°F setting is much safer than the higher temperature. (One blast of 140° water will scald a person's skin in a mere ten seconds.)

JOB	DIY	CALL A PRO
Clean chimney		✔
Install skylight		✔
Hang exterior shutters	✔	
Fix broken windows	✔	
Build outdoor shed	✔	
Install house siding		✔
Build deck	✔	
Insulate attic	✔	
Install acoustical tile ceiling	✔	
Wallpaper	✔	
Paint interior	✔	
Install wall paneling	✔	
Install/repair electrical fixtures		
• door chimes		✔
• dimmer switches	✔	
• nonworking outlets		✔
• track/recessed lighting		✔
Clean carpet	✔	
Install wall-to-wall carpeting		✔
Install hardwood floor		✔
Refinish hardwood floor	✔	
Install vinyl or tile floor	✔	
Install kitchen cabinets		✔
Install kitchen countertop		✔
Install new faucets	✔	
Install hot water heater		✔

And it will take you only about five minutes to change the temperature setting. Simply remove the cover plate that's on the front of your heater with a screwdriver. Change the setting (also with the screwdriver) so that the arrow points to 120. Then replace the thermostat cover.

Choose the Right-Size Heater
Save 15%

When you have to replace your hot water heater, you might also consider changing the size. A small-capacity heater may cost less up front, but you'll spend extra if it has to work overtime to keep up with your family's water needs. That could drive up your hot water costs by as much as 15 percent.

So make sure you get the right size for your household. For a family of three or fewer, a 50-gallon size is recommended. Families with four to seven people should have an 80-gallon unit, while a household with more than seven people needs a hot water heater with a 100-gallon capacity.

Drain Regularly
Save 10%

The most important maintenance job on a hot water heater is often ignored by homeowners. According to home energy experts, you should drain sediment from the bottom of the heater every few months.

To drain the hot water heater, unscrew the bottom cap, attach a hose, and drain off the "dead" water at the bottom of the heater, along with any sediment or mineral deposits that may have built up. That way, you remove the water and sediment that can prevent your heater from operating at peak efficiency. It takes about 20 minutes and should be done every three months. Failing to regularly drain your unit can add about 10 percent to your annual hot water bill.

Blanket It
Save 15%

Most newer heaters (those purchased within the past five years) have interior insulation to keep water hot. But if your heater is older, you can buy a specially fitted insulating blanket for about $10 at any home improvement center.

Alternative method: Wrap a piece of wall or ceiling insulation around the heater and seal it with duct tape. Either way, you can reduce your costs by up to 15 percent because the water stays hot for longer periods and doesn't need to be reheated as often.

INSULATE FOR SAVINGS

To insulate a hot water heater for energy savings, use R-11 fiberglass and duct tape. Cut the insulation and tape it as shown, leaving openings for the controls and drain faucet. (Be sure that you don't cover the flue collar on a gas heater.)

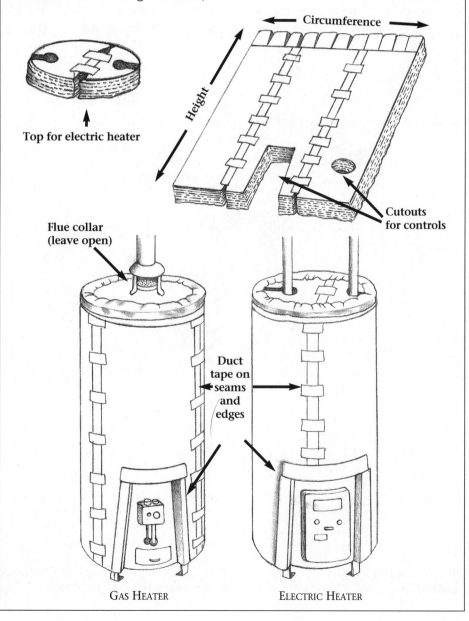

Top for electric heater

Circumference

Height

Cutouts for controls

Flue collar (leave open)

Duct tape on seams and edges

GAS HEATER

ELECTRIC HEATER

Wrap Your Pipes for Energy Savings

Hot water cools as it travels through the pipes in your house—and that means you're wasting the energy needed to heat it. To prevent cooling, wrap all exposed hot water pipes with insulated pipe wrap, available at any home improvement center for about $5 per three-foot section. Depending how much pipe you can wrap, you may cut your need for additional hot water (and its cost) by about 15 percent.

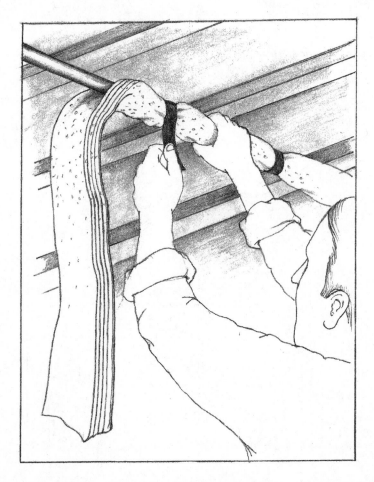

Save on energy costs by wrapping all hot water pipes that run through unheated spaces. Wrap with insulation secured with electrical tape.

ROOFING

If you need a new roof, you may have noticed that replacement costs have gone . . . well, through the roof. For most homes, a new roof costs between $3,000 and $6,000. And those costs can soar above $15,000, depending on the size of the roof, the materials used and whether or not the worn roof must be removed. Even minor repairs can cost several hundred dollars.

But here's how to squeeze the most out of your money while getting a roof that will stand the test of frost, sun, wind and time.

Revise Your Roof
Save 10%

Depending on your climate, light-colored roofing can make a big difference in helping to keep a house cool in the summer. (A dark-colored roof helps warm the house in winter—but the benefit is very minimal.) So if your next roofing job calls for new shingles, choose white, light gray or a light pastel color—especially if you live in a warm climate. Also, make sure that there's good ventilation in the attic or crawl space and insulation in those areas.

With a lighter-colored roof and improved ventilation and insulation, you can reduce your summer cooling costs by 10 percent or more and make your home more comfortable during hotter months.

Lend a Hand
Save 50%

If you're moderately handy, you can lend a hand to the contractor and cut your costs by as much as 50 percent, depending on the extent of your "sweat equity."

For example, if your current roof must be removed before you install the new shingles, consider having the contractor tear off the old roof and haul away the debris. Have the contractor install the sheathing and building paper and stack the new shingles on the roof. Then you can install the new shingles yourself—saving up to 50 percent!

Even a novice do-it-yourselfer can patch a roof, hang downspouts,

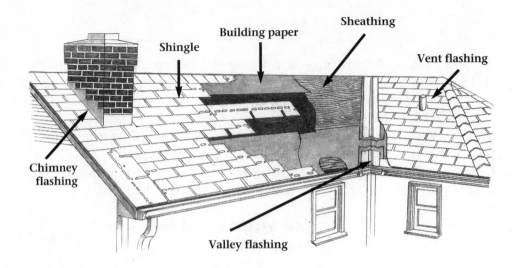

You can save hundreds of dollars on a new roof if you have a contractor start the job, then finish it yourself. Hire the contractor to do the sheathing and to tack on the building paper; then install the flashing and shingles yourself.

install cooling vents or even shingle the entire roof, according to our experts. Your public library has plenty of books with detailed information on these jobs. You can also rent how-to videos at many video stores (the series by "Hometime," a PBS program, is particularly good) or even get some tips from clerks at your neighborhood home improvement center.

Even if you're new at the fix-it game, there are still plenty of chores you can do to save the contractor time (and to save you money), such as disposing of garbage and other gofer jobs.

When taking bids from roofers, find out what type of discounts are given for your participation. Discuss chores that fit your abilities and get approximate time estimates for doing them.

Foil the Heat
Save 15%

If you're building a new home or getting a new roof on an existing home, ask the roofing contractor about placing a radiant barrier over the roof sheathing. This barrier is usually a reinforced layer of foil

SAVE A ROOF—AND A BUNDLE OF CASH

Reshingling a whole roof is an expensive proposition, but you can postpone the cost by doing some springtime caulking and patching. Here's how.

Add years to the life of a roof by doing minor, low-cost repairs on shingles. If wind has lifted or curled asphalt shingles, use a caulking gun to secure them with quick-setting shingle cement.

If an overlapping shingle is torn, coat the underside with roofing cement and press it flat. Nail both sides of the torn shingle, then cover with more cement to seal.

With well-ventilated attic space, light-colored shingles and reflective foil under the shingles, your house will stay cooler in summer—a good way to save on air-conditioning costs.

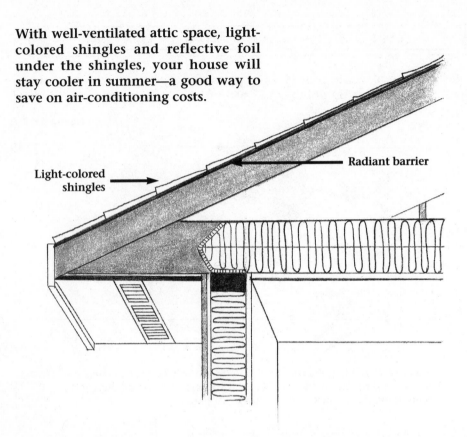

Light-colored shingles

Radiant barrier

that is stapled to the roof's plywood deck. The reflective material (such as Thermaseal, Homasare and other products) prevents 95 percent of the heat from the roof's surface from entering your home. This simple installation can cost as little as $200 for an average-size roof. A radiant barrier reduces cooling costs by as much as 15 percent a year because your attic stays cooler.

During the winter months, the radiant barrier has the opposite effect—helping to keep warmth in the attic space—so you save on heating bills as well.

PEST CONTROL

Whether you're trying to rid your dog of fleas or rid your house of termites, pest control measures can take a big bite out of finances.

Here's how to stretch your dollar when you want to eliminate pests from your home.

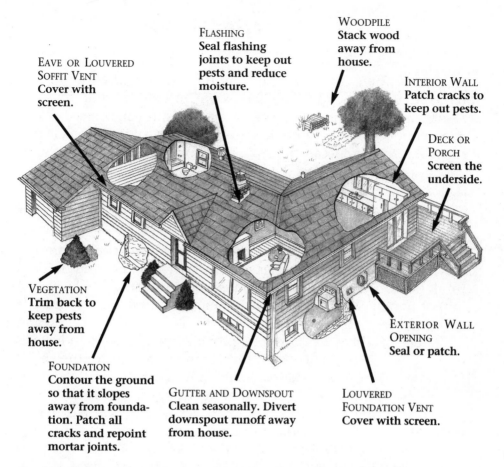

FLASHING Seal flashing joints to keep out pests and reduce moisture.

WOODPILE Stack wood away from house.

EAVE OR LOUVERED SOFFIT VENT Cover with screen.

INTERIOR WALL Patch cracks to keep out pests.

DECK OR PORCH Screen the underside.

VEGETATION Trim back to keep pests away from house.

EXTERIOR WALL OPENING Seal or patch.

FOUNDATION Contour the ground so that it slopes away from foundation. Patch all cracks and repoint mortar joints.

GUTTER AND DOWNSPOUT Clean seasonally. Divert downspout runoff away from house.

LOUVERED FOUNDATION VENT Cover with screen.

To prevent expensive damage from insects, rodents and other pests—and to control the moisture that attracts them—take these low-cost precautions around your house.

Nuke Roaches with Cukes
Save $300

Instead of spending the typical $25 a month on a professional exterminator (who sprays potentially harmful chemicals in your home), you can keep cockroaches away the natural way—by placing slices of cucumbers in cupboards and other roach-filled areas.

The cukes contain a chemical component that's been found to repel roaches, according to studies. Bay leaves may also do the trick, so sprinkle them liberally in those dark areas where roaches hide.

Treat Exterior Wood
Save $800

Treating a home infested with termites can cost anywhere from $800 to $2,500, depending on the extent of damage. But you can prevent termites in the first place by making sure all exposed wood surfaces connected to your home are treated with an insect repellent.

For about $25, you can have an exterminator spray newly built

---

DO YOU HAVE TERMITES?

Although termites exist in every state but Alaska, they're most prevalent in Florida and other warm-weather states. And don't think that only homes with wood exteriors are susceptible. Termites can make their way through concrete foundations to feast on wood beams inside.

"If your neighbor has a termite problem, you're likely to have one, too," says Joel Paul, director of communications for the National Pest Control Association. Here's how to be sure.

Look for the insects. They swarm in clusters from February to May, depending how early spring arrives where you live. Termites will spend only a few minutes flying around, but if you spot them when it's happening, you'll know they're in your vicinity. Besides swarming around the base of your home, they can also be seen around trees.

Check the exterior of your home. Termites betray their presence by narrow dirt tunnels, or tubes, that rise from the ground. If you see these telltale tunnels, they're a sign that subterranean termites are moving up into the house. (The other variety is the dry-wood termite, which lives in the wood rather than in the soil. You might have this kind of termite even if you don't see the tunnels.)

Avoid storing firewood within ten feet of the house. Termites in the firewood can easily travel to a wood-frame house. Also, if you scatter decorative wood chips around, they should be no closer than three feet from the foundation. (For borders next to the house, stick with decorative stones.)

wood decks with a pesticide that prevents termite infestation. It's advisable to do this when you're constructing an addition. Any wood structures connected to your home should be termite-proofed with a treatment.

To deter termites, also be sure that there is at least 18 inches of space between the soil and wood. If you're designing an add-on wood porch, for instance, it should be at least 18 inches above the ground.

Go Over-the-Counter
Save $1,000

Termites aren't the only wood-scarfing critters in your home. Carpenter ants and powder post beetles also destroy wood. Any time you see sawdust on top of wood surfaces—indicating damaged joists and subfloors—you need to take action quickly.

But don't assume the damage is caused by termites. So before spending the money for a professional extermination, do your own detective work and determine what kind of wood-munching pest is causing the damage. If the problem is caused by carpenter ants or powder post beetles, you can use Dursban, a product manufactured by the pest control division of Dow Chemical Company.

Use Powder Power
Save $30

It takes at least three "flea bombs" every few months to adequately control fleas. But each bomb costs about $10. There's a better way to go. For the price of just one bombing, you can buy a year's worth of an even more effective flea controller: diatomaceous earth. Just spread some in the nooks and crannies of your home, and the fleas will stay away. You can purchase DE (as it's called) at garden supply stores.

It works because its crystalline structure cuts through the waxy coating on fleas as they walk across it, causing them to dry out and die. But be sure not to use the type of DE available at pool supply stores; it's ground so fine that it may be dangerous if inhaled.

Hint: If you have pets, it's a good bet that your home has fleas. To be sure, walk across the floors (particularly carpeted areas) wearing white socks. The fleas will go for the socks, since they're attracted to warmth and vibrations. If your socks are dotted, your home has fleas, so it's time to buy some DE.

Get an Exterminator with a Warranty

If you need a professional exterminator, you'll probably have many questions—on what was found, how it's treated and the expected results. But before signing on the dotted line, be sure to ask any exterminator: "What kind of warranty do you offer?"

Look for the company that offers you the longest warranty, with no charge for an annual visit during that warranty period to recheck your home. In addition, the pest control company should be willing to promise in writing to treat and/or repair damage caused by these insects after service begins—at no charge to you.

HEATING AND COOLING

No matter where you live, the largest slice of your energy costs goes toward heating and/or cooling your house; for some folks, one-half of every dollar spent on electric or gas energy goes toward keeping their homes heated or air-conditioned.

But don't think that your local power company has all the power to determine how much you spend. There are ways to lower your heating and cooling costs, without affecting your comfort.

Insulate Your Attic
Save 30%

You can reduce your heating and cooling costs between 20 and 30 percent by investing a few hundred dollars in insulation. An entire attic can be done in one afternoon: This is one of the easiest home projects you can do.

Insulation comes in various forms. The types that can be installed by the home handyperson include rigid boards and rolled batts. (You can also have foam blown in between the rafters—but this is a job for an insulation contractor.) Insulating power is measured by R-value; the higher the number, the more effective the insulation. To find out what R-value is recommended in your area, ask the salesperson at your home improvement center. A typical attic can be insulated for $250 to $500.

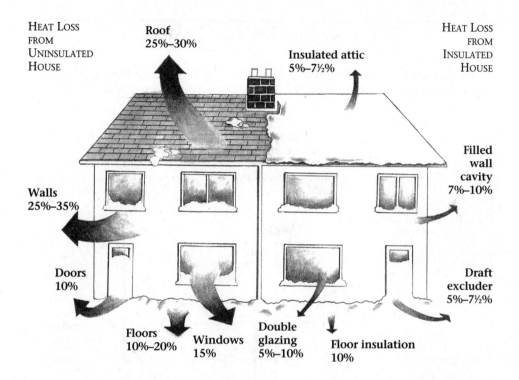

Heat Loss from Uninsulated House

Roof 25%–30%

Insulated attic 5%–7½%

Heat Loss from Insulated House

Filled wall cavity 7%–10%

Walls 25%–35%

Doors 10%

Draft excluder 5%–7½%

Floors 10%–20%

Windows 15%

Double glazing 5%–10%

Floor insulation 10%

Insulation can make a drastic difference in heating bills. By insulating the attic and walls, heat loss is reduced by 25 percent or more.

Seal the Right Windows
Save 10%

Poorly sealed windows that are located near your thermostat give the thermostat a false reading. Your furnace will continue to work even though other areas of the house have reached a comfortable temperature. All windows within 15 feet of a thermostat should be caulked, weather-stripped and locked tight.

For the same reason, you shouldn't place lamps too close to an air-conditioning thermostat. Heat from the lamps gives the temperature sensor a false high reading, and the air conditioner will stay on even though the room is generally cool enough.

Buy Oil with Your Buddies

There *is* power in numbers when it comes to buying heating oil. If you have neighbors who also use heating oil, you can form a fuel-

STOP THE ENERGY LEAKS

By caulking, insulating and taking a few other energy-saving precautions, you can save hundreds of dollars on your energy bills.

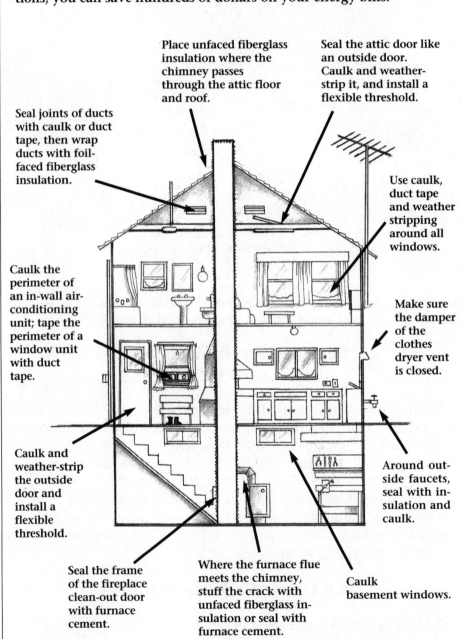

Place unfaced fiberglass insulation where the chimney passes through the attic floor and roof.

Seal the attic door like an outside door. Caulk and weather-strip it, and install a flexible threshold.

Seal joints of ducts with caulk or duct tape, then wrap ducts with foil-faced fiberglass insulation.

Use caulk, duct tape and weather stripping around all windows.

Caulk the perimeter of an in-wall air-conditioning unit; tape the perimeter of a window unit with duct tape.

Make sure the damper of the clothes dryer vent is closed.

Caulk and weather-strip the outside door and install a flexible threshold.

Around outside faucets, seal with insulation and caulk.

Seal the frame of the fireplace clean-out door with furnace cement.

Where the furnace flue meets the chimney, stuff the crack with unfaced fiberglass insulation or seal with furnace cement.

Caulk basement windows.

buying club and save 5 to 25 cents per gallon. For the typical consumer, that translates to savings of up to $170 per year.

It works like this: Neighbors pay $5 to $25 a year for membership in the group. Since heating oil companies offer lower prices for volume orders, your group negotiates directly with the dealer.

To organize a fuel-buying club, contact your local consumer affairs office or heating oil companies in your area.

Close the Fireplace
Save 20%

When it's not in use, your fireplace is little more than a vacuum made from brick or stone, sucking heat or air-conditioning out of

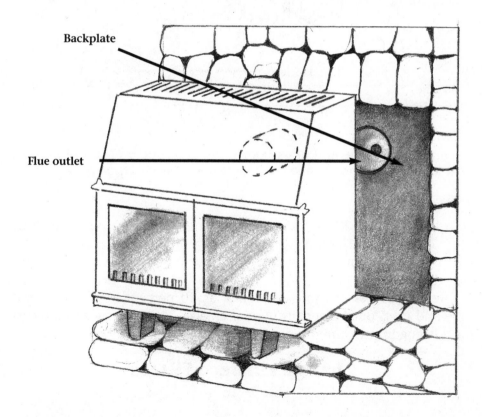

You can close off the chimney to cut heat loss—but still use your fireplace. Install a freestanding heater, with a backplate to close off the fireplace opening.

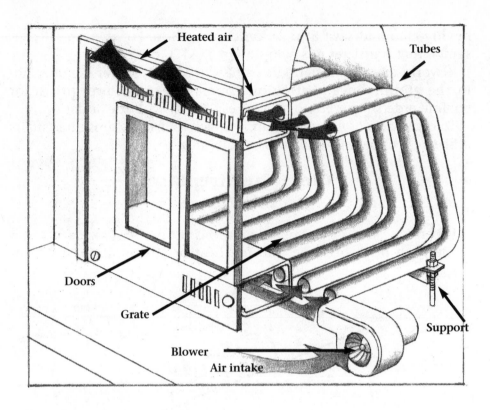

A combination tube and glass door insert for your fireplace eliminates heat loss through the chimney and increases fireplace efficiency.

your home. If you leave the damper open when the fireplace isn't in use, you're paying about 10 percent too much in energy costs. So when wood isn't burning, don't burn your money—keep the damper closed.

You can save even more—as much as 20 percent—by installing a tube and glass door insert in your fireplace. These items, available at most home improvement centers, start at about $100.

Change Furnace Filters
Save 15%

It costs less than $1 to buy a new filter for your furnace, but that simple chore can save you hundreds of dollars over time. Filters should be changed every four months—and always before the winter heating season begins—in order to keep your furnace at peak efficiency.

Failing to change filters can clog vents, waste energy and result in you paying about 15 percent too much in energy costs.

Put a Dent in Vent Use

You may unknowingly be wasting hundreds of energy dollars a year—simply by using kitchen and bath ventilating systems. In just one hour, these odor-removing fans can also blow away a houseful of heated or cooled air (which means you have to heat or air-condition your house all over again). So if you must use vents to remove odors, turn them off after two or three minutes.

Cut Your Spending on

APPLIANCES

- How to Shop for Savings
- Service Contracts and Warranties
- Refrigerators and Freezers
- Air Conditioners and Fans
- Washing Machines
- Clothes Dryers
- Dishwashers
- Ranges and Cooktops
- Home Entertainment Systems
- Personal Computers

GET A BARGAIN ON TODAY'S TECHNOLOGY

Appliances are designed to make our lives easier. So why is it so hard to read those monthly utility bills or to believe all those zeros on price tags in appliance showrooms?

No doubt about it—refrigerators, washing machines, dryers, TVs, personal computers and other appliances improve the quality of your life. But you'll also notice that they add to your bottom line—sometimes more than you'd like.

Popular wisdom says it's all part of the trade-off. Well, popular wisdom is wrong.

You *can* enjoy today's technology without having to pay today's sky-high costs. There are scores of ways to cut your spending when you're buying and operating appliances—and not sacrifice a lot of time, convenience or energy.

In about five minutes, for instance, you can slash the cost of running your freezer by $60 or more a year. (All you need are a few plastic bags filled with plain tap water.)

By spending about $5 for materials from any electronics store, you can enjoy the same kind of "stereo TV" quality that costs your neighbors hundreds of dollars more.

As for energy savings, you *can* run appliances more cheaply.

And the next time you go shopping for high-quality appliances or electronic equipment, you can pay just a fraction of what the price tag demands.

HOW TO SHOP FOR SAVINGS

Did you ever notice that there's a big difference in price for the same item from store to store? Even the same item in the same store changes price from week to week.

WHERE YOUR MONEY GOES

- Americans spend nearly $90 billion a year redesigning their kitchens.
- Microwave ovens, once considered a nice luxury, are now called "the most important lifestyle necessity" by affluent Americans. More than 80 percent of families earning more than $100,000 annually say they "can't live without" their microwaves, according to a poll by the Roper Organization. The only other appliance to earn this honor is the telephone answering machine (although VCRs and home computers are also considered very important).
- Women look for practicality when buying appliances. But men prefer kitchen appliances with a high-tech look. Children and teens are drawn to appliances with special features such as freezer water dispensers.

That's because there's not one set price for that new TV or dishwasher you want but rather a range of prices. Although the salesperson isn't about to admit this, buying appliances is much like buying a car. There's a sticker price—the top-dollar asking price—and a separate, lower amount that the salesperson can accept and still make money. Since the markup may be as high as 100 percent or more, that refrigerator with a price tag of $700 cost the store only about $350. So the salesperson has a lot of room to bargain.

Getting that discounted price depends on several factors: inventory and demand, competitors' pricing, the buying "season," whether or not you want "extra features," the salesperson's quota and his ability to meet it that month. But perhaps the most crucial factor is knowing some tricks of the retail trade.

Case in point: Let's say you want a new appliance. You probably go to a nearby retailer and begin looking at the inventory that suits your budget. There you encounter a friendly salesperson who immediately starts pointing out all the special features. You may think he's just a helpful chap who's doing his job by "explaining" the product, right?

Perhaps . . . but more likely, he's trying to gauge your lack of knowledge about that item, a common practice in retail sales. The less you know about it (which he can determine by your reaction to his sales spiel), the theory goes, the more likely he can sell you—and for top dollar. Once convinced you know little, he'll probably move on to another common strategy—trying to convince you that you need a more expensive item.

But by having a few tricks up your sleeve, you can slash your spending the next time you're shopping for appliances. Here's how.

Ask for a Discount
Save 15%

You wouldn't think of paying the full asking price for a new car or a new home. So why do it for a TV or refrigerator?

The fact is, you could get up to 15 percent knocked off the price tag—simply by asking. Insiders tell us that some salespeople will lower the price—as long as you have a good reason for "deserving" a discount.

Good reasons include:

- Having seen the item on sale at that store for a lower price. Many people don't realize that you can ask for and get a sale price even when the item is not on sale.
- Being a return customer who's been satisfied with your previous purchases.
- The promise of "bringing in" more business for that particular salesperson in exchange for a deal. (*Example:* Tell him that you intend to recommend his store to other people. And it's true: Every satisfied customer brings in more customers by word-of-mouth recommendations.)

Prove You've Shopped Around
Save 20%

If the item is on sale and you still want to cut your spending, fret not. All you have to do is clip newspaper ads—and you may save 20 percent or more the next time you walk into an appliance store.

Salespeople religiously follow pricing strategies at competing stores. That means they know you can probably get it for less at another store. But they won't admit it—unless you have proof. So here's your strategy.

- Next time you shop for any appliance, read the ad pages of local newspapers and magazines every day for two weeks. Pay special attention to papers from Friday to Sunday, when most appliance sales are advertised.
- Clip ads for the appliance you're shopping for. Those ads with the lowest prices go on the top of your clipping file.
- Carry that file with you when you head for the appliance store.
- If the salesperson doesn't offer you a lower price, show him the ads with the better deals.

For instance, if you're shopping for an $800 refrigerator, you might find advertisements for that item ranging from $650 to $850. If you visit a store where the sticker price for the unit you want is $700, show the $650 ad.

"Can you meet or beat this price?" you ask. If the salesperson can't, ask to see the manager. If the manager can't give you a discount, head for another store.

Look for Stores with a "Can't Be Beat" Policy

As long as you do your homework (clipping ads), you can be sure you'll get the lowest price if you visit retailers with a "guaranteed" lowest price policy. The deal is, they'll meet or beat any advertised special.

In fact, some retailers even give you an additional 10 percent discount if you find the same item for less (so look for such claims in advertisements or on store signs). But once again, you have to prove there's a lower price—by having the advertisement in hand when you visit the store. Simply saying that you've "seen it cheaper" isn't enough.

Ask about Accessories

Buying an electric range? Seal the deal if the salesperson throws in, at no charge, a $20 range cord (which connects the range to its power source). Buying a VCR? Ask for a complimentary multi-pack of videotapes. Getting a computer? Schmooze for some free software.

In most cases, salespeople make no commission on these small items—ranging in price from $10 to $100—and are more than willing to give them away if they think it will close the deal.

But since they usually don't offer these "freebies," you have to make the first move—after you've negotiated your best deal and the salesperson still isn't sure he's got the sale.

"Tell you what," you say. "I'll take the VCR at that price if you throw in two multi-packs of videotapes." He gets his commission at a price that pleases his manager; you get $20 worth of tapes that you'd probably wind up buying anyway.

Buy Last Year's Model
Save 25%

If you're not a slave to state of the art, you can nearly always get discounts ranging from 10 to as much as 25 percent by buying close-outs or last year's models. It's a good way to cut $50 to $125 off a $500 purchase.

Each year, newer models tend to have higher prices—usually between 5 and 10 percent—yet the actual features don't change much from year to year, if at all. In one comparison-shopping trip, for example, we discovered that one name-brand refrigerator that had retailed for $799 one year was selling for $899 the next year—for almost the identical model.

Here's what you do.

- Call area retailers when you're ready to buy. Tell them the item that you're looking for and ask when the new shipments are coming in.
- Go to the store about a week before the expected arrival. You'll likely encounter salespeople who are under orders to "unload" old merchandise to make room for the new.
- First ask the salesperson to show you closeouts. These items may have discontinued colors, features or other small differences that don't jibe with the new models arriving next week. Sometimes they're just hard-to-sell items. As a result, they're discounted up to 25 percent off regular prices.
- If there are no closeout items, pick what you like from the "old" inventory and ask for 15 percent off the sticker price for a quick sale. He'll probably tell you the item is already discounted, but in most cases, you can still get even more off the price by politely pressuring.

SUPER SAVINGS FROM YESTERYEAR

Last year's appliances usually cost a lot less than just-arrived-from-the-factory models. To find out how much less, we compared sample prices for a dishwasher, range and refrigerator early in the year—when the previous year's models were still in the stores. The features on the new models and the old models were almost exactly the same. But look at the difference in price!

APPLIANCE	LAST YEAR'S MODEL ($)	CURRENT MODEL ($)	SAVINGS ($)
Dishwasher	659.99	699.90	39.91
Range	799.99	879.97	79.98
Refrigerator	799.97	899.97	100.00

"Argue" Your Way to 20% Off

A surefire way to get a discount is to make the salesperson think that he's about to lose your business (and his commission). One way to do this is to let him think you're interested in another item not carried in his stock.

One way to get this across is by playing "good cop/bad cop" with your spouse.

Let's say you're shopping for an electric range at Kitchen Kubbyhole. You discuss the range you liked in the last place you visited—Chef's Cornerstore—while your spouse favors the one the salesperson is showing you now. The stronger you argue for the Chef's Cornerstore product (point out features as well as price), the harder the salesperson will try to sway you to your spouse's "thinking." Finally, he'll realize he has to lower the price to clinch the sale.

The next time you shop at Kitchen Kubbyhole, try this.

YOU (TO SPOUSE): I don't know; this model is nice, but I like the Energ-eze we saw at Chef's Cornerstore.

SPOUSE: Yes, but this one has the self-cleaning feature.

YOU: Maybe, but it costs $120 more—and simply having a self-cleaning oven isn't worth that kind of money! Besides, the one we

---

ASK TO BE PREFERRED—AND PAY 35% LESS

Many retail chains keep records of "preferred customers," or customers who have consistently purchased from their stores or sent business their way. These pampered patrons are sent special invitations to preferred-customer sales, usually held two to four times a year, that entitle them to discounts not available to the general public. Find out from the salesperson how you can have your name added to this privileged list.

---

saw at Cornerstore had a second timer. And this one doesn't. If we got $70 off (the value of the feature in question), then maybe . . .

By now, the salesperson will probably bite—and offer you a discount of 5 to 10 percent. Show a little more interest, but keep leaning toward the competition while your spouse pushes for the item he's showing. Eventually, you'll probably get a price break close to what you asked for.

Have a Friend in the Business?
Save 50%

You can get the biggest savings of all with a little help from a friend, provided he's in the appliance sales business. Employees at large chain stores usually get substantial employee discounts: They can buy appliances at cost or slightly above. Since that amounts to only about one-half of the retail price, you'll get major savings if you know the salesperson and you can make the purchase at his employee rate. (Or you can buy it slightly above that rate and give him a commission.)

Example: A refrigerator that retails for $999 might be purchased on employee discount for $500. If you pay $600, you've given your friend $100 for his trouble, and you've still cut your spending by 40 percent. If your friend doesn't ask for his "cut," you get the fridge for 50 percent off retail!

But it isn't fair to insist: Some companies frown upon excessive purchases by their employees, and you might put your friend in an awkward position if you push for this deal.

Use Private-Label Cards
Save 20%

One of the easiest ways to save is to get a private-label credit card instead of using your usual credit card.

More and more retailers are offering private-label cards, which usually mean interest-free financing and no down payment. That gives you an interest-free payment plan. By using the private-label card instead of a regular credit card, you could save $100 or more in interest charges. (Most credit card companies charge annual interest rates between 15 and 20 percent on the unpaid balance—which quickly adds up if you pay off the balance in installments.)

SERVICE CONTRACTS AND WARRANTIES

You know the scenario: After you've decided which product you want to buy and you've settled on a price, the salesperson leans over confidentially and says "But between you and me, here's what manufacturers are doing nowadays." Then he proceeds to spin a story about the many things that can go wrong with your glittering new purchase—and how much it will cost to fix. The windup comes when, pulling out some more papers, he urges purchase of a service contract. "Added insurance," he explains.

Why do salespeople push so hard for you to buy these service contracts? Because they're easy money for the retailer—and the salespeople usually get a hefty commission for selling them. But is a service contract really worthwhile?

To answer that question, here's some advice from savvy shoppers.

Start a Breakdown Fund
Save $100

Many consumer advocates advise against buying a service contract—which can cost more than $100 for between three and five years of "protection" that you usually don't need.

Instead of buying a service contract, set up your own "breakdown" bank account. Every month, put away $10, just as you would for a Christmas club. At the end of five years, you'll have $600. If you need

SAVE $150 OR MORE BY NOT PLAYING THE NAME GAME

Some brands, as we all know, cost a lot more than others. But what are you really paying for? A classier "look" and label—or a better piece of equipment? While there are some differences in quality, they may not be as significant as the salesperson would like you to believe.

That's because many appliance companies manufacture multiple brands. While the pricier brands may have more bells and whistles, the "insides" are often very similar—if not identical. For instance, General Electric also manufactures Hotpoint appliances (as well as RCA televisions). That General Electric refrigerator may cost you an additional $250 or more compared with a similar-size Hotpoint—even though there is little or no difference in the actual mechanics of the two.

Others playing the name game:

- Frigidaire, owned by A. B. Electrolux of Sweden, also makes Gibson, Tappan, Kelvinator and White-Westinghouse.
- Whirlpool also puts out KitchenAid, Roper and Estate.
- Admiral division of Maytag manufactures Crosley, Magic Chef, Maytag, Jenn-Air, Montgomery Ward and Norge.
- Philips also makes Magnavox and Sylvania.
- Matsushita makes Panasonic, Prism and Quasar.
- And Sears's Kenmore line can be made by any number of companies: Amana, General Electric or Whirlpool.

To find out the price differences, we shopped around retail stores for some well-known brands of ranges, refrigerators, washers, dryers

repairs, you'll have money to cover them; if not, the money can collect interest—or can be used to buy another brand-new appliance that you may need by then.

This "breakdown" fund is a better alternative because your money works for you—whether or not you use it to make appliance repairs. Besides, it's an easy way to build a tidy nest egg.

and dishwashers—and discovered that prices for similar models may differ by as much as $170. Models used for comparison all have similar features and capacity.

BRAND	PRICE ($)	SAVINGS ($)
Dishwashers		
KitchenAid (made by Whirlpool)	419.99	
Whirlpool	259.97	160.02
Dryers		
Whirlpool	329.97	
Estate (made by Whirlpool)	299.97	30.00
Ranges		
Roper (made by Whirlpool)	500.00	
Whirlpool	450.00	50.00
Refrigerators		
Frigidaire	689.99	
Kelvinator (made by Frigidaire)	519.97	170.02
Washers		
General Electric	369.97	
Kenmore (made by General Electric)	319.99	49.98

Still Want Insurance?
Look to the Manufacturer

Another alternative is to inquire about a manufacturer's service contract (as opposed to a service contract sold by the retailer). This is also called an extended warranty or a service agreement and may be offered by mail or telephone. It's sometimes cheaper than a retail-sold service contract. But even if it's not, the agreement is a better choice because the repair work is done by the actual manufacturer instead of by a local repairman, who may or may not have expertise in fixing your particular brand.

Check Your Warranty

Most appliances also have what's called an implied warranty that can last as long as four years, depending where you live. Unless the product is marked "as is" when you buy it, the Federal Trade Commission says that "almost every purchase you make is covered by an implied warranty."

There are two types of implied warranty. The warranty of merchantability promises that the product will do what it is supposed to do—the toaster will toast. There's also a warranty of fitness for a particular purpose, which means that the product is suitable for a particular use: A VCR with eight-hour capability will record for eight hours.

It's good to know about implied warranties in case the manufacturer tries to sock you with all repair bills. Implied warranties, however, are no guarantee that you'll automatically get a refund if a product is defective. The company may be entitled to try to fix it first if your product falls within your state's implied warranty time period.

REFRIGERATORS AND FREEZERS

Buying a refrigerator or freezer is a decision that can affect your pocketbook for decades. Shelling out for the unit itself is only the beginning. You also have to pay to run the unit for 15 to 20 years.

New efficiency standards, which took effect with 1993 models, reduce costs: A new 18-cubic-foot refrigerator, for example, must consume no more energy than a continuously lit 75-watt bulb. And standards will again tighten in 1998.

But even with all the advances, your refrigerator's consumption still is a significant part of your energy bill—as much as one-fifth of your total yearly energy charges.

So how do you chill your refrigeration spending?

Store Ice in Your Freezer
Save $60

An empty freezer costs more to run than a full one. Filling as much space as possible in your freezer—whether it's a separate unit or part of your refrigerator—makes it run more efficiently.

One low-cost way to cut your utility bill: Fill heavy-duty freezer bags with water and seal them tightly. Then place them in the empty spaces in your freezer. The water, of course, turns to ice, and the ice acts as supplemental refrigeration. So it's helping the freezer to do its job more efficiently. Depending on your local utility rates and the size of your freezer, you can cut your energy bill by as much as $60 a year.

Buying a Fridge?
Skip the Ice Maker

If you're shopping for a new refrigerator, save the extra $100 to $200 and buy a unit without an ice maker.

A refrigerator with an automatic ice maker may be convenient, but you'll pay dearly for it. Ice makers use an average 300 kilowatt-hours per year in energy costs—which costs you as much as $50, depending on your electric company's hourly kilowatt rate. What's more, statistics show that refrigerators with automatic ice makers need repairs twice as often as the same units without them.

If you've already bought a refrigerator with an automatic ice maker, you can still reap savings by not using it. Simply unplug the tube in the back of the machine and begin making ice instead.

Keep the Door Closed
Save $50

Each time you open your refrigerator door, you waste electricity. Studies show that the typical refrigerator in a household with children is opened about 40 times a day. The energy lost just to open the door that much can amount to $50 a year.

The obvious answer is to open the refrigerator door only when necessary—and to close it as quickly as possible. Of course, that isn't always easy with a houseful of kids. Some people find success by placing restrictions on the number of "allowed" door openings by kids or by hanging signs on the door, such as "Is opening necessary?"

Consider a Mini Door

If you're in the market for a new fridge, you may want to consider a unit with a separate "mini door" that allows access to a storage compartment of readily available food and drinks. The initial cost is higher for this feature—about $250—but if your family has the refrigerator open a lot, the mini door will pay for itself in energy savings in about five years.

Adjust the Thermostat
Save $25

A quick flick of your wrist, and you can be $25 richer a year—or pocket more than $300 over the lifetime of your fridge. The savings occur because most people set their refrigerator's thermostat close to 32°F.

But as long as the temperature is set no higher than 40°F, food stays fresh, and you use less energy. Just find the thermostat on the back panel of the fridge and turn it a few degrees higher.

Do Your Math
before Buying a Refrigerator

The EnergyGuide label on all refrigerators (as well as other appliances) is a good way to determine how efficient that unit is. But for calculating your total costs from purchase day to the time when it needs to be replaced, here's a handy formula.

Add the purchase price to the estimated long-term costs of the appliance. To calculate long-term costs, first determine what your annual energy costs are likely to be. (You can use the table on the EnergyGuide label as a guide.) Then multiply by 13, the average lifetime in years for a refrigerator. And then multiply that by 0.76, a "discount factor" that accounts for inflation and interest on savings. That number is your bottom-line lifetime cost: purchase price + (annual energy costs × 13 × 0.76).

So if you buy a refrigerator for $850 and it costs $72 a year to run (according to the EnergyGuide), you add $850 to the total of $72 × 13 × 0.76 for an estimated lifetime cost of $1,561.36.

Keep in mind, however, that the EnergyGuide costs tend to be conservative—and that they're calculated (like gas mileage on a car's sticker price) on the unit operating at its maximum efficiency. You may notice that your energy costs are much higher than the estimate.

DECIPHERING THE EnergyGuide Label

Estimate the yearly cost of a new appliance before you make a purchase—then compare. Here's how to read the EnergyGuide label found on new appliances.

Type of appliance and capacity

Name of manufacturer and the model number of the appliance

Estimated annual operating cost for this model only

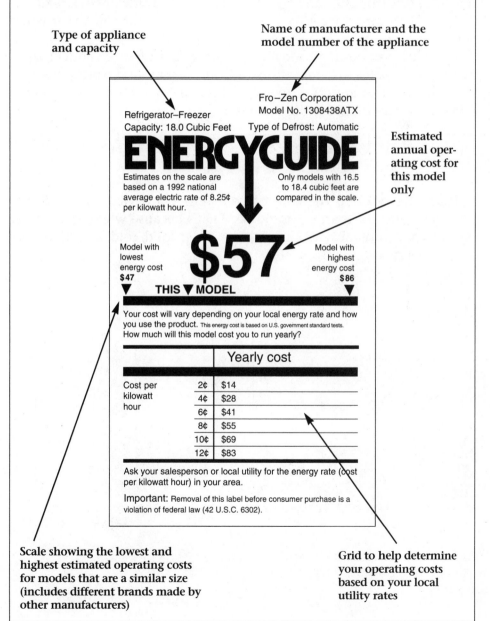

Fro–Zen Corporation
Model No. 1308438ATX

Refrigerator–Freezer
Capacity: 18.0 Cubic Feet   Type of Defrost: Automatic

ENERGYGUIDE

Estimates on the scale are based on a 1992 national average electric rate of 8.25¢ per kilowatt hour.

Only models with 16.5 to 18.4 cubic feet are compared in the scale.

Model with lowest energy cost
$47

$57

Model with highest energy cost
$86

▼ THIS ▼ MODEL ▼

Your cost will vary depending on your local energy rate and how you use the product. This energy cost is based on U.S. government standard tests. How much will this model cost you to run yearly?

Yearly cost		
Cost per kilowatt hour	2¢	$14
	4¢	$28
	6¢	$41
	8¢	$55
	10¢	$69
	12¢	$83

Ask your salesperson or local utility for the energy rate (cost per kilowatt hour) in your area.

Important: Removal of this label before consumer purchase is a violation of federal law (42 U.S.C. 6302).

Scale showing the lowest and highest estimated operating costs for models that are a similar size (includes different brands made by other manufacturers)

Grid to help determine your operating costs based on your local utility rates

Switch Off Moisture Reducers
Save $50

Many refrigerators have switches that, when turned on, reduce the moisture content in the crisper bins, so vegetables stay crisper longer. While this feature (usually a switch located on a side or back panel) is helpful, it can increase your energy costs as much as $50 a year when left on continuously.

Instead, save your money—and use the moisture reducer only when you notice condensation in your vegetable crisper (which is usually in the summer). Otherwise, keep the switch on the "energy saver" mode and pocket the savings.

Vacuum Coils Every Month
Save 25%

If you never clean the coils of your refrigerator, it may be 25 percent less efficient than it should be. That's because when its coils get dusty, your unit must work harder to keep food cold, and that uses more energy.

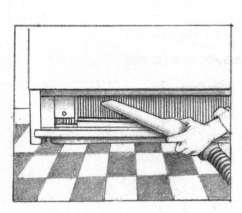

To get the most efficiency from your refrigerator, vacuum the coils.

Most experts recommend a monthly cleaning, done with a standard vacuum. But that may be difficult if the coils are located in the back of the fridge, where they're hard to reach. Still, a periodic cleaning can lower your operating costs. (In some models, you can reach the coils by removing the toe panel below the door. Then reach in with a long-handled wand to vacuum them.)

Make Sure the Seal Is Tight
Save $50

The rubber seal around a refrigerator door should close tightly. In fact, the harder it is to open your refrigerator door, the better the fit. A loose seal means that warm air is entering and cold air is escaping—a one-two punch that can raise your electric bill by as much as $50 a year.

So if your seal is loose, replace it. A handy do-it-yourselfer can do the job for about $15 in materials.

Cut Electric Bills with a Piece of Plywood

If your refrigerator is located next to the oven or stove, you're probably spending more than you should on energy. The heat from the range makes the refrigerator work harder to keep food cold, requiring more electricity.

The solution: Try placing a piece of plywood between the two appliances to absorb heat from your range. The savings could be about $20 a year.

Buy the Right-Size Fridge

The best way to spend too much on a refrigerator is to buy one bigger than you need.

You pay a higher price for a bigger unit. Although there's no set-in-stone ratio, you can figure that you'll spend at least $50 more for each cubic foot.

All that empty space—in both the refrigerator and freezer compartments—wastes energy. For a two-person household, a 12-cubic-foot model should be sufficient, unless you entertain a lot. Add 2 cubic feet for each additional member of your household, unless you have teenagers who consider your refrigerator their personal feeding trough. In that case, add at least 3 cubic feet per person.

Same goes with separate freezers: Families with more than two children and that buy a lot of food in bulk should consider 15- to 16-cubic-foot models, but smaller families would be better off with more compact 10-cubic-foot units. And be sure to keep that freezer in an unheated basement or garage to reduce energy costs.

Go for Simplicity
Save $500

The more basic your refrigerator is, the cheaper it is to buy and operate. The standard top-freezer/refrigerator combinations are between $200 and $500 cheaper than same-size side-by-side models or bottom-freezer models—and they use less energy.

IS A SIDE-BY-SIDE WORTH $400 MORE?

There's always the convenience factor to consider. But if you don't have to have a side-by-side freezer/refrigerator combination, or a freezer on the bottom of the refrigerator, you can save hundreds of dollars with a top-freezer unit. We priced three models of a popular-brand refrigerator, and here's what we found for similar-size units.

MODEL	PRICE ($)	SAVINGS ($)
Side-by-side refrigerator	1,199.97	
Refrigerator with bottom freezer	1,029.97	170.00 less than a side-by-side unit
Refrigerator with top freezer	799.97	400.00 less than a side-by-side unit
		230.00 less than a bottom-freezer unit

Cut Your Defrosting Costs
Save 45%

Manual defrosters cost 45 percent less to run than those that defrost automatically, according to the American Council for an Energy-Efficient Environment. That amounts to about $50 a year in savings for the typical consumer.

Buy in Summer
Save $100

Since the demand for refrigerators increases in the summer—when most breakdowns occur due to wear and tear—many retailers will offer attractive deals to steer you away from competitors. So if you're shopping for a new unit, hold off until summer, when sales are plentiful.

Double Efficiency
with a Chest-Style Freezer

Chest freezers are more efficient than upright models—in some cases, twice as efficient. A basic chest unit can save you about $40 a year in energy costs compared with a same-size upright model.

AIR CONDITIONERS AND FANS

Trying to keep cool can make you lose your cool—financially speaking. During the 3½-month summer season, you may pay as much as $200 more in electricity if your home has central air-conditioning. Even a single window unit air conditioner can add $30 or more to each month's bill, depending how often the unit is run. But you can chill those cooling costs without sacrificing comfort.

Leave On the Air Conditioner
Save $50

Most people assume that the less they use their air-conditioning, the more they'll save in operating costs.

Actually, if you live in a hot, muggy climate, you're better off leaving the air-conditioning running all night.

"Here in Florida, where it's very humid, people unknowingly waste a lot of energy when they shut off their air-conditioning at night and open all the windows," says M. Virginia Peart, Ph.D., associate professor of home economics at the University of Florida in Gainesville. "Opening the windows allows humid air to enter the house, so when the air-conditioning is turned on again, it has to work even harder to dehumidify the room—which uses a lot more energy than simply keeping it on continuously on a milder setting."

So if you're going to turn on the air-conditioning, leave it on—but on a milder setting during evenings. Using it for short periods isn't as comfortable and may cost you as much as $50 a year, depending where you live.

Don't Assume Bigger Is Better

Many people assume that the more powerful a wall unit they buy, the faster it will cool a room (and the less time and energy needed to run it).

Not exactly. The real purpose of an air conditioner is to remove humidity from the air, not to cool air. And the compressor of an oversize air conditioner may not run long enough to adequately dehumidify a room, which adds to your electric bill—as much as $200 over the unit's operating life.

Meanwhile, an undersize model may not cool the room well enough. So before you buy anything, measure your room. Then look for an air conditioner that has adequate power, as noted in BTUs (British thermal units), the standard measurement of energy use. Generally, an average-size room between 150 and 250 square feet needs a 6,000 BTU wall unit. A larger room needs more BTUs; a smaller room, less BTUs.

Look at EER Ratings
Save 15%

Like refrigerators and other appliances, air conditioners have energy efficiency ratings (EERs). The higher that number, the lower the cost of running the air conditioner. For air conditioners between 8,000 and 14,000 BTUs, the EER should be 9 or higher. They're at least 15 percent more efficient than those with lower numbers and can save you nearly $100 over the operating life of the unit.

Be a Fan of Fans
Save 90%

Most people believe that an air conditioner is the best way to beat the heat in the dog days of summer. Maybe, but the cheapest way to keep your cool is to run a fan—and not an air conditioner—as often as possible.

If you live in an area where hot days are followed by cool nights, humidity isn't usually an after-hours problem. So a fan can be just as effective for those dog nights—for as much as $30 less a month.

The American Council for an Energy-Efficient Environment reports that the standard human comfort range (while wearing light clothing) is between 72° and 78°F. Even at 82°—hotter than the average uncooled room during the height of summer—you get relief with a breeze of about 1.7 miles per hour, and electric fans easily attain that.

Another advantage of fans is their low purchase cost. While a quality air conditioner starts at around $350, a top-notch ceiling fan can be purchased for one-third of that price; other models start as low as $30.

Give a One-Two Punch
Save 10%

Running a fan while your air-conditioning is running can trim 10 percent or more off the energy cost of cooling your room with air-conditioning alone.

How? With a fan, the air conditioner can be placed on a lower setting. Ceiling fans are an excellent choice for this strategy, since they move large amounts of air continuously and cost just pennies a day to operate. A 36-inch fan is fine for a ten- by ten-foot room; larger rooms are better handled with a 42-inch or larger unit.

Use That Cool Fan
to Cut Your Heating Bills

Ever think of using a fan in winter? It can actually help you save on your heating bills by pushing down warm air that rises to the ceiling.

To get this benefit, be sure to buy a reversible fan. In winter, you can change the blade direction so that warm air blows down and around the room, which makes for more efficient circulation. When warm weather returns, switch the fan to a "cooling" mode again, so it draws warm air up toward the ceiling.

WASHING MACHINES

While technology has yet to invent a machine to locate all the socks that have vanished into that black hole of a laundry room, the chore of cleaning clothes has come a long way since Ma Kettle used to scrub clothes at the river's edge.

So has the price. Today's washing machines can cost as much as $800, depending on their features. But most of those fancy frills, such as electronic controls and extra cycles, are unnecessary. Often they're confusing to use, and they usually add to the operating cost of the machine.

The first rule for cutting your clothes-washing costs is to stick with the basics. A $250 machine may have very few optional controls and cycles, but it cleans clothes the same way as the top-of-the-line unit—and for less money. Here are some other tips for saving money.

Use Cold Water

Most of the costs to run your washing machine result from making the water hot. So doing your laundry in cool or cold water is the best way to save money operating your washing machine.

A "hot" load uses four times as much energy as a "warm" load and eight times as much as a "cold" load. You may decide to wash your whites in hot water, but other "hots" such as towels and linens can be cleaned just as well in warm (or even cold) water. And unless your load is very dirty, most clothes you normally wash in warm water can be cleaned just as effectively in cold water. (Just be sure to use liquid detergent for cooler-water washes, since some powders dissolve properly only in very hot water.)

And don't even bother with "warm-rinse" cycles, found on many newer machines. Experts tell us you never need warm water to rinse your clothes (no matter what temperature the wash). Depending how much you wash, you may be wasting $50 or more a year on this unnecessary feature.

SKIP EXTRA CYCLES—AND SAVE YOUR DOLLARS

Having extra cycles on a washing machine or dryer may sound appealing, but it can add as much as $500 or more to the cost of these appliances. Shopping around, we compared the prices of washers and dryers that had different extra-cycle features but were alike in all other respects. Here's what we discovered.

UNIT	PRICE ($)	SAVINGS ($)
Kenmore Washer		
11 wash cycles	489.99	
3 wash cycles	279.00	210.99
Whirlpool Washer		
7 wash cycles	399.97	
3 wash cycles	299.97	100.00
Kenmore Dryer		
7+ dry cycles	749.99	
2 dry cycles	239.99	510.00
Whirlpool Dryer		
6 dry cycles	479.97	
No optional cycles	249.99	229.98

Forget "Water-Saving" Machines
Save $300

Front-loading machines, like those in professional laundromats, are reported to be very cost-efficient. Don't believe it.

True, these machines use only one-half of the water of the more common top-loading machines. But what isn't as widely touted is their price—typically $300 more than the price for a similar-size top-loading machine. As if that weren't enough, insiders tell us that front-loaders break down nearly twice as often.

"SOFTENED" TOWELS ARE LESS ABSORBENT

Life is full of trade-offs, and the laundry is no exception. When it comes to towels, what you gain in softness you lose in absorption, and that can affect the bottom line on your washer operating costs.

"When you use a fabric softener on your towels, it does make them softer," says one expert. "But that 'softness' puts a coating on towels that also makes them less absorbent."

This can result in having to wash towels more often or spending more money to buy newer, more absorbent towels. Either way, fabric softeners add to your washing costs.

Furthermore, the front-loading machines made for consumer use save only a few bucks a year if you wash with cold water. That savings will never make up for the purchase price. So stick with the more popular top-loaders.

Go for the Mother Load
Save $50

If you're shopping for a new machine, you'll likely pay more for an extra-large capacity, but it's probably the most economical feature you can buy—especially if you have kids. Generally speaking, a two-person household is fine with a 10- to 12-pound-capacity washer, but larger families should look at machines that can handle 15 pounds or more.

The reason? When you wash large loads, you use water and energy more efficiently than when you put in smaller loads. Depending how often you do laundry, you can save $50 or more a year simply by washing the same amount of clothing in fewer but larger loads.

CLOTHES DRYERS

If you really want to cut your drying costs, all you need are two trees along with some rope and clothespins. But you can't beat a clothes dryer for convenience. So you'll be pleased to know that a clothes dryer is one of the less expensive appliances, both in purchase price and in operating costs. But here are two ways you can save some money running it.

Clean the Lint Tray

When the lint tray is full, your dryer has to work harder—and operate longer—in order to get clothes dry. If you clean the lint tray before each load, your dryer will operate a lot more efficiently—and your clothes will dry better.

Go Mid-range on Dryer Settings

You should set the drying control between the maximum and minimum settings rather than on the maximum. Unless you're doing a load of towels or other hard-to-dry items, your machine will operate for less time—and will usually do just as good a job. This amounts to pennies per load—but hundreds of dollars saved in energy costs over the life of your dryer.

DISHWASHERS

You might assume it costs a lot extra to have a dishwasher take the drudgery out of hand-washing dishes.

Not so. The cost of buying a typical dishwasher is about the same today as it was 30 years ago—usually less than $400 (although prices can be $600 or more). And despite what most people think, you use more water washing dishes by hand than with a machine (assuming you don't pre-rinse).

The amount of electricity a dishwasher uses is actually very low—typically around a nickel's worth per load. The real cost of running a dishwasher (aside from purchasing it) comes in heating the water. So . . .

Avoid the Frills
Save $100

Since most manufacturers use the same washing mechanism on their entire line, the difference in price—which can amount to $100 or more—is mostly for unnecessary frills.

But what about that pot scrubber feature? Though you may wish that you would never have to use elbow grease again, think instead

WHAT'S AN EXTRA OPTION WORTH?

That top-of-the-line dishwasher may have different cycles for scrubbing, rinsing, gentle wash and other options—but nothing comes free. When we compared dishwashers with the same brand names, we found that you might have to pay $100 or more for those extra features.

UNIT	PRICE ($)	SAVINGS ($)
Maytag Dishwasher		
5 wash cycles	469.97	
2 wash cycles	369.97	100.00
Whirlpool Dishwasher		
6 wash cycles	396.98	
2 wash cycles	259.97	137.01

with your wallet—these cycles just don't work as well as good ol'-fashioned muscle. It's better to save the money and scrub the pans by hand, since you'll do a better job for less money.

Even so-called energy features on dishwashers save an average of only $2 a year in operating costs.

Lower the Thermostat
Save 10%

Your dishwasher's service manual probably recommends that the water temperature be set between 140° and 145°F. What the manual doesn't mention is that setting your hot water heater thermostat that high can increase your annual utility costs between 2 and 10 percent compared with setting the thermostat at 120°. The lower temperature is fine for doing dishes, but you should use liquid detergent at this temperature, since it dissolves more quickly than powdered detergent. (And there's a side benefit: The lower temperature reduces the risk of scalding when you take showers or baths.)

In fact, if you're shopping for a new dishwasher, you'll notice that many models have a feature called a hot-water booster. This automatically increases water temperature for hard-to-clean loads, and you can switch it on as needed.

Use the "Light" Cycle
Save 50%

Most people use only one cycle on their dishwashers—the "normal" cycle. Usually, that means you're doing two washes with several rinses and using about ten gallons of water.

Yet unless your dishes are really dirty, they'll get clean by using the "light" cycle, which uses half as much water. That means one-half of the energy costs to heat the water. The difference may be only a few dollars a month, but it adds up over the years.

RANGES AND COOKTOPS

About the only way to make ranges and cooktops run less expensively is to keep them clean. Burners and ovens need to work harder when caked with burned-on food; the harder they work, the

DO YOU NEED THAT SOUPED-UP MICROWAVE?

If you're Chef Extraordinaire in the microwave department and you need a dozen or so temperature levels for your roast chicken . . . fine, spring for the high-priced microwave model. But if macaroni and cheese is more your line, you can trim about 25 percent off a new microwave price by going for a model that has just four temperature settings. Here are two prices we got from retailers on two popular brands.

UNIT	PRICE ($)	SAVINGS ($)
10+ temperature levels 1.4 cubic feet 800 watts	269.99	
4 temperature levels 1.5 cubic feet 800 watts	199.99	70.00

A RANGE OF RANGES

If you're shopping for a new range, you've probably noticed the new styles in electric cooktops, such as induction, halogen and solid disc units. The main selling points are that they're more attractive and easier to clean than the more common "coil" units. But there is a wide variety in their efficiency.

Induction cooktops have burners that look like circular patterns on ceramic glass. When a burner is turned on, a magnetic field is created that induces current and instantly generates heat.

With a selling price between $700 and $900 for most models, they're on the higher end of the price scale. And with induction units, magnetic cookware must be used. (To test your cookware, place a magnet on the bottom; if it sticks, it's okay. If it doesn't, you'll have to buy new cookware—an added expense.) But besides offering convenience, induction units are the most energy-efficient cooktops, saving about 20 percent in energy costs compared with coil units.

Halogen systems have halogen lights under ceramic glass. These lights turn on instantly, and only the cookware and food get hot—not the entire cooktop. Their control, speed and responsiveness make them similar to cooking with gas. They are the second most efficient units after induction, but since most halogen ranges start at more than $1,000, they're out of the price range of most consumers.

Also, repairs for halogen units cost twice as much as for other ranges.

Solid disc cooktops (also called European cooktops), in which electric wires are embedded in insulated cast iron, are slow to heat and are considered an energy waster. You'll pay about 20 percent more in energy costs compared with coil units.

The good news is that they are very easy to keep clean, and they maintain heat once warm. And with prices from $375 to $500, they're comparably priced with electric coil ranges.

more energy they use, and the higher your energy costs.

There are a few things you can do to cut your long-term spending if you're shopping for a new appliance.

Skip the Pilot Light
Save 30%

When shopping for a new gas range, look for models with pilotless spark ignition. In many cases, they cost no more than other models and are the most energy-efficient. In general, you'll slash your energy bill by 30 percent compared with other gas ranges.

See Your Food Cooking
Save $20

Another feature to look for when you're buying a new range or oven, whether gas or electric, is a window that allows you to see the food being prepared without having to open the oven door.

This is important because each time you open the oven, most of the heat escapes, and the oven uses much more energy to keep the cooking temperature constant. You'll pay between $25 and $60 more for an oven window, but a busy cook will save at least $20 a year in conserved energy, and this feature should pay for itself within two years.

FLATTEN COOKING COSTS WITH FLAT COOKWARE

No matter what type of cooktop you have, it's essential that the cookware you use be completely flat—without any ridges, bumps or other imperfections, says Leona K. Hawks, a home and equipment specialist at Utah State University in Logan and a member of the Association of Home Equipment Educators.

The flatter the cookware, the more evenly it cooks—and the less energy it uses. Concave or dented pots and pans require longer cooking periods and waste too much energy.

Also, use the right-size pot or pan: For the best cooking at the lowest cost, the cookware shouldn't extend beyond the heating element by more than one inch. Otherwise, you're using more energy than you should.

So put your pan on the burner that's closest in size. When you're cooking with oversize pans, such as large frying or sauté pans, cook on the largest element on your cooktop.

Buy in October
Save 20%

If you can hold out, try to buy your new range in October. That's because it's National Kitchen and Bath Month, and prices tend to be between 10 and 20 percent cheaper than the rest of the year.

HOME ENTERTAINMENT SYSTEMS

It seems as though it's no longer enough to simply watch TV or listen to music. You must, some say, *experience* home theater. But what may please the senses can cost big bucks: Big-screen TVs, stereo "surround sound" and high-tech VCRs don't come cheap.

But technically, a home theater doesn't have to put you in the poorhouse. You can't cut operating costs in any significant way, since most audio and video equipment uses the same (or a similar) amount of electricity. But here's how to make the most of your money if you're shopping for a new system or trying to bring new life to your current equipment.

Buy Mail Order
Save 50%

You can cut your spending between 25 and 50 percent by buying audio and video equipment through mail-order houses rather than at retail stores. For the best prices, contact several dealers—you'll find them in *Stereo Review* or *Video Review* advertisements. These magazines, available at most magazine stands, also do product comparisons.

After several phone calls (all through toll-free 800 numbers), you'll likely settle on the best price. To make sure you're also getting top quality and service, keep these considerations in mind.

- Call the manufacturer's toll-free number (you can get it through 800 directory assistance) to make sure the mail-order house is an authorized distributor.
- Insist on "factory sealed" cartons. Tell the dealer you will not accept boxes that have been resealed.
- Be sure you're not getting "gray market" goods by insisting that your items carry the original manufacturer's warranty.

• Request a 30-day return period that allows you to return merchandise for a full refund. (Some dealers will not allow returns on equipment that has been opened.)

Skip the Watts and Save the Dollars

As with other appliances, simplicity in a stereo system will save you hundreds when you're buying. For instance, spending $400 or more on a receiver may give you more sound than you'll find on a $200 unit, but it won't necessarily give you better sound. (The pricier unit, however, will give you more features—many of them unnecessary to most people.)

A lower-end unit typically has 25 or 35 watts of power; high-end units may have 100 watts. (Usually, the units with this much power also have separate amplifiers.) But unless you want the walls to rattle, or your hearing is exceptionally poor, you'll probably never need more than 35 watts.

The one feature you definitely want in a receiver—and you can find this feature in all units in all price ranges—is electronic digital tuning. This enables a station to be precisely captured, bringing you

---

MAKE SURE YOUR HI-FI SOUND DOESN'T COME AT A HIGH COST

Hi-fi VCRs have come down in price dramatically; the models you buy today may cost as much as $100 less than they would have a couple of years ago. For the serious home theater enthusiast, hi-fi VCRs offer great sound reproduction with less hiss and more authenticity than stereo. (For example, if you're watching a "shoot 'em out" on a hi-fi VCR, you'll hear the bullet being "shot" in one speaker and "pinging" in the other speaker. With a stereo VCR, you would hear the bullet "bang" from both speakers.)

Of course, the best hi-fi VCR is worth nothing if it's hooked to a monaural TV. So unless you're also going to invest in a TV with a high-quality sound system, don't pay the extra cost for a hi-fi VCR.

the best sound. Aside from that, a lot of what you pay for is fancy dials and snazzy readouts.

Buy the Cheapest CD Player
Save $100

All CD players use the very same technology, regardless of price or label. Yet you'll notice that the price difference between models can be as high as $100.

The difference comes in the number of added features (most of which you'll rarely use). Unless you need features such as faders (which allow you to fade in and out of songs that you're taping on cassettes) or a remote control, save your money and buy the cheapest reputable brand you can find.

Buy in the Spring
Save 20%

No matter the type of equipment, the best time to buy audio equipment is from February through spring, when new models are introduced and retailers are anxious to unload current inventories. You'll be in the best position to negotiate for a lower price with your retailer—as much as 20 percent less at some stores. Even mail-order houses will probably give you a bigger discount than usual, perhaps 10 percent off regular prices. If you're already on a mailing list, look for special spring announcements. If not, call a few mail-order houses for their catalogs and do some comparative shopping.

Get a Two-Head Model
Save $150

Perhaps the most basic question for those looking for a VCR is whether to get a two-head model or a four-head model. A four-head VCR may cost anywhere from $50 to $150 more than a similar two-head model. The only advantage of the more expensive model is that you get a cleaner picture when you pause the tape or run it in slow motion. But how often do you watch movies or TV shows in slow motion?

If you are like most people and use a VCR mainly for watching rented movies or taping your favorite TV shows, all you need is a basic (and cheaper) two-head model.

PERSONAL COMPUTERS

If you haven't purchased a home computer but plan to do so soon, congratulations. You've already saved yourself hundreds of dollars. Because of intense competition among manufacturers, prices are at an all-time low—and will likely continue to drop.

Here are some tips on saving even more.

Be One Step behind the Times
Save $1,000

You may notice that most home computers are advertised by "numbers"—such as 386/25 or 486/33. Generally, the first number represents the style of microprocessor; the higher that number, the more "high tech" the microprocessor is. The second number is the number of megahertz—or speed. A higher number of megahertz means it's a faster computer.

Many shoppers believe that they need a personal computer with the highest numbers they can afford because it's the "latest and greatest."

But by avoiding state-of-the-art systems (those with the highest numbers), you can save big. If the current rage in advertisements is 486 models, for example, shop for yesterday's "star" 386. The only difference is that the 386 is slightly slower.

Besides, unless you need a home computer for desktop publishing or another specialized function, there's no reason you need a top-of-the-line unit. Even the most basic model will do everything a typical family needs.

Stay Out of the Fast Lane
Save $350

Memory is measured by two numbers—RAM and MB. RAM, or random-access memory, is the computer's short-term memory, while MB, or megabytes, is its memory storage. You'll probably want to shoot for 120 MB or more and about 2 MB of RAM. (But find out whether the RAM is "expandable"—which means you can upgrade your computer by adding more RAM.)

If speed isn't a big consideration, you can get a good value on a slower computer. For instance, you can save as much as $350 buying a 386 rather than a 486—and the 386 may have more memory as well.

Buy Mail Order
Save 50%

No appliance has better deals through mail order than the home computer. You can get as much as one-half off the retail price for the computer itself and about one-third off for software. And since few companies actually make their own computers—most buy them from original equipment manufacturers and attach their logos—you don't have to buy a big name for top quality.

To find out about mail-order houses, read some computer magazines such as *PC Home Journal, PC Source* and *PC World* (or *Macworld,* for those interested in Macintosh systems).

But if you buy by mail, be certain that you get the same manufacturer's warranty you would get from a store. Also, find out if you can get the telephone support you'll need. Probably most important, find out how you could have your computer repaired if it breaks down. You want to be able to take it to a local authorized dealer or repair shop rather than ship it somewhere. If you have to ship your computer across the country, you could lose weeks of user time and end up paying round-trip shipping charges.

Buy from Smaller Companies
Save 20%

Rather than shell out top dollar for an IBM or Packard Bell unit, be sure to investigate computers made by lesser-known companies. Though generally not stocked in large retail outlets, Dell, Leading Edge, Gateway and Zeos are among the highly competitive companies with good value at low prices. Call 800 directory assistance to get toll-free numbers for these companies, so you can comparison-shop by phone.

Schmooze Free Software
Save $150

One advantage to buying retail is that you can usually get software at little or no cost as part of an overall package. Sometimes you can get $500 worth of free software on a $1,000 package. Granted, you wouldn't necessarily buy that $500 worth of software, but you would probably shell out $100 to $150 for some of it. Even if your "package" doesn't offer free software, salespeople will often throw it in to close a deal.

Buy Used
Save 35%

You can typically knock 35 percent off your spending by buying a "used" computer. However, not all used units are alike: Some are truly used, and you're better off not buying these. At today's prices, you can spend a couple of hundred more and get a much better new machine.

Another problem with used computers is that they have extremely limited warranties—as little as one week, and usually from the seller (as opposed to the manufacturer). Generally, you should stay away from these "deals."

But you can get a good buy on used computers that were demo models or that are labeled as "manufacturer refurbished." This means that a customer didn't like the machine or that the distributor went out of business owing the manufacturer money, so the maker reclaimed all the unsold (and unused) computers in inventory. With a little hunting for this labeling, you can cut one-third off your spending and get a great computer, too.

Cut Your Spending on

FURNITURE AND DECORATING

- New Furniture
- Used Furniture
- Buying Quality: Hard Furniture
- Buying Quality: Upholstery
- Fabric
- Bedding
- Floor Coverings
- Window Treatments

LIVEN UP YOUR
LIVING QUARTERS FOR LESS

If you want to see the most common way that people cut their furniture spending, go to your nearest college campus. Within these ivy-covered halls of education, you'll find old milk crates being used as coffee tables, concrete blocks and boards acting as entertainment units and pillows thrown on beat-up old mattresses to make sofas.

Or you can take a lesson from really educated people and cut your spending without settling for less. In this chapter, we'll tell you how to get a beautiful coffee table, quality storage units and a great sofa—along with other fine furniture—for hundreds or even thousands below the standard retail price.

Furnishing your home on a budget doesn't mean you have to sacrifice comfort, beauty or quality. With good planning, creative thinking and smart buying, you may be able to make your home even more beautiful and comfortable than ever before—and spend less in the process.

NEW FURNITURE

As you may have noticed, furniture isn't cheap. Even the low-quality stuff is pretty darn expensive. So it's important to stretch your money as much as possible whenever you buy a new piece. Here's how.

Hire a Decorator to Take You Shopping
Save 60%

Professional designers and interior decorators have access to wholesale furniture showrooms that the general public never sees. At these showrooms, the interior designer or decorator gets bargain-basement prices for top-quality goods. That's because they have resale licenses—or the equivalent. They can buy goods at wholesale prices and resell those goods at any markup.

So you can get a great deal by "hiring" the designer to go shopping with you. The designer buys the goods for you at the discounted rate,

166

WHERE YOUR MONEY GOES

- Americans spend more than $26 billion a year on furniture. That amounts to about $310 for households where the head is under 35 years old; $443 for those 35 to 44; $426 for those 45 to 54; and $316 for those 55 to 64. People over age 65 spend only $128 a year furnishing their homes.
- The typical mattress and box spring set costs $800 and lasts anywhere from seven to ten years.

---

then resells the goods, either with no markup at all or with a small commission.

Most designers charge between $25 and $50 an hour for these shopping trips. If they add a commission, it's usually less than 10 percent.

Even if there is a commission, you still get the goods at 40 percent or more off the retail price—and you get professional decorating advice to boot. And if you concentrate on buying only floor samples, which are discounted even more, your savings can be as much as 60 percent, adds New York City interior designer Steve Lyons.

To learn about designers in your area who are available for these shopping trips, call the American Society of Interior Designers referral hotline toll-free at 1-800-775-ASID.

Assemble Furniture Yourself

One of the newest trends in furniture is ready-to-assemble items (RTA in the trade). With this furniture, you assemble various sections and pieces to make a wall unit, sofa, table or whatever. Instructions are usually quite simple, and most of the assembly tools are provided.

This type of furniture was popularized by stores such as Workbench. Probably the ultimate RTA store is now Ikea, a Swedish-based furniture "superstore" that sells everything for your home, from couches to coffee cups.

These items are mass-produced and have low shipping costs (most come in flat boxes when unassembled). So RTA goods cost anywhere from 15 to 40 percent less than similar ready-built items made from the same types of materials.

What you gain in savings, however, you may sacrifice in quality. Joints are usually held together with screws rather than more elaborate fastening systems such as dovetails, and the furniture is usually made from soft pine and composite wood such as plywood and particleboard rather than solid, whole wood such as oak and maple. But if you're looking for an inexpensive way to furnish a child's bedroom or for "interim" furniture that your family will outgrow, you can drastically cut your costs with RTA merchandise.

Haggle for a Discount
Save 15%

Retailers may deny it, but the fact is, furniture prices are negotiable. Since most furniture store salespeople work on commission, you can usually wheel and deal for a better price, so don't just assume you have to pay the sticker price.

Before haggling, do some comparison shopping. If you can prove you've seen the item you want for less money at another store, many retailers will match or beat the price of their competitor. Even if you haven't seen the item cheaper, you can usually negotiate some "bonus" such as free delivery and setup.

If you're paying with cash or a personal check, as opposed to a credit card, you're in an especially good negotiating position: It costs the store money to process any kind of credit card charge.

DON'T FALL FOR THE LIST LINE

When you're shopping for new furniture, you may notice that retailers make their furniture look cut-rate with stickers that advertise 30 or 40 percent off "list" or "manufacturer's suggested retail price."

But you're still not getting a bargain. Most stores sell their wares at prices that are 2½ to 3 times the wholesale price—but they'd like you to think you're instantly getting furniture that's marked down about 30 percent from the list price. In reality, the furniture you buy from a retailer at 30 percent off is probably being sold about 180 or 200 percent above wholesale.

Whatever you do, don't assume that sticker prices are carved in stone. Consumers are often successful at negotiating a 10 to 15 percent reduction in the price shown on the tag. Retailers rarely cut any more off, however.

Let the Store Play Inspector

When buying retail, you may be given the option of having the furniture delivered from the factory directly to your home. The furniture salesperson may explain that this is a "matter of convenience."

For whom?

This option may *sound* easier. It may even be less expensive, because you save $35 or so in setup and delivery charges. But direct shipment isn't doing you a favor. In fact, it's actually done to protect the store.

By accepting factory delivery, you (rather than the store) may have to pay shipping costs, which can amount to several hundred dollars, depending what you order. Shipping usually costs between $50 and $90 for the first 100 pounds and $30 to $45 for each additional 100 pounds.

Even if the store does pay the shipping costs, by accepting factory delivery you are responsible for inspection and setup of the furniture. That means if you get the wrong order or the goods arrive in damaged condition, *you* must pay freight damage claims.

Instead, always have the store accept delivery. That way, it's the retailer's responsibility to make sure everything is okay before your merchandise is delivered to you.

Say No to Suite Talk

Retailers love to move entire sets of furniture—the complete bedroom suite, the matching sofa and loveseat, the entire dining room set. It's great for them but not so great for you.

For one thing, the "one-look" period room is a thing of the past. Newer styles suggest a more eclectic look for most rooms. And the savings are actually minimal. You'll notice that there is a very slight discount—or none at all—for buying a complete set. Instead, you pay approximately the same amount as you would if you were to buy each piece individually.

The problem: Most people don't need the complete five-piece bedroom or four-piece living room set. So resist the pressure: Purchase only the pieces that you need. Don't be sold on the advantages of a complete, matched set.

Play Hardball with Add-Ons
Save 15%

Another ploy used by furniture salespeople is to lure you into the "add-on" sale. When you want to buy just a table, he tries to sell you a lamp to go with it. Or you buy a chair, and he schmoozes with you until you're almost convinced that you need a matching ottoman.

If you need these items, fine: But tell the salesperson you want them for 20 percent less than the sticker price. After all, you've already spent a great deal on items that will pay him a handsome commission. He may initially balk at your 20 percent suggestion and counter with a 10 percent price break. Compromise at 15 percent, and you've saved $30 on a $200 ottoman.

If you don't need these items, however, stop the salesperson as soon as he begins the add-on come-on. Most salespeople are drilled to excel at this tactic, and once he starts, you may find it very hard to say no.

Buy Straight Legs
Save 40%

Furniture with "fancy" shapes is more expensive than goods with straight lines and simple designs. If you favor tables and chairs with curved legs, for instance, you should realize that they're more expensive than the same items with straight legs. Since furniture with more elaborate details takes longer to manufacture, figure you'll spend anywhere from 10 to 40 percent more.

Order from the Manufacturer
Save 70%

North Carolina is the furniture-building capital of the United States, with nearly 400 manufacturers based in or near the cities of Hickory and High Point. It's also the best place in America to buy furniture.

Many manufacturers in the Tarheel State operate giant furniture outlets that sell top-quality furniture directly to the public at savings

CAROLINA BECKONING?
HERE'S WHAT YOU NEED TO KNOW

Whether you are planning to drive to North Carolina to buy furniture or simply want your fingers to do the walking, the first step is to know the offerings of the furniture discounters—which you can find out from their catalogs.

For a list of dealers in the Hickory area between Winston-Salem and Asheville—and also a list of the brands they sell—get your free *Furniture Shopping Guide* by calling 1-800-849-5093. Or get complete information on outlets in the Hickory area by writing to the Chamber of Commerce, P.O. Box 1828, Hickory, NC 28603.

For catalogs and information on furniture discounters in the High Point area, which is located off I-85 southwest of Greensboro, write to Southern Trade Publications, P.O. Box 18343, Greensboro, NC 27412. (Please include $1 for postage and handling.)

If you're ordering furniture by phone, be prepared to pay a deposit of 25 to 30 percent of the total price on large orders. For single pieces or small orders, you may be asked to pay in full before delivery. If possible, pay with a credit card; that way, if there's a problem with your order, your credit card company may help with its buyer protection plan.

When your order arrives, you may need to pay the shipper with cash, money order or a cashier's check; some do accept credit cards, however. Be sure to ask when ordering. Don't sign or pay the balance until you've thoroughly inspected everything. If goods are flawed or damaged, you can refuse to accept the shipment. But if you accept shipment and then find a problem, you could end up paying the high cost of return shipping.

of 70 percent below list price. Need a place to stay while you shop? Scores of hotels are located near these outlets, and many offer discounts to travelers who are scouting for furniture deals. Many people simply rent trucks and travel to North Carolina to go furniture shopping, picking up furniture at manufacturers' prices while avoiding sales taxes in their home states.

THE OFFERINGS OF NORTH CAROLINA

Quality and price aren't the only benefits of buying furnishings from North Carolina. These discount superstores also offer a selection that's second to none. Here's a sampling of the name-quality furnishings you buy from these stores—either in person or by phone.

Action by Lane Recliners

American Drew

American of Martinsville

American West Collection
  (by Lexington)

Athens

Athol Tables

Barcalounger

Barn Door

Bassett

Berkline

Berkshire

Bernhardt

Bevan Funnel

Blacksmith Shop

Bob Timberlake Collection
  (by Lexington)

Broyhill

Builtright Chair Company

Carlton McLendon

Carolina Mirrors

Carsons

Casa Bique

Catnapper

Century

Chapel Hill Chair

Charleston Forge

Chatham County

Classic Leather

Clayton House

Clayton Marcus

Cochrane

Corporate Office Furniture

Councill Craftsmen

Cox

Craftique

Crawford

Denny Lamps

D & F Wicker

Dixie

Dresher

Emerson

Fashion Bed Group

Five Rivers Craft

Flexsteel

Florida

Furniture Guild

In some cases, you can also shop the manufacturers without ever traveling. Your local retailers probably get most of their goods from North Carolina. Stop by any store that handles the furniture you like,

Glencraft Leather

Hammary

Hekman

Henry Link

Hickory Crest

Hickory Hill

Hickory-White

Highland House

Holiday House Sleepers

Hooker

Howard Miller Clocks

Jasper Cabinet

Johnston Casuals

Keller

Kimball Victorian

Kincaid

Kingsdown Bedding

Knob Creek

LaBarge

Laine

Lane

La-Z-Boy

Lea

Leathercraft

Lexington

Link-Taylor

Madison Square

Murphy

Nathan Hale

North Hickory

Null Industries

Parliament

Peters-Revington

Pulaski

Raleigh Road

Regency House

Richardson Brothers

Riverside

Sealy

Serta

Sherrill

SK Furniture

Southwood Reproductions

Stanley

Stanton-Cooper

Stearns and Foster

Superior

Thayer Coggin

Vanguard

Vaughn

Venture

Waterford

Weiman

Wellington Hall

Wesley Allen

Woodmark

Young-Hinkle

write down the styles and model numbers, and call North Carolina to order the furniture by phone. Or you can look up the price of the selected furniture in the manufacturer's catalog. Placing your order over the phone is a great way to get quality goods at a fraction of the retail price. However, not all retail discounters will accept telephone orders.

Pass on the Fabric Protection Warranty
Save $100

When you're buying new upholstered goods, the salesperson will probably try to sell you a fabric protection warranty for $25 to $100. Don't buy it! Most natural fabrics such as cotton and linen have already been treated at the mill, while man-made fibers repel stains without any further treatment.

If you want added protection, simply buy a can of Scotch-gard or a similar product at any store and spray the upholstery yourself. After all, that's basically what the manufacturers or retailers do—but they charge a high price for doing it.

Shift Your Pieces before You Shop Around

Some folks aren't lacking in furniture—they just have it in the wrong location. A low chest that looks all wrong in the living room may be the perfect night table in the bedroom. Those chairs that don't go in your redone kitchen may be great on the porch or in the dining room. Something as simple as moving a coffee table at a 45-degree angle can completely change the look of a room.

"People usually have more of what they need than they realize," says Lauri Ward, a designer who specializes in rearranging furniture. "Most homes are like a giant jigsaw puzzle—all the pieces are there. They just need to be put together right."

So before buying, try some rearranging. You may find that you have all the furniture you need. To stock up on new ideas, buy some home-furnishing magazines, so you can find out what arrangements you like. Then sketch the room and relocation of furniture to help you visualize the new look before you actually start moving pieces.

USED FURNITURE

You don't have to be an MBA to know that you can really cut your spending if you buy furniture at garage sales, flea markets, auctions and consignment shops. A piece of furniture is a lot like a car—

the moment it leaves the showroom, it depreciates in value. But even once-used furniture can have a very long life—so buying used gives you the most value for your money. Here's how to get even better deals when you're shopping for used furniture.

Arrive at Sunrise
Save 10%

The early bird catches the deal at flea markets. Dealers usually arrive before dawn, and their best goods are often picked over by savvy shoppers by the time the gates officially open.

As a general rule, the better deals are outside the flea market, in the parking lot. Dealers will often give a reduced price to early birds in order to avoid having to haul their goods to the booths inside the flea market.

The best strategy is to arrive an hour before the flea market opens, then negotiate a bargain to help the dealer avoid excess hauling. At the very least, you should aim for a 10 percent price reduction.

Wait Two Weeks
Save 20%

There's a growing trend to sell used furniture in consignment shops that specialize in home furnishings. These stores differ from thrift shops because the quality of goods is better. And the pieces you find in consignment shops are usually in better condition than those you find elsewhere. You'll also pay somewhat higher prices for consignment goods than you would for thrift store items. That's because the consignment shop pays "donors" a cut of the sales price. (The cost is usually worthwhile, however, because of the higher-quality goods.)

Even so, you can cut your consignment shop spending as much as 20 percent simply by playing the waiting game. Consignment shops want to move merchandise quickly, and when an item has been in the store a long time, the shop will begin to lower the price. Generally, prices drop anywhere from 10 to 20 percent if an item doesn't sell within two weeks. So if you can wait, you usually get a better deal.

This strategy is best used for items that won't attract a lot of attention from other customers or that aren't in demand—such as patio chairs being sold in October. Don't wait too long on a great find, however, or someone else will buy it first.

Bargain at Garage Sales
Save 20%

A garage sale is a great place to pick up furniture bargains. Unfortunately, many people don't realize just how good the bargains are. One common misconception of garage sales is that you have to pay the asking price.

No way! Garage sales are the best places to bargain for used furniture. The items offered are unwanted, which is why they're up for sale. So don't assume that you need to pay top dollar simply because that bureau once belonged to beloved Aunt Bessie. Heck, if it's not sold, it will probably belong to the garbage collector.

Negotiate your brains out! Many people holding garage sales purposely overprice their stock, thinking they'll be "bargained down." (Those who are experienced at garage sales always price their items high.) So if you're interested in something that's selling for $50, offer to "take it off their hands" for $35, and you'll probably get it for $40. Generally, for items under $50, you should make an initial offer of 25 percent under the asking price; for items above that amount, offer two-thirds of the asking price. Either way, you can usually buy it for 20 percent less than what's marked.

Get Goods for Free!
Cruise before Trash Pickup

No doubt the cheapest way to get quality used furniture is to rummage for it. Cruise through affluent neighborhoods in your area the night before "bulk" garbage is collected. Provided you have a pickup truck—or you can use a friend's for an evening—all you really need is some luck. An especially good time to make a rummage trip is right before the quarterly or annual "pick-up-anything" day. Most municipalities announce certain days when they'll collect anything, however large or small, and if you browse along slowly, you may spot some great furniture that you can pick up for nothing.

People routinely discard old items that no longer fit the decor or that have a few stains and scratches. But *old* often means *quality*—and a little paint or sandpaper or some basic carpentry can renew the splendor of these old pieces.

Affluent neighborhoods are your best bet because the quality of throwaway items tends to be better. Spring and fall seem to produce

USE THE RIGHT SALE
TO SELL YOUR THROWAWAYS

If you just discard used furniture that could be sold, you're not getting the full value from it. Here are some ways to cut your spending on the back end—by selling the goods you own for what they're worth.

Garage sales are easy to hold. All you need is a front yard or driveway. The only drawbacks are that garage sales are often seasonal—you don't find many in midwinter in northern states—and time-consuming, since garage sales can last all day. Also, people tend to expect great deals, so you may not get the price that you really want.

Consignment shops are good for those who want to unload only a piece or two, and you'll probably get better prices than you would at a garage sale. There are some disadvantages, however: You have to transport the item to the store, and it could take weeks or months before you get paid once the item is sold. Also, you have to split the profit from the sale with the consignment shop owner.

Flea markets have the advantage of drawing serious customers who come specifically to buy, so there's less browsing. While a flea market is the best place to wheel and deal, you really have to be a serious dealer to take a booth. Or you have to transport your items to the market, where they can be viewed for possible purchase by dealers.

Auctions, like flea markets, draw customers who are serious buyers rather than browsers, and the quality of goods tends to be better. But you may not be eligible to place your goods in an auction unless you have a lot to unload: Some auctions want only "quantity" sales, such as a complete houseful of furniture. Also, you pay the auctioneer a commission for selling the goods.

the best finds—probably because that's when people are doing heavy-duty cleaning in their homes. So if items are out by the street waiting for the next morning's trash pickup, help yourself.

BUYING QUALITY: HARD FURNITURE

You'll feel more confident that you're getting a bargain—whether you're buying new or used furnishings—if you can judge quality. This is especially true when you're looking for "hard" furniture pieces such as chests, bureaus and other non-upholstered items.

You can never assume that more expensive furniture is also better quality. Even "junk" furniture can be expensive, relatively speaking. Since it's not always easy to separate superiority from schlock, here are some tips to help you get the most value for your money— whether shopping at a first-rate retailer or strolling through your neighbor's yard sale.

Look at the Back

In good furniture, the back panel is usually finished rather than bare wood. That panel should be inset and screwed into the frame. Inferior pieces, by contrast, typically have unfinished back panels that are nailed, stapled or just glued to the frame. Also, in cheaper construction, that back panel is flush with the frame rather than inset.

Make a Point to Look at the Joints

To spot quality in case goods such as bureaus, chests and similar pieces, look at the construction of the joints. To do this, simply remove the drawer and look at the way it is fastened on its sides.

Lower-quality merchandise is usually just butted together and stapled or nailed. It's likely to fall apart too easily. So even if you pick up an inexpensive item, you're really getting no deal at all if it's made this way.

Quality goods have more detailed joinery. It's worth paying more for them because you may get a lifetime of use out of those pieces of furniture.

If you're buying a dresser with drawers, look for the dovetail joint. The corner is cut so that interlocking, wedge-shaped "fingers" of wood hold the front, back and sides together. A dovetail is the strongest joint for drawers. In all likelihood, it will never loosen during the entire life of the furniture.

Nearly as good is a mortise-and-tenon joint: The end of one part of the frame is fashioned into a tenon (a rectangular peg) that fits into a similarly shaped notch (the mortise) in another part of the frame.

Also look for the French dovetail: A wedge-shaped tongue of the side piece fits into a vertical groove in the front piece. Usually, the type of joining can be detected by carefully examining the inside and outside of the drawer where the pieces are joined.

In chairs, look for double dowel joints where the back and front of

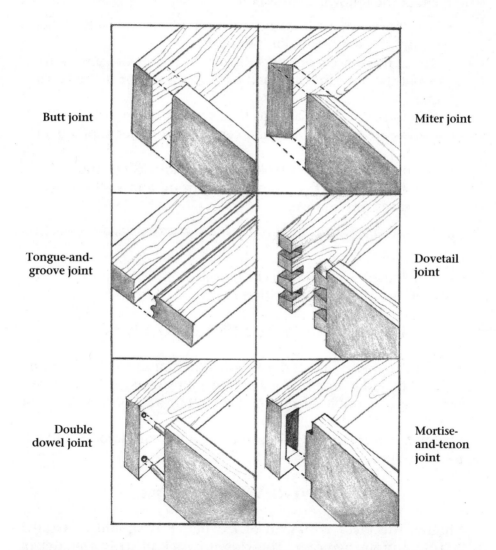

Butt joint

Miter joint

Tongue-and-groove joint

Dovetail joint

Double dowel joint

Mortise-and-tenon joint

To determine the quality of wood furniture—and to find out whether a piece is likely to last—be sure to examine the joints before you buy. Butt joints and miter joints are the weakest. Dovetail, double dowel and mortise-and-tenon joints are stronger. A well-made tabletop should have tongue-and-groove joinery.

FOR SOLID FURNITURE—USE THE PRESSURE TEST

"Bargain" furniture is no bargain if it won't stand the test of time. To make sure you're getting a piece of furniture that will last, check the following stress points.

- Press down on a top corner or push against the side. If the furniture "gives," you don't want it.
- Open any drawers or doors. If they fit snugly but also move smoothly, it means the wood has not warped or swelled over time.
- If a cabinet or sideboard has long shelves, make sure that the shelves are supported in the center with either supports or braces.
- Buying a dining room table? Lift the table leaves and try to "wobble" them. If the hinges are strong and well secured, the leaves won't move.

---

the seat are joined to the sides. (The dowels are inserted into holes for stability, as shown in the illustration on page 179.)

Go Outside to See the Real Finish

A finish that looks rich and lovely in the dim light of a furniture store may be muddy in a true light. To get a really good look, carry a drawer or any movable furniture to a well-lit area of the store—or even better, go outside.

What you're looking for is a finish that is clear and smooth and has a pleasing color.

Test with Water Drops

Whether the piece is stained or lacquered, it should be treated with a final protective coat. The gloss (or lack of it) is a matter of personal preference, but the protective coat should be tough enough to resist moisture. So place a few drops of water on it to see if it beads up. If the water "puddles" on the surface of the piece, it's not properly protected.

Feel for Roughness

Generally, better pieces go through a series of finishing steps that include sanding, waxing, glazing and even buffing. The result is a smooth surface that's also hard and even. Less expensive pieces, however, are usually treated with a coat of polyurethane and may have bubbles, pockmarks or cracks. The surface of a cheaply finished piece usually feels rougher.

WOODEN IT BE NICE

Despite advertising that touts "the timeless beauty of solid wood," there's surprisingly little solid wood in most of today's furniture. Veneers, plywood and particleboard are commonly used by manufacturers in both the visible and invisible parts of most wood furniture.

That's not necessarily a problem. Plywood, for instance, is actually stronger than solid wood and better than solid wood for some uses. Still, you should know what you're really getting. Here's how to tell.

Solid wood means that all visible parts of the item are made from pure oak, pine, maple or another type of solid wood. But the back, bottom and inside components of drawers and other "hidden" parts can be made from anything else the manufacturer chooses to substitute.

All wood is a confusing term. Although you may think you're getting a quality piece because it's marked this way, in reality, all wood simply means that all the parts of that piece of furniture once came from a tree. That means anything that contains particleboard, plywood or some other composition board can be listed as all wood.

Veneer means that a thin slice of wood has been glued to a base (usually plywood or particleboard), so the piece has an expensive look without being expensive to manufacture.

Laminate refers to a man-made product, such as Formica, that can sometimes resemble wood. It doesn't contain any real wood, however.

Check the Label

In newer furniture, premium finishes are usually labeled "hand-rubbed." That means the finish was built up in layers, and each layer was sanded before the next was applied. So for the best-quality new furniture, look for the label that says "hand-rubbed."

BUYING QUALITY: UPHOLSTERY

Most people judge sofas and chairs by their outward appearance—how they look. Actually, better pieces are determined by their "guts."

When you're considering a price-versus-quality trade-off in upholstered furniture, keep this in mind: A poorly made $600 sofa that lasts only six years costs you $100 a year. Though a quality, well-constructed sofa may cost $1,000, it's a bargain if you know it will still look good after 20 years. That's an average cost of just $50 a year.

So here's how to tell if an item you're considering has the fortitude to withstand years of wear and tear.

Choose Small Patterns
Save 10%

Upholsterers need to use more fabric to match complicated patterns, and that drives up the cost of upholstered furniture. By sticking with small patterns or solid colors, less fabric is wasted. You'll usually find that an upholstered piece with a small pattern costs about 10 percent less than the same chair or sofa with a large pattern. There's nothing different about the quality of fabric or construction—just less waste in the manufacturing process.

Don't Fall for a Lame Frame

The easiest way to gauge a frame is to pick up one end of the furniture. It should feel solid. If the furniture wobbles or makes creaking sounds, it suggests that the wood wasn't dried properly before assembly and that the piece doesn't have strong-enough joints for its weight.

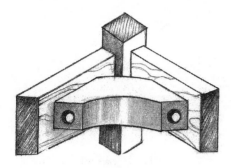

A well-built table or chair has corner blocks inside the frame at each of the four corners. Be sure to check the underside of a piece of furniture before you buy—and make sure there are no signs of cracking or splintering around the joints.

Frames on better furniture are made from seasoned hardwood—not pine—joined by dowels or with interlocking pieces. If the joints are just butted and glued or stapled together, you can count on problems. Also, look on the underside to find out whether corner blocks are screwed into position for added strength.

Check Out the Legs

Quality of construction is also evidenced by the way the legs are joined to the rest of the frame. They should be not separate pieces but rather a continuation of the front or back frame. Unless you're buying chairs, be wary of legs that are screwed into the frame. Also, a good-quality chair should not have legs that are held on by metal plates.

Turn the chair over, or feel underneath the corner joints, to find out what kind of construction has been used.

Weigh the Cushions

Generally, the lighter the cushions are, the cheaper the goods. A standard two- by two-foot sofa cushion that's six inches thick should weigh no less than two pounds; anything lighter suggests inferior quality.

Most manufacturers now use polyurethane foam as the filling in cushions because it's strong and resilient. Older quality pieces, however, are often filled with either a down material or a solid piece of polyester wrapped around a more dense piece of foam. (Cheaper goods may have shredded foam, which doesn't hold its shape as well.) Whether the cushion is new or old, if it's better quality, the material should be enclosed in its own sewn ticking.

$199 $499

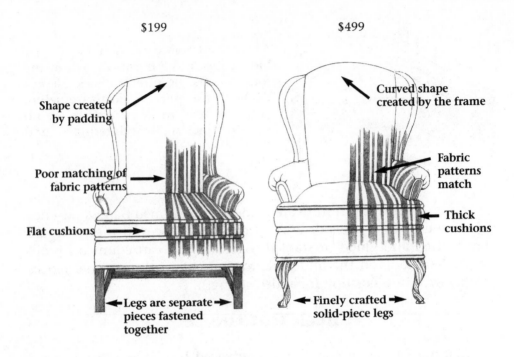

Shape created
by padding

Curved shape
created by the frame

Poor matching of
fabric patterns

Fabric
patterns
match

Flat cushions

Thick
cushions

←Legs are separate→
pieces fastened
together

←Finely crafted→
solid-piece legs

Special design features and tailoring add to the price of an armchair. Here are the differences that can boost the retail cost by $300 or more.

The filling material should be listed on the "under penalty of law" tag on the cushion.

Don't Be Foiled by the Coils

Those who shop for the very best quality upholstered goods look for individual round coils that are funnel-shaped, spaced closely together and hand-tied eight ways. But hand tying is labor-intensive and drives up the cost substantially.

It's not worth the additional cost. Sinuous wire springs, also known as zigzag or seamless springs, last just as long as the more ballyhooed eight-tied coils. And if you go for the sinuous wire construction, you can save as much as $250 off the price of a sofa.

But don't neglect to check the quality of webbing that holds the coils or springs. It should be interwoven, with webbing that's closely spaced. The less "air space" between the crisscrosses in the webbing, the better the quality.

Check Out Leather

If you're in the market for a new sofa, don't ignore leather uphol-stered goods. While a leather chair might cost one-third more ini-tially, studies show that it tends to last four times longer than a fabric-covered piece. So quality leather is a better value.

But it has to be good quality to be worth the extra price. When shopping for leather, unzip the cushions to examine the underside. You want "aniline dyed," meaning that the leather is a uniform color all the way through. If the leather on the underside is lighter or darker than the surface color, the piece probably isn't worth the price. Also, look for items marked "full grain" or "full top grain." These are both natural looking and very durable.

FABRIC

Purchasing furniture with a top-quality frame means little if the fabric covering is second-rate. Since the actual fabric—rather than the frame—takes most of the abuse from use, you want to be sure the fabric will hold up.

Here's how to tell if the fabric on your upholstered furniture (as well as draperies and linens) is a good value for the money.

Hold It to the Light

The easiest way to tell if the fabric is of good quality when you're buying new furniture is to hold a swatch of it to the light. (At most furniture stores, they'll give you a separate swatch to examine as a sample.) The tighter the weave, the better the fabric is. Either no light or only tiny pinpoints of light get through. But if there's no swatch available, here are some other ways to inspect the fabric.

Give It a Rubdown

Dampen a clean white handkerchief, then give the fabric a good rub. If any color comes off on the handkerchief, the fabric is inferior quality.

Next scratch the fabric with a fingernail to see whether threads stretch or pull easily. Then rub a pencil eraser along it to see if bits of fabric pill or form tiny balls. If so, you definitely don't want that piece of furniture.

Look at the Backing for Up-Front Info

You can also check the strength of the fabric with a simple pressure test. Hold the swatch tightly between your hands, with your thumbs about two inches apart. Press down on the fabric as hard as possible with your thumbs. If yarns slip or separate, construction is weak.

Is It Woven or Printed?
Here's How to Tell

A woven pattern will last longer than one that's printed. You can tell the difference by looking at the back of the fabric. If you see the pattern clearly on the back, it's woven and of better quality. If the pattern on the reverse side is faded or a solid color (and the design isn't evident), the fabric is printed.

Don't Let Softness Fool You

Natural fibers such as cotton and linen are softer and take colors better, so people assume these fabrics are a better choice. Actually, they tend to wear out more quickly.

For lasting value, you're better off with man-made fibers such as nylon, olefin and polyester—or a blend of man-made and cotton fabrics. To see what you're getting, check out the label.

BEDDING

Considering the fact that you spend one-third of your life in bed, this is probably the most important furniture item you purchase. Beds vary greatly in price. For a frame, foundation (or box spring) and mattress, you can pay as little as $150 or as much as $2,000. But no matter what your budget, here's how to get the best bedding at the lowest possible price.

Buy from a Volume Dealer
Save 40%

As with anything else, buying bedding from a volume dealer can save you big. But with everyone claiming to buy in volume, how can you tell you're really getting the best price?

One way is to buy from North Carolina. The same great deals you can get in living room, dining room and other types of furniture are available for bedding. That's because these Tarheel State furniture marts and warehouses truly deal in volume mattress sales. (In fact, some claim to be the nation's largest volume dealers of Sealy and other top name brands.)

Their volume buying means you can buy the same mattresses for 40 percent less than retail, even when you include shipping costs. Simply go to any nearby retailer and decide what you want. Then call a dealer in North Carolina and order that mattress by phone. It will be shipped to your home.

To learn more about buying from North Carolina discounters, check page 170.

Shop during White Sales
Save 20%

Although there's no "official" furniture sale season, you may notice that many items—particularly bedroom furniture—tend to be discounted during the traditional white sale seasons.

From December to February, and once again from June to September, many department stores and furniture retailers discount mattresses, box springs and even bed frames by taking 5 to 20 percent off regular prices. (You may also find similar savings on table and floor lamps, floor coverings and assorted pieces of living room and dining room furniture.)

Use a Pad to Prolong Mattress Life

For a mere $35, you can buy an extra-thick mattress pad that can add at least three years of life to your mattress. (Most people have standard mattress pads, which cost about $20 but are not as effective as the extra-thick ones.) The best time to get a pad, of course, is when you buy a new mattress. But extra-thick pads also help prolong the comfort and life of a basically sound but worn mattress that's showing its age.

Another way to help extend the life of your mattress is to turn it over once a year. This helps prevent sways and wear and tear on one end of the mattress. To turn it, simply flip it over so that the "below" side is now on top.

Look into Private Labels
Save 25%

Although name-brand bedding is more popular, you can usually get a similar-quality mattress or box spring through a lesser-known company—and save 25 percent or more in the process. Retailers tend to showcase the Sertas, Sealys and other high-profile brands because of their popularity, but private-label goods are usually just as good. They may not be displayed, so ask your retailer, since lesser-known brands are often kept in the "back room."

Measure the Thickness to Avoid Hidden Cost

Sometimes, there's a "hidden" cost in bed buying. If you purchase a mattress that's three to five inches thicker than other mattresses, you may need to buy new bedsheets. Same goes with European bedding (like that sold in Ikea), which is measured in centimeters rather than inches.

Either way, you need special sheets to fit these mattresses correctly, so keep this in mind before buying.

Count the Coils

The more coils a bed has, the longer it will keep its shape—and the longer it will last.

Full-size mattresses should have at least 300 coils, queens should have 375 or more, and kings should have at least 450. If the bed has anything less, you're not getting good value. Read the manufacturer's description to find out.

Listen for Creaks, Feel for Sways

In any price range, you're likely to find some beds that are far more comfortable than others. And the only real way to find the one you like is to try them out. Don't hesitate to lie down and roll around. You can't assess comfort and support simply by sitting on the edge of the bed.

Get a pillow and lie down in the position you normally sleep in. Then roll from the center to the edges. The support should be the same at all points, without any creaking or swaying. Finally, lie on your side for several minutes: If your hip and shoulder aren't comfortable, try another bed.

Check the Covering

It's not only what's inside a mattress and box spring that makes them good. Make sure you check the covering for these features.

- Look for a sturdy ticking with a pattern that's woven, not printed.
- Check for handles on the sides for easy turning.

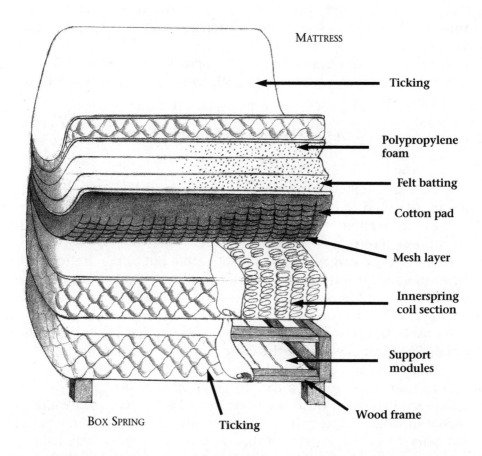

You can get great bargains in bedding, but be sure to check the manufacturer's description before buying a box spring and mattress. Here are the components of a good-quality box spring and mattress.

- Small metal vents on the sides help disperse heat and allow air to circulate inside.
- Plastic corner guards help protect the bed from scratches and nicks.

FLOOR COVERINGS

Choosing a floor covering can be one of the toughest decisions a homeowner can make. There are so many choices—and each one has its advantages and disadvantages, especially for "high-use" rooms such as the kitchen and bath.

And no matter what you choose, it will probably be expensive. You can spend more than $1,000 to buy and install floor coverings for a couple of rooms. And once it's down, it's down! It can cost dearly—in money and hassles—to rip up and replace that floor if you change your mind.

While you're the best judge of the right kind of flooring for your home—be it carpet, wood, ceramic tile or sheet goods—here's how to buy it for less.

Ask for Last Year's Lot
Save 50%

Each year, slight improvements are made in sheet goods, which are mostly used as flooring in kitchens and bathrooms. Examples of these improvements may include thicker padding, a slightly different design or new colors.

Often these changes are barely noticeable but allow the retailer to boast of added features, much like a car dealer. And as with any other business, when the new stuff comes in the showroom, the old inventory goes to the back room.

By asking for last year's inventory, you can get top-quality sheet goods for about one-half of the current retail cost. After all, who cares if a floor is last year's model?

For instance, we found a pattern we liked in a retail showroom for a new kitchen floor. Unfortunately, it cost $38.50 a square yard. But mixed in with inventory from the previous year was the same pattern for only $18.50 a square yard. The only difference was that the cheaper version had a slightly darker color (signifying to the retailer that it was the previous year's model), which was barely noticeable.

The retailer explained it was on sale because it was from an old lot number—a numerical system used to make sure that similar-looking rolls are made from the same dyes. (If you want patterns to match, you always need to make sure the separate rolls come from the same lot number.) By purchasing the pattern with last year's lot number, we paid $18.50 instead of $38.50 a square yard—saving 52 percent.

One caution: Make sure you buy enough from the same lot number—otherwise, you may not get a perfect match with the newer pattern if you have to go back for more.

Piece Together Remnants
Save 25%

It's always cheaper to piece together several smaller remnants than to buy one large piece. For instance, let's say you need to cover a 20- by 12-foot room. If you buy two 10- by 12-foot remnants, you can save anywhere from 25 to 40 percent compared with buying one 20- by 12-foot piece—even when it's discounted.

That's because smaller remnants are usually leftovers from jobs. Since they're often too small to cover complete rooms, they're sold as filler.

After laying our kitchen floor with the discounted pattern that cost $18.50 a square yard, we decided to include an adjacent hallway. We found a 12- by 8-foot remnant for $95—about $9 a square yard. So we saved an additional 50 percent off our already half-off purchase! (Again, be sure that the remnants have matching lot numbers.)

Buy in the Spring
Save 10%

Many home improvements are considered seasonal. Building decks, for instance, is considered a warm-weather project, while interior jobs (including installation of new flooring) are considered cold-weather tasks. So when spring comes, it's time to spring into action—and look for sales on tile, carpet and sheet goods.

While there is no "official" sale season for flooring, many retailers (especially larger home improvement centers) seem to have their biggest discounts when they try to clear inventory to make room for spring and summer merchandise. With most homeowners thinking about yard work and other outdoor jobs—and not floors—you can usually buy new flooring at discounts of 10 percent or more off the usual prices. You'll notice even greater savings at specialty stores such as Color Tile and at carpet centers.

Paint the "Fifth Wall"

Most people assume a floor needs to be stained, carpeted or covered. But why not cut your spending—and decorate it with paint?

Wood, cement and terrazzo can all be painted, and so can some tile and sheet goods. In fact, the perfect way to spark up a kid's room, play area, family room or kitchen is by painting whimsical designs in wild colors.

And you don't need to be concerned about wear and tear. You can

---

GET CREDIT FOR YOUR ORIENTAL RUGS

Handmade oriental rugs don't come cheap—but it could be money well spent. Besides getting a beautiful floor covering, you're also making a good investment. But you have to make sure the rug is handmade—either by buying from a very reputable dealer or by getting an outside appraisal from an expert. Only the handmade rugs have the legendary durability of true orientals.

Besides long wear, there's another plus to buying handmade oriental rugs: They tend to increase in value. Many stores allow you to trade in an oriental and to receive the same price you paid as credit toward the purchase of a new rug. In other words, if you paid $2,000 for your rug and "move up" to one costing $3,500, you can pay only $1,500 with your trade. Just make sure your trade-in agreement is with a reputable dealer who has been in business for a long time.

Whether or not you have a trade-in agreement, however, you should always keep the receipt for a handmade oriental rug. Prices start in the high hundreds for a small doormat-size rug—and can go as high as tens of thousands of dollars for an oriental that covers an entire room. If you ever redecorate or decide you want a different rug, you may be able to take your receipt to a dealer and get full credit toward the purchase of a new one.

BUYER BEWARE! IF IT SOUNDS
TOO GOOD TO BE TRUE . . .

One of the oldest rip-off scams in the carpet biz is to advertise a really low price for wall-to-wall carpet in an effort to get you into the store.

The reason for the "bargain"? The price is quoted for a square foot—not for the standard square yard. Keep in mind that there are nine square feet in a square yard when you do your math.

---

create a tough, long-lasting surface—for hundreds less than traditional flooring. Just be sure to use oil-based enamels, because they last longer. And after you've painted the floor, cover it with several coats of polyurethane, so your new design lasts.

Opt for Area Rugs
Save 15%

Yard by yard, you get more for your money buying area rugs instead of wall-to-wall carpeting. Generally, you can get an oriental-style rug for about 15 percent less than you'd pay for a wall-to-wall carpet of similar quality—even if you get free installation of the carpet. You'll save even more—between 20 and 35 percent—buying a single-color carpet remnant rather than wall-to-wall. (*Exception:* Authentic oriental rugs, which are handmade, are very expensive.)

Area rugs do need padding, which can mean additional cost. However, many carpet stores will gladly give you the padding for free or for a nominal amount, such as $5. So be sure to ask.

Go with a Wider Roll

If you do want wall-to-wall carpeting for a big room, look for carpet that comes in 15-foot rolls instead of the usual 12-foot width. If you get the wider carpet, you'll reduce the number of seams—and if your room is narrower than 15 feet, you'll eliminate the need for any seams. This can lower your installation costs by anywhere from $50 to $150, depending on the size of the job. Besides, the carpet will last longer, since the seam areas tend to wear out quickly.

KNOW YOUR AREA RUGS

Area rugs run the complete price range, from thrift shop bargains to antique, handmade orientals. No matter how you cover your floors, any area rug should be laid over a protective non-skid pad to extend its life and protect you from dangerous falls. But apart from that common factor, there are many differences.

Hand-tufted rugs are soft, dense and usually made from wool. While the price depends on the pattern, they usually cost between $20 and $50 per square foot. By comparison, most wall-to-wall carpeting costs that much per square yard. (And since a square yard is nine square feet, a hand-tufted rug can be nine times more expensive.)

Handmade oriental rugs are created by hand-knotting thousands of pieces of wool yarn around cotton warp thread. Quality is measured in knots per square inch. The typical rug has 80 to 150 knots per square inch, but top-quality merchandise has as many as 600. Most handmade oriental rugs now come from India, Pakistan, Iran, Romania, Turkey and China. Price is determined by country of origin (Iran is the most expensive); cost can range from several thousand to tens of thousands of dollars.

Machine-made oriental rugs are similar to their handmade counterparts but have less detail and a much lower price. Starting at around $150 for an 8- by 11-foot rug, machine-made orientals are among the most popular of area rugs. To tell whether an oriental is machine-made or handmade, look at the underside: In the machine-made rug, the knots are looser but more evenly spaced.

Kilims and dhurries are usually reversible and have no pile. (They're also called flat weaves.) Starting at around $15 for a small area rug, they are among the least expensive rugs because they're mass-produced. They also tend to wear out the fastest.

Rag rugs and braided rugs are popular for country interiors because of their rustic charm. Most are machine-washable. You can buy mass-produced rag and braided rugs starting at around $70 for an 8- by 11-foot size. For a little more money and a lot more pizzazz, check with local weavers, who often make uniquely designed rag rugs from scraps of fabric.

Stick with a Darker Color

If you're stuck on color choices, keep this in mind: While lighter colors tend to make rooms look larger, they fade faster and make a carpet look old before its time. Besides, the lighter the shade, the more it shows stains and dirt. So you're making a better investment in long-lasting carpet if you choose a darker color.

WINDOW TREATMENTS

When it comes to both cutting costs and enhancing a room's beauty, simple window treatments tend to be the best. In fact, many people now believe that the less attention placed on window treatments, the more elegant the room will appear. Here are some ways to cover your windows with style while stretching your budget.

Use Swags

A swag is a piece of fabric that decoratively hangs above a window. Traditionally, it's been used on top of draperies to add elegance to the window treatment and hide the curtain rod. But if you use a swag as the only window treatment, you'll let more light in the room—not to mention save on expensive curtain fabric.

For less than $10 in fabric and assorted small hardware, you can dress a window with an attractive swag "topping"—and save the $200 or so it costs for a set of quality draperies. Multiply that amount by the number of windows in your house, and you have ample opportunity to save hundreds of dollars.

Do Your Own Customizing
Save 55%

Probably no window treatment is less expensive than a simple white roller shade—and there's none more boring. But instead of spending $40 or more on a fancier type of window covering, you can easily "customize" a roller shade for a few bucks. Just glue a covering on the shade to complement the room.

First buy a basic white roller shade, which usually costs about $8 for a standard window. Spend another $10 or so on vinylized wallpaper or fabric. You can glue or staple most coverings to the roller shade. (Also, some stores sell laminating kits to make the job easier.) If you're gluing, use non-staining diluted white glue.

Go with Store-Bought over Custom
Save 30%

If you don't need custom draperies, you can save 30 percent or more by buying ready-made sizes at the store. Most people buy custom draperies because of length problems (store-bought sets may be too long or short).

If you're handy with a sewing machine, you can shorten them. But you may be able to avoid the custom costs if your sofa is in front of the window—it will help hide store-bought draperies that aren't long enough.

Opt for Plastic over Metal
Save 50%

If you like the look of mini-blinds, go with those made from plastic instead of from metal. They're just as durable, easy to clean and attractive as the original Levolor metal mini-blinds, but you can get them for about one-half of the cost.

Camouflage instead of Cover

If a window lacks a good view and you want to focus attention on the interior, you can camouflage it instead of covering it. For instance, if you want privacy *and* sunlight, a collection of glass bottles will catch the light beautifully. If the window faces north or is in shade, you can move a fish tank in front of it.

A window treatment can be practical as well. For an attractive "window garden" for houseplants, install shelf standards on each side of a window—then brackets and shelves. If you really want to cut costs, the shelves can be painted boards from a wooden skid—available for free at any home improvement center. Arrange houseplants on the shelves for a year-round indoor garden.

Cut Your Spending on

REAL ESTATE

- Paying Less on Your Mortgage
- Applying for a Mortgage
- Building a Home
- Existing Homes
- Negotiating and Bidding
- Steals and Deals
- Real Estate Agents and Agencies

MAKE YOUR DREAM HOUSE COME TRUE

It doesn't matter whether your American dream is styled contemporary or colonial, Cape Cod or Chicago greystone. Buying or selling a home is usually an unsettling experience.

As if all those zeros in the purchase price weren't enough, there are also inspections, mortgage points, escrow taxes, title searches and other fees that can add tens of thousands to the actual "price" of buying a home. Then there are the lifestyle considerations: the quality of your child's education, neighbors who will play a key role in your life (for better or worse) and the travel time to work, school and shopping centers. Even the air, water and earth surrounding your home can determine your family's health.

Not that sellers have it that easy, either. When you're selling, you must endure a parade of strangers peeking through every nook and cranny of your home, and then you have to pay a real estate agent a commission that rivals the gross national product of some Third World countries.

But whether you're buying or selling, it doesn't have to cause that much pain—at least to your wallet.

PAYING LESS ON YOUR MORTGAGE

For many people, a house is one of the biggest investments of a lifetime. But what does it really cost to own your own home? That will depend on how large a mortgage you need, the rate of interest and how long you take to pay. You can cut your spending in a major way if you carefully choose your mortgage before you sign on the dotted line. But even if you already have a mortgage and are making your monthly payments, you can save a lot of money over the term of the loan. Here are some choice money-saving tips on choosing a mortgage and paying it off.

WHERE YOUR MONEY GOES

- Because property taxes shot up in the late 1980s and early 1990s, the typical homeowner ended up paying 50 percent more in property taxes.
- Middle age brings some high housing costs. Those between the ages of 35 and 54 spend the most on mortgage payments and other basic household costs—more than $11,000 a year. The average spent by other age groups was $9,300.
- The typical homeowner pays more than $5,100 each year on interest for his mortgage.

Deal with a Mortgage Company
Save $500

Since mortgage companies deal only in mortgages (as opposed to car loans, money market certificates and other services), they tend to offer better rates than banks. Generally, you'll pay one-fourth to one-half percentage point less by getting your loan through a mortgage company as opposed to a bank. That means if banks are typically offering rates of 8 percent, you can usually get a loan for 7.5 or 7.75 percent at a mortgage company. On a typical loan, that translates to savings of about $500 a year.

What's more, mortgage companies are just as reputable as commercial banks. Most simply "sell" your loan to pension funds, credit unions and other financial institutions for a commission, and you make your payments directly to that organization.

Pay More Each Month
Save 50%

No matter who holds your mortgage, the real key to cutting your spending in half is to pay it off as soon as possible. Depending on your rate, you could literally halve your total costs over the life of the loan simply by paying more up front each month.

Most people try to do this by opting for a 15-year mortgage over a more traditional 30-year loan. Although the monthly payment is

(continued on page 202)

HOW MUCH DO YOU
WANT TO PAY THE BANK?

If you choose a 30-year mortgage, your required monthly payments will be lower, and as a result, your income will qualify you to carry a larger mortgage. If you go with a 15-year mortgage, you will pay more each month, but you'll build equity quicker and save on the total amount of interest you pay. So which kind of mortgage should you choose?

Most experts recommend that if you can afford it, go with the shorter mortgage. However, if you're paying for a "starter" home that you plan to leave in a few years, a 30-year mortgage may be better because your monthly payments will be considerably less.

Use the tables on the opposite page to compare a 30-year mortgage with a 15-year mortgage. To figure out the total interest on a 30-year mortgage, find your monthly payment in the table. Then multiply by 360 (the number of months) and subtract the principal. For total payments on a 15-year mortgage, find the monthly payment, multiply by 180, then subtract the principal. The difference is how much you'll save if you take a 15-year instead of a 30-year mortgage.

For instance, here's a comparison between 15-year and 30-year schedules for a $100,000 mortgage at 8 percent interest.

	15-YEAR MORTGAGE	30-YEAR MORTGAGE
Monthly payments ($)	955.65	733.76
Number of payments	180	360
Total paid during the term of the mortgage ($)	172,017.00	264,153.60
Principle paid ($)	100,000.00	100,000.00
Interest paid ($)	72,017.00	164,153.60

Conclusion: On this $100,000 mortgage, you can cut your spending by more than $92,000 if you can pay $222 more each month.

MONTHLY PAYMENTS: 30-YEAR MORTGAGE

RATE OF INTEREST	AMOUNT OF MORTGAGE ($)						
	70,000	75,000	80,000	85,000	90,000	95,000	100,000
6%	419.69	449.66	479.64	509.62	539.60	569.57	599.55
6.5%	442.45	474.05	505.65	537.26	568.86	600.46	632.07
7%	465.71	498.98	532.24	565.51	598.77	632.04	665.30
7.5%	489.45	524.41	559.37	594.33	629.29	664.25	699.21
8%	513.64	550.32	587.01	623.70	660.39	697.08	733.76
8.5%	538.24	576.69	615.13	653.58	692.02	730.47	768.91
9%	563.24	603.47	643.70	683.93	724.16	764.39	804.66
9.5%	588.60	630.64	672.68	714.73	756.77	798.81	840.85
10%	614.30	658.18	702.06	745.94	789.81	833.69	877.57
10.5%	640.32	686.05	731.79	777.53	823.27	869.00	914.74
11%	666.63	714.24	761.86	809.47	857.09	904.71	952.32
11.5%	693.20	742.72	792.23	841.75	891.26	940.78	990.29
12%	720.03	771.46	822.89	874.32	925.75	977.18	1,028.61

MONTHLY PAYMENTS: 15-YEAR MORTGAGE

RATE OF INTEREST	AMOUNT OF MORTGAGE ($)						
	70,000	75,000	80,000	85,000	90,000	95,000	100,000
6%	590.70	632.89	675.09	717.28	759.47	801.66	843.86
6.5%	609.78	653.30	696.89	740.44	784.08	827.55	871.11
7%	629.18	674.12	719.06	764.00	808.95	853.89	898.83
7.5%	648.91	695.26	741.61	787.98	834.31	880.66	927.01
8%	668.96	716.74	764.52	812.30	860.09	907.87	955.65
8.5%	689.32	738.55	787.79	837.03	886.27	935.50	984.74
9%	709.99	760.70	811.42	862.13	912.84	963.55	1,014.27
9.5%	730.96	783.17	835.38	887.59	939.80	992.01	1,044.22
10%	752.22	805.95	859.68	913.41	967.14	1,020.87	1,074.61
10.5%	773.78	829.05	884.32	939.59	994.86	1,050.13	1,105.40
11%	795.62	852.45	909.28	966.11	1,022.94	1,079.77	1,136.60
11.5%	817.73	876.14	934.55	992.96	1,051.37	1,109.78	1,168.19
12%	840.12	900.13	960.13	1,020.14	1,080.15	1,140.16	1,200.17

PAY MORE NOW, SAVE A LOT MORE LATER

Even if you have to pay more money each month, the key to saving on your mortgage in the long run is to pay for as few months as possible. Here's a comparison of your total costs on a typical $100,000 loan at 7.5 percent.

Loan length	15 years	30 years
Monthly payments ($)	927.01	699.21
Total costs ($)	166,861.80	251,715.60

higher, your bottom-line costs can be nearly half as much because you're paying the loan for one-half of the time.

But if you can't afford a 15-year mortgage or already have a 30-year loan, you can still save tens of thousands of dollars—simply by paying more in principal and interest each month. If you have a $100,000 loan at 7.5 percent, adding a mere $25 extra to your monthly payment of $700 can save you nearly $30,000 over the life of your loan; paying an extra $100 a month can save you $81,200.

Pay on Schedule

Most mortgage payments are due on the first of each month, but customers are allowed a few days' grace period. You'll notice on your statement that you pay dearly for late payments (after the 15th of the month in most cases).

But what you may not know is that there is no benefit to you by paying early. If your check goes in early, it just allows the bank to get extra interest on your money for a few days.

Don't Pay Extra for a Biweekly Program

Many mortgage companies tell customers that they can "save" thousands of dollars in interest if they choose to pay biweekly instead of monthly. On a biweekly program, you make a payment every two weeks that is equal to one-half of your total monthly mortgage payment. You end up making 26 mortgage payments a year, or the equivalent of 1 extra monthly payment annually.

Trouble is, the mortgage companies usually charge between $200 and $350 for joining a biweekly payment program. Don't buy it! If you want to pay off faster, just add to the payments on your principal, and save yourself that additional cost.

APPLYING FOR A MORTGAGE

If you're taking out a mortgage, there are a lot of variables to consider. Besides the term of the mortgage and interest rates, there may be points, application fees and payments to an attorney or a real estate agent. But here are some ways to cut those costs.

Don't Double-Pay Points

Besides the actual percentage rate, another key factor in applying for a mortgage is the number of points you have to pay. A point is 1

TO BUY OR NOT TO BUY?

Of course, before you begin looking at any house, you need to evaluate whether it's better to buy or to rent. Here are some guidelines to help you make that choice.

Consider renting if:

- You know you will be moving within the next year or two.
- Rents are low, interest rates are high and you have a small down payment.

Consider buying if:

- You can negotiate a deal to buy property at 15 percent or more below fair market value.
- You plan to stay in the area, need some tax relief and/or want to accumulate equity over the long term.
- You want the security of owning your own home.
- You want to be totally responsible for the care and maintenance of your home, without relying on a landlord or absentee owner.

CHOOSING A MORTGAGE

With so many different types of mortgages, it may seem hard to determine the one that's right for you. The interest rate is the most important factor, of course. But you should also consider how long you expect to live in the house, and you need to make a realistic estimate of how much you expect your household income to increase in future years.

No matter what "bracket" you're in, it helps to have an overview of the different forms of financing. Here they are.

Fixed rate. If you want to be certain that your monthly payment won't change during the term of your mortgage, you should consider a fixed rate mortgage. Remember that if mortgage rates go down, you will continue to pay interest at your fixed rate. Of course, if prevailing rates go up, you'll have a bargain for the term of your loan.

Fixed rates, which come in 15-year, 25-year and 30-year loans, are often advised for those who plan to stay in the same house for a long time.

Adjustable rate. Initial rates on adjustable rate mortgages (ARMs) are often as much as two to three percentage points lower than the rates advertised for fixed rate mortgages. The reason for the low "teaser rates" is a lower risk factor for the lender. If rates go up and you have an ARM, you'll pay more.

If you choose an ARM, your interest rate could go up or down at agreed-upon intervals (every six months or annually) during the term of your mortgage. So your monthly payments could increase or decrease once or twice a year, depending what's written into the mortgage agreement. Your new rate on the adjustment date will be tied to a national financial index.

ARM mortgages are good for people who don't plan to stay in a home very long, such as buyers of "starter" homes. But if you go with an ARM, make sure your mortgage has two "caps"—that is,

percent of the loan amount—so if you're applying for a $157,000 mortgage, for example, one point is $1,570.

For most mortgages, you'll have to pay anywhere from one to three points; usually, the overall interest rate is 0.25 percent less for each

limits on how much your mortgage can increase at the specified interval.

The first cap is for the interest rate. The most common cap is two percentage points, so if the rate starts at 5.75 percent, it can't go above 7.75 percent on your first adjustment date. (It can increase another two percentage points on the next adjustment date.)

The second is a life-of-the-loan cap—the maximum number of percentage points the interest rate can change from the initial rate. If you start with a rate of 5.75 percent when you take out the loan and you have a six-point life-of-the-loan cap, the interest rate on your mortgage would never go above 11.75 percent. (But for this reason, the initial loan rate is often called the teaser rate.)

Balloon mortgages. If you have one of these mortgages, payments of a fixed amount are made until a given date, which is usually three or five years in the future. On that date, the entire balance of the loan is due and payable, which means the homeowner must either sell or refinance before the loan comes due. These mortgages usually offer below-market rates. But you have to make that big payment on a predetermined date. So these mortgages are attractive primarily to those who plan to sell before the balloon is due.

Seller financing. Whenever the pace of the market slows down, seller financing crops up. As an enticement to buy, the seller may offer to carry a "purchase money mortgage" at an interest rate substantially below the going rate among banks, mortgage companies and other conventional lenders.

One benefit of seller financing is that loan qualification requirements are less stringent than those used by institutional lenders. Also, the seller may ask for a lower down payment, and his interest rate may be lower than what banks and mortgage companies are offering. Most seller financing is done with a balloon clause, however, so the buyer must refinance, sell or pay off the balance of the loan within a certain time frame.

point you pay up front. That means if the going rate for mortgages is 8 percent with one point, you can probably get a 7.75 percent rate with two points or a 7.5 percent rate with three points.

Whether you go with the lowest rate and highest points or

highest rate and lowest points isn't that crucial. You'll end up paying just about the same amount—within a few dollars—in the long run.

What's more important is that you don't double-pay points. Some banks and mortgage companies quote competitive rates and points but then tack on a separate origination fee (sometimes called a processing fee) that amounts to $1,000 or more. If your mortgage calls for a processing fee, make sure that you're paying one point less than you would pay for a competitor's loan. Otherwise, you're paying the same fee twice.

Waive the Application Fee
Save $500

Most lenders require that you pay a fee for applying for a mortgage. This application fee is not the same as points, nor is it an origination fee. Instead, it's a "standard" cost—ranging from $250 to $500—just to process the application form.

But in very competitive mortgage markets, when houses are selling slowly and interest rates are low, some lenders will waive application fees if you have a steady income and an excellent credit rating. If your lender will waive the application fee, you may save as much as $500.

Have the Lender Do His Own Homework
Save $650

Another fee that could be avoided is the lender's attorney fee. Some banks and mortgage companies require that an attorney review the mortgage papers—but even so, they make you foot the bill.

Don't give in on this one. Since it's their papers that are being drafted and their interests that are being protected, insist that any attorney fees come out of their pocket. A lender who wants your business may waive this fee, which can be anywhere from $200 to $650.

Use an Agent as Your Lawyer
Save $500

When you decide to use a real estate agent, you're saving some money in closing costs—automatically. Without an agent, you (as the buyer) have to hire a lawyer to draw up the papers for closing—a move that can cost you $500 or more. Since a real estate agent will do that for you, that's just one expense you don't have to worry about.

Building a Home

How do you gauge costs when you're having a home built for you? Home building may seem like an expensive proposition, but you can get a good-quality home at less cost if you know where to cut corners. Here's how to make sure you're getting the most for your money.

Do Your Own Customizing
Save $20,000

Just about everyone dreams of building his own custom home. But the more "custom" it is, the more you have to pay.

Just to design a home, architects are normally paid 10 to 15 percent of the approximate construction costs. That means the design alone for a new home costing $150,000 (without the land) may be $15,000 to $22,500—before the first brick is laid.

Want to pay a mere fraction of that? Then do your own customizing. Simply buy a set of standard building plans for any size home you want to build. You can get these plans from an area builder. Or look for advertisements in home improvement magazines. Once you have the basic plans, hire an engineer or a construction consultant to make any changes you want. You'll end up with a complete, customized design for a new home that meets all your needs. And the cost will be about one-tenth of what an architect would charge.

A complete set of these building plans costs between $250 and $500, and construction consultants charge about $50 an hour for their work. In most cases, that means the total redesign for your own customized home would amount to about $1,500.

Build Up, Not Out
Save 20%

In selecting a design, keep this in mind: Depending on its size, a new ranch house can cost as much as 20 percent more than a two-story home that has the same square footage.

That's because a larger foundation is needed for the ranch-style, and pouring a foundation is a major construction expense. So for maximum space at the least possible cost, build up instead of out.

Don't Get Soaked
with Water and Sewage Fees

If you buy a tract in an established development and build on it, expect to pay more—and get more. Developers usually provide municipal water and sewage hookups; if not, figure on spending an additional $3,000 to $10,000 for municipal hookups.

If you're buying in a more rural area, you'll probably have to drill or maintain your own well for water—and you'll probably be entirely responsible for the septic system.

Be sure that any tract of land you buy qualifies for a standard perc. That means that drainage is sufficient for a typical septic system, rather than a more elaborate and expensive "sand mound" or another specialized system. The difference can be costly: A specialized system may be priced around $7,000.

Shop Around
Save $40,000

All builders are not the same: You'll find a wide range in estimates for the same job—as much as $40,000 difference.

Price is a big factor, but it shouldn't be the only one. The best way to shop for builders is to visit their offices and inspect homes they've built for other clients. Ask for the approximate cost per square foot for the type of home you're considering (such as ranch or colonial).

While you're at the office, look at floor plans and drawings of what is being built on speculation (or "spec"). Some builders will follow only certain designs—and the "on spec" designs are the ones they use.

Also, get asking prices for new construction that's being done by that builder. When you have the figures at home, compare prices by calling some of the other builders in your area.

Be Your Own Contractor
Save 25%

It's a major hassle searching out plumbers, electricians and other subcontractors to build your home. And then you have to make sure

HOW TO SHOP FOR A BUILDER

For anyone building a new house, it's essential to get a reliable builder who will complete the job in the agreed-upon time. So before you even get an estimate, do your "homework" carefully to make sure the builder you choose is the one you want. Here are some questions to ask before you sign with the builder of your choice.

- Is the builder an established member of the community in which you want to live?
- Does he belong to the local home builders association?
- Does the builder have a good credit rating?
- What type of customer service program does he offer?
- Will you get warranty protection?
- What houses has the builder constructed previously? Are they attractive? Are the people who purchased them satisfied? If not, why not?

they complete the work on time and meet their estimate. But if you're willing to undertake this chore, acting as your own contractor can trim as much as 25 percent off your total building costs—or about $37,500 from a $150,000 home.

Be warned, however: This is not a job for the novice. You need to have some idea of construction and be willing to devote about 20 hours a week to your "contracting" duties. But if you're an accomplished do-it-yourselfer with enough free time, acting as your own contractor not only saves you tens of thousands of dollars but also will guarantee that the job gets done to your specifications. There are plenty of books and videotapes giving complete instructions on how to act as your own contractor.

Save Cash with "Cozy"

No matter the design, the larger the home you build, the more it will cost. The problem is, many people overbuild—constructing more rooms than they actually need.

Construction prices are determined on a square-footage basis, so if your builder charges $75 per square foot (which is about standard), a four-bedroom, 2,100-square-foot dwelling will run approximately $157,500, excluding land. Add just one more room—about 250 square feet—and the price goes up nearly $20,000. So keep this in mind when you're planning your design; otherwise, you could be adding 15 percent or more for each additional room.

Control Those Upgrades
Save 20%

One common builders' practice is to offer upgrades during construction—better windows and flooring, oak moldings (instead of pine) and other options that increase your overall price. While these better-quality items are appealing, they can add 20 percent or more to that phase of construction.

If you decide to go with an upgrade, negotiate for a better price. Sometimes these upgrades are a way for the builder to unload excess inventory—at your expense.

EXISTING HOMES

Generally, it's cheaper to buy an existing house rather than build a new one: That is, you can generally get more house for your money if you buy the older home. You eliminate many of the expenses that come with new construction.

Unfortunately, you can also inherit a lot of old problems. Your savings can quickly diminish if you need to make a lot of repairs after you sign on the dotted line. A professional inspection is always suggested (and mandated in many states). But the following are some potentially costly areas that may sometimes be overlooked.

Get Proof the Roof Is New

Most people fail to get a roof inspection, an oversight that can cost them dearly a few years down the road. Replacing a roof costs anywhere from $3,000 to $15,000, depending on its size and materials.

Be suspicious of any roof older than 15 years, and be especially wary of older slate roofs because they're extremely expensive to replace. If the roof seems to be in poor condition and the seller claims it's new, be sure to get written proof, such as a contractor's receipt.

If you don't hire a professional inspector (which costs $100 to $350), do your own inspection by climbing on the roof and looking for any split, cracked or misshapen shingles as well as any dips or bumps in the roof. (*Caution:* Climbing a steep roof can be risky—so get someone else to do the job if it has a steep pitch.) If you find any signs of these problems, ask the seller for a new roof.

If the seller won't pay for the whole job, you can offer to split the cost of a new roof and deduct your cost from the purchase price. Negotiate that as a condition of purchase.

Check for Mildewed Walls

Any signs of mildew or wetness on basement walls or floors indicate moisture problems. This means that even a slight rainfall can cause water in your basement, which can eventually ruin your foundation (and, more immediately, ruin your possessions). Heavy rainfalls can mean real trouble.

Since walls can be cleaned and dried before a buyer comes to inspect a home, also keep your eyes peeled for appliances such as washers and dryers elevated on bricks or other platforms: This means the seller is aware of the problem and has done nothing about it. If left to you to remedy the problem, figure on paying $3,000 or more. You'll spend at least that to have the basement sealed and drains or a sump pump installed.

Kitchen Old? Mention It

When you see an old and outdated kitchen or bathroom, it means that the seller should be cutting thousands of dollars from the price of the house. So if you're looking at homes with outdated cabinets, fixtures, tiles and flooring in the kitchen and bath, mention it to the seller.

Conventional wisdom says a kitchen and a bath that are ten years old or more lower the home's value between $5,000 and $10,000 compared with the same home with newer fixtures. And that's true even if the old fixtures are in great condition. Real estate experts say that savvy buyers who make an issue of an older kitchen and bath generally walk away with a $5,000 discount.

How to Spot Fix-Up Costs

A house may look like a bargain . . . until you inspect it carefully and add up all the must-do repairs. But if the needed repairs are minor, add up the additional costs and get the seller to trim his price. Or make sure you deduct these anticipated expenses before you make an offer.

BASEMENT AND GARAGE
Inspect the foundation, and ask for a professional opinion if you see cracks. (The house may have structural problems.)

ELECTRICITY
Test all the switches, outlets and fixtures. If some don't work, the electrical system may need costly repairs.

PLUMBING
A dripping faucet or running toilet may be a minor problem . . . or a sign that the whole plumbing system needs repair.

KITCHEN AND BATHROOMS
If these high-use areas need work, get an estimate before you make an offer on the house. Renovations may be expensive.

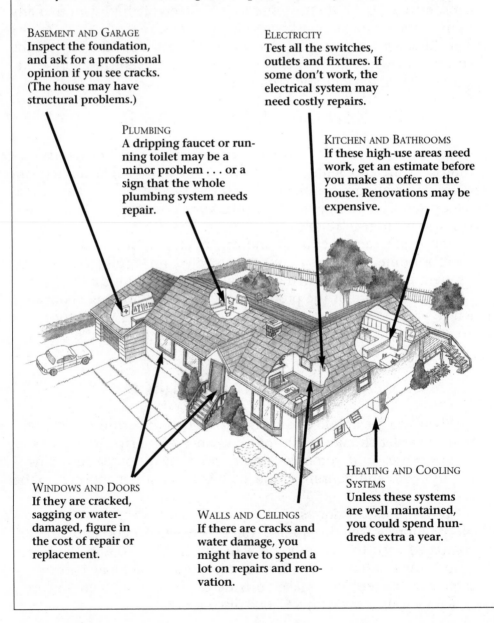

WINDOWS AND DOORS
If they are cracked, sagging or water-damaged, figure in the cost of repair or replacement.

WALLS AND CEILINGS
If there are cracks and water damage, you might have to spend a lot on repairs and renovation.

HEATING AND COOLING SYSTEMS
Unless these systems are well maintained, you could spend hundreds extra a year.

DRIVEWAY
Look for potholes and cracks. Extensive re-sealing can be costly.

TREES AND SHRUBS
Check for signs of disease such as blighted leaves, dead branches and trunk damage.

ROOF
Inspect for torn or lifted asphalt shingles. Look for gaps and holes in gutters and flashings. Make sure the roof line is straight, not sagging.

DECKS AND PORCHES
Inspect for loose or sagging railings and cracked or water-damaged floorboards.

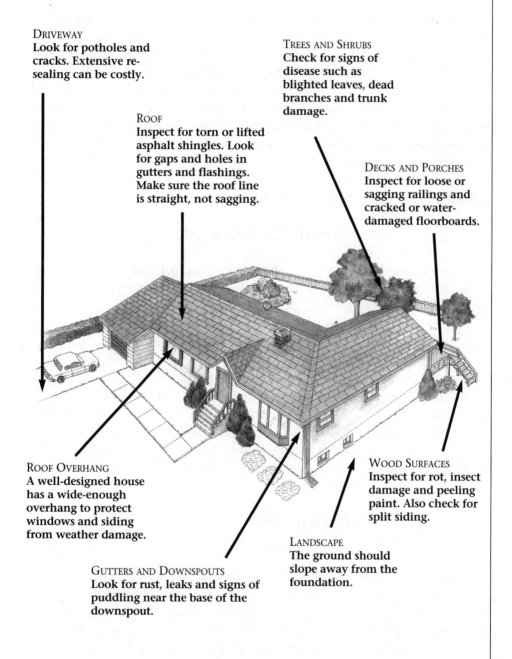

ROOF OVERHANG
A well-designed house has a wide-enough overhang to protect windows and siding from weather damage.

WOOD SURFACES
Inspect for rot, insect damage and peeling paint. Also check for split siding.

GUTTERS AND DOWNSPOUTS
Look for rust, leaks and signs of puddling near the base of the downspout.

LANDSCAPE
The ground should slope away from the foundation.

Review Electrical Codes

Another common oversight by home buyers is failing to check with the local municipality about electrical codes. Old and outdated electrical systems don't adapt to today's lifestyle and can be expensive to replace—as much as $2,000, depending where you live.

Call the municipality in which the house is located. You can find out what the electrical codes are. Also, you can find out whether the house needs 60-, 100- or 200-amp circuits. If you're looking at a house that doesn't meet today's codes, insist on the seller making improvements. And if the house has fuses instead of circuit breakers, you can also insist that a breaker box be installed. Otherwise, you'll have to make renovations down the road.

Read the Furnace

When you're looking at homes, take one minute to "read" the house's heating and cooling system, and you may save yourself thousands in years to come.

Service technicians routinely place dated tags or stickers on a furnace whenever they've done repairs or maintenance. Read the service record, and you'll have a complete maintenance history of the furnace. (The tag may show the furnace's fuel efficiency as well.)

You should be suspicious of any furnace older than 15 years (and try to get the seller to kick in for a replacement). But age isn't everything. With proper care and annual cleanings, a furnace can last much longer. Checking out the furnace history is worthwhile, especially when you consider that a single repair visit can cost $100 or more and a new heating system can cost over $3,000.

Do Your Own Repairs
Save 50%

While major jobs such as framing, home rewiring and basement waterproofing should be left to the pros, novice do-it-yourselfers can do the labor on projects such as painting, hanging moldings, laying tile and drywall and replacing faucets—and cut their costs in half.

Your public library has books that give step-by-step instructions for most household chores, and most of these jobs can be done with a

RENT TO OWN YOUR HOME

Renting a house with an option to buy is a no-lose way for you to test the waters of home ownership without having to dive in over your head.

Here's how it works: Let's say an owner can't sell a house or an apartment because of the slow market. If you're interested in the house but not sure you want to buy it, you may suggest a long-term lease (two or three years) at a slightly higher rent than what it would normally bring. According to an agreement that you sign up front, one-third of that money can be applied toward a down payment if you decide to buy at the end of the lease.

So if the home would normally rent for $700 a month, you might agree to pay $750. That's a slightly higher rent—but you also agree that $250 of each month's rent can go toward your down payment if you decide to buy.

As part of the lease with an option to buy, you have a pre-signed agreement on your option price. For example, if the asking price for the property is $119,000, you might have an option to buy at $110,000. If home values go up during the two years of your lease (let's say to a market value of $125,000 for your home), you can exercise your option and buy it at $110,000, with the seller providing you with a down payment of $6,000. So you get the property for $21,000 less than its market value!

On the other hand, if home values go down during your lease and your place is worth only $100,000 at the end of two years, you can walk away.

If you're looking for an option-to-buy situation, look for single-family homes with a "For Rent" sign on the lawn. (Since these properties are for rent, the owners either are trying to sell with little luck or want to wait until the market improves.) You might also get this deal on a "spec" home that hasn't been sold (ask the developer). Condominiums and cooperative conversions needing tenants may also offer a lease with an option-to-buy arrangement.

basic set of tools. If specialty tools are needed, you can usually rent them at a tool rental shop for less than $20 a day.

NEGOTIATING AND BIDDING

No one can force you to pay more than you want to pay for a home. That's important to remember when it comes to negotiating, because sometimes you may feel as if you're being forced to bid ever-upward. To put yourself in the best negotiating position, you should always be willing to walk away from a deal that isn't right— and that's your ultimate playing card. But first play the other cards in your hand to get the price you want. Here are some tactics to help with the art of the deal.

Listen for Problems
Save 30%

Information is the trump card in many real estate negotiating situations. But the information you want is more than you'll find on the listing sheet. Keep your ears open in supermarket aisles or on Little League bleachers to seek out gossip about sellers.

The best deals usually happen when a seller needs to sell as quickly as possible because of personal problems such as divorce, job layoff, impending foreclosure or a death in the family.

What's a Home Really Worth?

To cut your spending when buying a home, you need to know how much that house is really worth before you begin bidding—because of course you want to bid below that figure. Professional appraisers calculate the real worth by comparing the house in question with similar properties that have been sold during the past year.

The easiest way for you to get this information is to ask your real estate agent for the "comparables" file—that is, the homes in the neighborhood that are of comparable size and similar construction. Each listing sheet will have all the information for a current for-sale listing, plus the actual selling price, the date of sale and the length of time on the market.

If your real estate agent won't give you this information, usually it's because the asking price on the house you're considering is too high. (Don't forget—the real estate agent is acting on behalf of the

Don't Forget to Ask . . .

Before you even begin to negotiate, you should ask some important questions about the property. Listen carefully to the answers and adjust your offer accordingly, suggests Barry Miller, president of the Buyer Broker Council in Denver.

How long has this property been on the market? A real estate agent can answer this question by referring to the listing sheet. Be sure to ask the agent if the property was listed previously with another broker. If so, the seller is probably getting impatient and will be likely to consider a low offer.

Has the price been reduced? If the answer is yes, then find out how much it has been reduced and when the reductions occurred. This information is part of the listing history of a property, but not every agent will tell you unless you ask specifically.

Even though price reductions usually indicate an anxious seller, bear in mind that they don't automatically spell bargain. A lot has to do with how the asking price compares with the prices of similar homes that are up for sale. In other words, if the seller started at an overly optimistic level, the readjusted price may actually be fairly realistic.

What did the seller pay for the property . . . and when? This information is a matter of public record. If your agent says "I don't know," insist that he find out. Either the seller can tell your real estate agent or someone in the real estate agent's office can look up the price in the town records or the local newspaper.

Is there a seller's property condition disclosure form? A number of states now require sellers to disclose known faults or problems in the structure or working systems of a property. If there is no written disclosure form, ask the real estate agent to question the seller about each likely area. Also, ask the owner if there are any known deed restrictions, since this information can affect property value. (One type of deed restriction, for instance, would prohibit the owner of the property from dividing the property or using the home for certain kinds of business activities. This information would appear on the title report the owners had ordered when they purchased the home.)

MAKING AN OFFER
ON A HANDYMAN'S SPECIAL

So you've got your eye on a handyman's special, and you've estimated the out-of-pocket expenditures necessary to bring the place to your standards. What should your offer be?

Here's a formula that works in most market situations.

1. Estimate what a similar home in "good" condition would cost in the same neighborhood.
2. Subtract the estimated costs of repair and refurbishing.
3. Make an offer at least 15 percent below this figure.

For example, if a similar house in mint condition goes for $120,000 and you estimate that you'll need to spend $20,000 in repairs for your fixer-upper, offer $80,000 (or less). If you go up to $85,000 in your negotiating, you'll be buying at 15 percent below market value, which most real estate pros consider a fail-safe bargain.

But keep in mind that a handyman's special isn't a home that needs a new paint job or minor repairs. It's a structure that needs significant work, such as complete new "mechanicals" (such as plumbing or electrical) or foundation work.

seller, not the buyer!) But you can still find out what you need to know. Neighbors can usually tell you exactly how much homes in their area have sold for.

If the neighbors don't know, you can go to the county courthouse and ask a clerk where the deeds are kept. You'll be able to look up the home you're interested in by looking up the address. The deed lists all the times the house has been sold, and it shows the price of each transaction.

Seek a Seller Who Has Already Bought

If a seller has already signed a contract to buy another home before selling his current dwelling, you're in a great position to negotiate. Even a few months of paying two mortgages can spell financial trouble for him. The longer he has two houses—and two mortgages—the bigger the motivation to sell the property.

So if you learn that the seller has already bought another house, make your first offer at least 20 percent below the asking price. Even though it's less than the seller hoped to get, you'll be saving him from the agony of all those double mortgage payments in the months ahead.

Seller Being Transferred?
Save 15%

If someone's selling because he's being transferred, your ears should perk up: This could be the opportunity for a real bargain.

Usually, the person who's being transferred needs to move fast. An-

(continued on page 222)

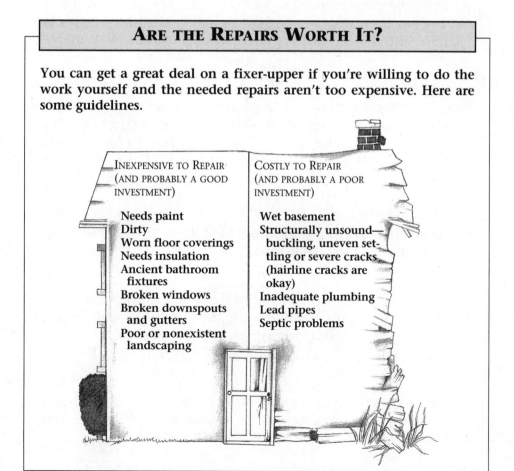

ARE THE REPAIRS WORTH IT?

You can get a great deal on a fixer-upper if you're willing to do the work yourself and the needed repairs aren't too expensive. Here are some guidelines.

INEXPENSIVE TO REPAIR
(AND PROBABLY A GOOD
INVESTMENT)

Needs paint
Dirty
Worn floor coverings
Needs insulation
Ancient bathroom
 fixtures
Broken windows
Broken downspouts
 and gutters
Poor or nonexistent
 landscaping

COSTLY TO REPAIR
(AND PROBABLY A POOR
INVESTMENT)

Wet basement
Structurally unsound—
 buckling, uneven set-
 tling or severe cracks
 (hairline cracks are
 okay)
Inadequate plumbing
Lead pipes
Septic problems

Negotiating the Price: A Scenario

Most home purchase negotiations are resolved in the third or fourth round. But here's an example of a sticky situation, where a couple negotiates its way to a good deal. Similar strategies can help save you thousands of dollars when you go to buy.

The Situation

George and Frederica Sand want to buy a house from Bob and Clara Schumann. The real estate agent is Ann Goodfellow.

The property is a three-bedroom, two-bathroom ranch-style home with a two-car garage, situated on one acre. The original price was $235,000, but after five months on the market, the property has been reduced to $229,900. In general, the real estate market has been sluggish, with more sellers than buyers. It's late October, and the end-of-the-year slowdown has already begun.

Round One

The Sands want to buy a house under $200,000, even though they have been qualified by a mortgage lender to go as high as $210,000. After studying six similar homes, they come up with a probable market value of $205,000 to $210,000 for the Schumanns' house. They make a written offer of $189,000. Ann Goodfellow warns them that such a lowball offer might anger the sellers.

George: "Try it."

The Schumanns: "Absolutely not! Tell them to come back when they can make a reasonable offer."

Round Two

Three days later, the Sands schedule another inspection tour of the house. The day after the tour, they make another offer of $193,000, with a closing date six months in the future.

The Schumanns: "We'll sell at $225,000. Not a penny less."

Round Three

A week goes by. Ann Goodfellow calls the Sands to say that the Schumanns really want to sell. They plan to close on the house they are buying in 30 days. Why not make another offer?

The Sands offer $198,000: "This is our absolute top-dollar price."

The Schumanns: "We'll take $210,000 with a 30-day closing date. And that is absolutely *our* last word."

Round Four

The Sands: "We'll go to $200,000 if they'll throw in the draperies, the washing machine and dryer and the dining room chandelier. But the closing has to be 60 days."

The Schumanns: "We'll give them the extras, but only if they give us $208,000. We can't afford to go any lower."

Round Five

The Sands tell Ann Goodfellow that they'll stretch to $202,000 and rush to a 30-day closing, since they're qualified at their mortgage lender. They tell her to point out that the quick closing is saving the Schumanns a full month's worth of carrying costs.

The Schumanns: "Make it $207,000, and we'll throw in the riding mower."

The Sands: "Too much."

Round Six

The buyers and sellers are $5,000 apart; neither will budge. Ann Goodfellow knows her listing on this property will expire in two weeks. If she doesn't make this deal, the Schumanns will probably try to sell "by owner" or hire another broker. At 6 percent, the commission on a sale at $207,000 would be $12,420.

With this knowledge and the facts of the deal in hand, Ann makes an appointment to talk with her office manager, who suggests that they trim $3,000 from the commission. Ann presents the deal to the Schumanns. They can now afford to make a counteroffer at $204,000 without losing anything.

The Schumanns: "Try it."

The Sands: "$204,000 is still too much."

Ann Goodfellow: "Don't lose this house over $2,000. That's only $14.68 more per monthly mortgage payment."

The Sands look at one another. They're tired of house hunting, and they do like this property. "Fifteen bucks a month," they say. "Why, that's just a night at the movies!"

The Sands agree to $204,000. Everyone is happy.

other factor in your favor: The seller's employer may be paying the difference between the actual selling price and the appraised value of the home—which means the seller can accept a lower price with no financial loss. Your offer, in this situation, should be about 15 percent below the asking price.

Breaking Up Is a Break for You

When you hear about a divorce, it's a signal that a house may go on the market soon—and the couple will want to sell quickly. When you know that a couple is splitting up, you should start your bidding at 15 to 20 percent below the asking price and negotiate persistently. The actual decision to sell may take some time—since real estate can be a real bone of contention in a divorce settlement. But the answer is worth waiting for: Divorcing couples often sell their properties below market prices.

Heirs Are Eager Sellers
Save 30%

The heirs to family property may want to sell quickly in order to divide the assets. Follow the obituary column in the local newspapers, find the houses of the deceased, and if you see something that you like, contact the heirs to find out if they're interested in making a quick sale.

If the heirs live in the house, they may be unwilling to sell. But if the house was occupied by a widow or widower who lived alone, the children probably want to sell the house as soon as possible. This is your chance!

Obituary notices usually list the residence cities of surviving relatives. A week or two after the funeral, call a relative of the deceased (you're best dealing with grown children who live in another city). Mention that you may be interested in the property if it's for sale, and leave your name. Then wait. If the heirs call you back within a few days (and they usually will if they have no intention of keeping the home), you have the makings of a great deal.

Offer 30 percent below the asking price. That may sound like low-balling, but next of kin who live away from the area usually want a quick sale and don't want to deal with the hassles of selling a home.

Focus on Misfits
Save 20%

If you don't mind being different—or at least living that way—the misfits of the marketplace could be your low-cost doorway to home ownership. Consider a truly unusual home such as a converted schoolhouse or a home that does not fit into its surroundings, such as a 1960s split-level on a street of stone and glass contemporaries or a single-family home in an area of twins. These kinds of "misfits" are either grabbed up quickly or take long to sell.

Be warned: Patience is power in this arena. When buying an unconventional property, it's a good idea to wait until it has been on the market for at least six months before making your first offer. And then your offer should be at least 20 percent below the asking price.

Don't worry about insulting the sellers. They know their property is "extraordinary," and they probably had trouble setting the asking price. Once negotiating starts, it might take you several months to convince the sellers to sell at your price. But the longer it takes, the more eager they'll be to sell, even at a lower price. So hang in there.

NEIGHBORHOOD PROBLEMS TO WATCH OUT FOR

A house may seem like a bargain . . . until you find out more about the neighborhood. Before you make an offer, be sure to run down this checklist. It could make a big difference in what you decide to spend.

- Have real estate taxes been increasing steadily during the past few years?
- Are the prices of homes decreasing in the neighborhood?
- Have lots of families been moving away?
- Is there heavy traffic or lots of noise?
- Do you see litter or signs of pollution?
- Are there factories or heavy industry in the immediate area?
- Are businesses closing down?
- Do you see vacant houses or buildings?
- Is there increasing crime or vandalism in the neighborhood?

Go for the Extras
Get Back Thousands

What transforms an ordinary purchase into a great deal is usually the stuff beyond land and buildings. It's extras such as appliances, draperies, selected pieces of furniture, lighting fixtures, lawn furniture and lawn maintenance equipment—which can add thousands to your bottom line.

The best strategy for getting these extras is to avoid asking for them too early (a common problem among buyers). Instead, make your first low offer without extras attached. With each negotiating round (and each increase in your offering price), ask for something you want.

When the seller eventually says "That's it! This is my price—take it or leave it!" you can take it (if it's within your fair market value range)—but conditional upon getting the extras you want. Few sellers refuse, since they're getting their price.

STEALS AND DEALS

Misery, it seems, is in good company. Besides the divorces, deaths and other personal problems you hear about, there are also plenty of hard-luck tales in the filing cabinets of banks and even the federal government.

But the bad news for the previous owners of the homes is good news for you. By keeping an eye on Uncle Sam's bonanza sales and watching the local paper, you'll see plenty of opportunities to get a great deal on a home. In fact, it may be just around the corner.

Buy from Uncle Sam
Save 50%

Because of the savings and loan bailout, the U.S. government unwillingly acquired billions of dollars' worth of real estate held by owners who could no longer meet their bank payments. As a result, Uncle Sam is now the largest real estate owner in the nation. But Uncle Sam doesn't want all that property. That's why the federal government is trying to sell thousands of foreclosed properties once owned by failed lending institutions.

Since Uncle Sam has better things to do than act as a real estate agent, you can buy these homes for a song—sometimes less than one-half of their appraised value.

The Resolution Trust Corporation (known by its initials RTC) is the government agency responsible for selling off the real estate acquired through the savings and loan bailout (among other things). Houses and apartments are available in virtually every style, size and price range. To get the phone number for your local RTC office or for the office in the town in which you're planning to relocate, call 800 directory assistance and ask for the toll-free number of the RTC.

The office will send you, without charge, updated notices of new properties on the market. You'll also receive information about price reductions and auction dates. And if you do decide to make an offer, the RTC office will even help you qualify for financing. Most properties at these auctions sell well under market value. However, you'll be expected to pay 10 percent or more of the selling price at the auction, so you'll need a certified check that you can "sign over" to the auctioneer.

You can also call your local office of the U.S. Department of Housing and Urban Development (HUD) to find out about government sales of property in your area. HUD is listed in the Blue Pages of your phone book under "U.S. Government."

As you might expect, the quality of properties offered through these sales can vary widely. Many of these houses are in need of repair or are located in bad neighborhoods. However, some are beautiful homes in excellent neighborhoods whose owners happened to fall on hard financial times. With patience and fortitude, you can pick up a nice house at a great price.

See What Local Banks Are Unloading

Besides Uncle Sam's bag of houses, banks and other lenders also carry foreclosed properties on their books. These institutions definitely want to get rid of these REO (real estate–owned) properties at a decent price, but the longer they hold a property, the more it costs them in maintenance and other fees. And that property produces zero income as long as it remains unsold. So the banks are usually less likely than traditional sellers to quibble over price.

Most real estate agents, and nearly all bankers, are happy to inform you of REO properties. If you find one you like, bid as you might in a Mexican flea market—at about 30 percent below the

AUCTION ACTION: SEVEN STEPS TO BOMBASTIC BIDDING

Going to a property auction isn't enough to get you a good deal. You have to do some homework beforehand, too. Here's what you have to know to improve your chances of getting a great deal.

Know the name of the game. Auctions are run by auction companies. These companies take care of the business of advertising, setting up the auction, selling the property and following through. They are hired by the sellers, and they work for the sellers' interests.

There are three ways to run an auction. Ask the auction company which is being used.

If it's an absolute auction, no minimum bid is required. The property will be sold to the highest bidder, no matter what the price.

If it's an absolute auction with a minimum bid, the seller sets the bottom price. The property will be sold only if the auctioneer gets a bid at that price or higher.

And sometimes it's a reserve auction. There's no printed minimum bid, but the seller reserves the right to accept or reject the highest bid. If the auction advertising reads "Sales subject to confirmation by the seller," it means you're going to a reserve auction. Even if you have the high bid, you might not get the property.

Read all about it—beforehand. Many multiple property auctions will offer a brochure describing properties to be auctioned (with addresses) and the specifics of the sale, such as property condition and any special financing opportunities. You should get this brochure and read it before the auction.

Choose and inspect. Referring to the auction brochure, select

asking price. Since the property holder is a bank or lender rather than an individual homeowner, any offer is likely to be considered. The only way to test for bottom dollar is to start bidding at ridiculously low prices.

Watch for advertisements in your local newspapers that list a bank or lender as the seller. Some lenders, both large and small, have set up special departments to market their REOs without listing with a

those properties that interest you and make appointments to inspect each one. Make sure that the structure is sound and that all systems are in good working order. (If you can't evaluate the property yourself, take along someone who can.) Estimate how much cash you'll need for repairs and refurbishing.

Qualify for a mortgage. Whether you work with financing arranged by the auction company or seek out your own lender, you must know how much mortgage you can carry before you start bidding.

Set a ceiling. Using one card for each property, write down its address, some particulars for easy identification in case you get your properties confused and your absolute top-dollar price. Don't bid above this price—no matter what!

Register your money. Either in advance or early on the day of the auction, you'll have to fill out registration papers and show your deposit money to representatives of the company running the auction. Your best bet is a certified check made out to yourself. If you buy, you can sign that check over to the auction company. If not, it's easy to cash in the certified check and get your own money back.

Use your paddle . . . within limits. At the registration table, you'll get a paddle with your bidder number printed on it. Raise it, and you've made a bid. If bidding gets frenzied and passes your top-dollar figure, sit on your paddle.

If you're lucky enough to be top bidder, be sure to get written confirmation of what you've bought. A "ring person" will come by to confirm your name and address. Before you give him that information, restate the figure you bid and request a written voucher that you own the property at that price.

broker; some even offer special financing deals such as below-market mortgages. Since you may be expected to pay a significant portion of the purchase price if you win the bid, you'll need a certified check to hold the purchased property.

But be sure to thoroughly inspect these properties—or better yet, hire a professional inspector. These houses are nearly always sold "as is" and may require extensive work.

Deal with a Distressed Developer
Save 25%

Watch for advertisements from builders offering "closeout specials" or similarly worded deals. These "specials" are usually the last few units in a development or perhaps a particular model that is no longer being built. Either way, you can buy a home this way for 10 to 25 percent below the market value of similar homes.

Builders reduce prices because they want out—and you can usually save thousands if you make a low offer on one of the last homes in the development. What's more, you can also ask for (and likely get) extras such as upgraded carpeting or other flooring, custom painting and additional kitchen appliances in exchange for taking the unit off their hands.

Some builders offer special financing concessions—such as a lower first-year interest rate on your mortgage (called a buy-down). Sometimes the builder is so eager to wrap up the deal that he'll pay all closing costs, mortgage points and fees.

REAL ESTATE AGENTS AND AGENCIES

Two things you always need to remember about real estate agents: If you're buying, they're working for the seller. If you're selling, they're working for themselves.

That's not to say that real estate agents don't want to sell your house. They do, because that's how they make money. But here's how to make sure you're not the one who pays for their time and efforts.

Negotiate a Commission
Save $1,500

With so many real estate agencies vying to list the same property, sellers don't have to pay the standard 6 percent commission fee usually quoted. Although most agents don't want you to know this, their commission fees can be negotiated.

And they should be. By striking a deal to pay the agency only 5 percent of the sale price instead of the usual 6 percent, you can save paying out an additional $1,500 on a $150,000 sale. (The real estate agency still gets $7,500—not exactly small potatoes.) So before signing on the dotted line, negotiate with several agents—and use the one who takes the lowest commission.

A Tip for Sellers: Get a Short Contract

When you're selling, the longer your house takes to sell, the more it costs you. Each month it remains on the market means another

---

IF YOU'RE SELLING . . . WHAT TO LOOK FOR IN A REAL ESTATE AGENT

How do you judge a real estate agent before signing on the dotted line? Some factors to consider when you're trying to sell your house:

MLS membership. Look for an agent with membership in the local MLS—Multiple Listing Service. If an agent is a member, it means that he shares listings with other agents. And that means more potential buyers will be looking at your home.

A good track record. Ask your agent for his selling-to-listing ratio—and the time frame of these sales. Real estate agents might brag about having an 80 percent "sold" ratio, but it means little if it takes an average of one year for properties to sell. Look for agents who have a high "sold" ratio (about 75 percent or higher) within the first three or four months of the contract.

High visibility. People trust the familiar, so choose a real estate company with a lot of visibility. You can tell. The highly visible agency will have a frequent display of listing signs in your area, large and noticeable newspaper advertisements and special fliers, usually available in local businesses. Many high-profile real estate firms have invested in TV "infomercial" shows as well.

Salesmanship. Your home will probably sell itself, but the agent can get the job done more easily if he is an expert salesperson. Look for a real estate agent who has a good "sales" personality—someone who's aggressive but not overbearing, personable but not wimpy, sharp but not a know-it-all. Above all, it should be someone who—in your estimation—can match the right buyer with your house.

mortgage payment and lowers your chances of getting top dollar.

Of course, every seller wants a quick sale. But often it takes a motivated real estate agent to get you one. One way to motivate the agent is to get a short-term contract. Ask for a three-month contract instead of the standard six-month contract.

Then add an incentive: You can offer the agent a "bonus" of $500 or $1,000 if the property is sold within six weeks or so. The money you spend for a bonus is small potatoes compared with the mortgage payments you'll have to make if the house stays on the market for many months.

Cut Your Spending on

CARS

- Used Cars
- New Cars
- Leasing
- Service and Maintenance

DRIVE A HARD BARGAIN ON YOUR NEXT VEHICLE

It's downright amazing how we can shop so sensibly for certain products and become so smitten by others. We conduct research, scour advertisements and think nothing of visiting a half-dozen stores to save a few bucks on the purchase of a pair of shoes.

But when it comes to buying a car—and shelling out the average $17,000 for a new one—our brains turn to mush. Too bad, since car buying is an opportunity to cut costs significantly, sometimes by thousands of dollars. But instead, many of us get overwhelmed by the bewildering number of choices, intimidated by pushy salespeople or confused by complicated financing options.

Purchasing the right car at the right price takes time and careful planning. But the rewards can be substantial for the careful shopper. You can save up to 25 percent off the list price of new cars and make great deals on used cars. Best of all, the car of your dreams might just be a down-to-earth possibility.

But you need to develop a strategy—a battle plan, if you will—that will help significantly cut the cost of buying a car without making you settle for less than you want.

USED CARS

The first rule of saving money is to think used. The moment you drive your new car off the dealer's lot, it's worth about 20 percent less.

Cars depreciate faster than three-day-old fish—and it never stops. So buying used makes good financial sense. By knowing what to buy, and how to buy it, you could get a used car for thousands less than others spend for the same vehicle.

232

WHERE YOUR MONEY GOES

- The typical family spends about $5,000 a year to own and operate its automobiles. That amount includes over $1,000 a year for gas and oil.
- One in 14 Americans buys a new or used car annually.
- About two-thirds of those who buy cars take out a loan to pay for them. Men are more likely to finance through a credit union or the auto manufacturer. Women are more likely to go to a bank or to finance with the car dealer.

Buy a Three-Year-Old
Save 50%

A car depreciates about 28 percent in the first year and another 20 percent in the second. So by the time a car is in its third year, it's worth about one-half of its original value.

But a quality car that's been driven an average amount still has a lot of life in it—assuming it's been well maintained. Since most people drive between 15,000 and 20,000 miles a year, a three-year-old car probably is still good for another 60,000 miles or so. And a three-year-old Mercedes or Volvo—cars that usually have a very long engine life—can get 200,000 miles or more.

Search for Surplus
Save 50%

Each year, there are scores of opportunities in your area to buy a well-maintained, late-model car for up to one-half of what you'd have to pay a dealer for the same car. You simply buy surplus.

Airport limousine services, for instance, usually keep their vans for only two or three years—and then sell them at huge discounts to anyone savvy enough to seek them out. (Be warned, however, that most are six- to ten-passenger monsters that guzzle gas.) Rental car companies and corporations also sell their fleets of cars, vans and trucks after only a few years (or a certain number of miles).

The only problem in getting these cars is finding them. Since the savings are so great, these special sales aren't widely advertised. You have to periodically call these businesses to find out when their auto surplus sales are being held. Or religiously check the classified section of your newspaper under "Government Notices" (for municipal sales) or "Auctions." The time is well spent, since most of these cars were well maintained, even though they may have a lot of miles.

Look for a Leaser
Save 25%

Another way to save money is to check auto dealerships for cars that just came off lease agreements. The savings aren't so dramatic (although the need to "move them out" is), but you may pay nearly 25 percent less than you would for a comparable used car—and probably get more for your money.

Under lease agreements, dealers insist that the operators keep the vehicles serviced regularly. What's more, the terms of the lease generally mandate that the operator can't drive more than 15,000 miles a year, so you can get a low-mileage, well-maintained car.

Cut Out the Middleman
Save 15%

Unless you're buying a previously leased car from a dealer, you're usually better off buying a used car directly from the previous owner.

All things considered, you'll usually pay about 15 percent more for a used car on a dealer's lot than for the same vehicle being sold directly by the owner. Dealers charge more for two reasons: because they have to due to overhead (such as advertising, sales commissions, inventory and the lot itself) and because they want to—because they want to make as much as they can.

Besides saving you money (and allowing you to bargain with someone whose skill levels are more on par with your own), personal contact with the real owner gives you the opportunity to get honest answers to questions you might have. The downside, however, is you won't get the standard three-month warranty that comes with dealer-sold used cars.

But make sure your questions require more than a yes or no an-

HOW TO SELL YOUR CAR

You're usually better off selling a car yourself than trading it in when you purchase another vehicle from a dealer. Dealers tend to lowball you on trade-ins; when they offer what you want, it's usually because you didn't get a particularly good deal on the purchase of the other car.

To make the most money for your car, wash and wax the exterior and fix all small nicks and scratches. Be sure to use dealership paint made specifically to match your car.

Clean battery terminals with a solution made from two parts baking soda to one part water. Also clean engine and oil grease with products made for that purpose; they're available at any auto parts store. And make sure you vacuum, dust and polish the interior.

Set your price by checking out ads in your local newspaper. Assume buyers will negotiate, so price accordingly. (Many people price 10 percent above what they expect to get.) Place an ad in the newspaper during weekends—Friday, Saturday and Sunday—and use power phrases such as "one owner," "trouble-free" and "low mileage."

When people want to test-drive the car, record information from their driver's licenses or some other form of identification (just in case they're car thieves). Accept only cash or certified check as payment.

swer. For instance, asking "What were the car's major problems?" is better than "Did the car have any major problems?"

Protect Your Money
Don't Buy the Privacy Line

Even if you're buying a used car from a dealer, insist on talking to the previous owner. Dealers are reluctant to allow this: They may claim they bought the car at an auction and don't know who the previous owner is or say they're hesitant to bother their "established" customers because it's a violation of privacy.

BEFORE YOU BUY, BE SURE TO CHECK . . .

Even if you can't have a mechanic help check out a used car, there are a number of tests you can do yourself—no matter how little you know about cars. Here's what to check to make sure the car you're looking at isn't headed down the road to financial disaster.

- Kneel by each fender and look down the length of the car. If you see ripples in the metal, it means the car has been in an accident. *Significance:* Pass on cars that have been in serious accidents. Often they cannot be fixed properly, and even slight damage can lead to serious bodywork problems.
- If rust is starting to show on the body, trouble is sure to follow. If you notice that paint on the inside of doors or under the hood is different from the outside paint, the car has been repainted. In a late-model car, this can mean the car was damaged in a storm or an accident.
- Check the tires. If there are a lot of uneven wear patterns, it could mean that the car needs an alignment—or that the frame has been bent, which is serious trouble. (To gauge the need for an alignment: Vibration in the steering wheel indicates the front wheels are out of balance; an overall bumpy ride while driving suggests the problem is with the rear wheels.)
- Take the car for a test drive. Expect to notice some smoke from the exhaust in the first few minutes (as the car warms up). But if the smoke continues—especially when you hit the gas pedal—that could mean problems, depending on the smoke's color.

  - White smoke indicates a transmission problem. A transmission is always expensive to repair—and sometimes the

Don't buy it. Any dealer who won't reveal the name of the car's original owner could have something to hide. It's your money on the line here, and with all the good used cars available, you'll be able to find a dealer who will comply with your request.

After that, it's essential to talk to the previous owner who sold the car to the dealer. After all, he's got nothing to lose by being up front about the car's history. Besides asking the owner all your questions about the car's defects, ask for the odometer reading when it was sold

problem can't be properly fixed with a simple repair job. Don't buy the car.

- Blue smoke suggests an oil problem. This also means trouble.
- Black smoke usually means that carbon deposits have built up (usually from stop-and-go driving). But this is not a serious problem.

• Check the brakes by driving the car to about 30 miles per hour and slamming on the brakes. The car should stop quickly and in a straight line. If it doesn't, don't buy.

• After a test drive, place a sheet of dry newspaper under the car. If you notice oil droplets on the newspaper, there's an oil leak. Also, place your finger inside the tailpipe (while the car isn't running). If your finger comes out oily, that suggests the car is an oil burner.

• Look under the hood for excessive dirtiness, which could mean an oil leak. Also check belts and hoses; if they're tight and in good shape, it indicates the owner cared for his car.

• Check the steering. If the car tends to wander during a test drive, it could signal a variety of troublesome problems.

• When you're driving a car that has an automatic transmission, press your left foot on the brake pedal and your right foot on the accelerator. If the car moves forward even though you have your foot on the brake, it is a sign of slippage—and means you should pass on the car.

• If the car has a manual transmission, make sure you drive on a hill to check for clutch slippage. (You'll hear the engine revving excessively—or the tachometer will show high revolutions per minute.)

to the dealer; if it's lower now, the dealer tampered with it—an illegal way to induce you to pay more for the car. (Reputable dealers rarely do this—but it does happen sometimes.)

For the Best Deal, Go to the Glove Box First

Forget about kicking tires and looking under the hood (as though you know what you're looking at!). Smart buyers of used cars head for the one place that reveals the true story about a used car—the glove compartment—for the service and maintenance history of the vehicle.

More important than how many miles the car has is how well it's been cared for: A well-maintained car with 60,000 miles is usually a better deal than a poorly cared-for one with 25,000 miles.

Whether you're buying from a dealer or a private party, be sure to look at the owner's manual, where service checks are usually logged. Find out what problems were addressed (and, hopefully, corrected). You're also looking for records of routine maintenance, such as oil changes every 2,500 to 3,000 miles.

(With a car that was formerly leased, expect to find a thorough history. Dealers tend to have rigid rules about servicing leased vehicles. If a dealer is hesitant to show you the maintenance history of a leased car, it's probably because it's a lemon—not because this history isn't available.)

Are They Lying?
Look inside the Driver Door

To be sure the owner or dealer is giving you accurate registration information—including the identification number and model year— be sure to check the label on the inside of the driver's side door. It's very difficult to tamper with that label, which says when and where the car was manufactured. However, if that sticker looks as though it's been fooled with, pass on the car.

Take Your Mechanic

Whenever possible, take your mechanic car shopping with you. A mechanic knows what to look for—and may detect problems that you could miss before you sign on the dotted line.

But perhaps even more important, there's the intimidation factor. A seller is more likely to be willing to negotiate when someone knowledgeable has his head inside the hood, looking for problems— especially when that someone has been introduced as an "insider," such as your buddy or brother-in-law.

Even if you can't take a mechanic, at least talk to one. He'll be able to tell you, from experience, which used cars are the most trouble and which are good buys.

Go for a Deluxe Model
and Stretch Your Savings

You're usually better off paying a few dollars more for the deluxe model of the make you've chosen. Since that car cost more when it was new, chances are that the previous owners took better care of it. Besides, deluxe models tend to have all sorts of extra and special features. Some experts even believe that deluxe models last longer than the economy versions of the same type of car.

Start 15% under Price

Perhaps the most essential aspect of buying a used car is gauging the selling price of a used car. Many people rely on car guide books, such as the *National Automobile Dealers Association (NADA) Official Used Car Guide* or the *Automobile Red Book;* both are available at libraries. But a more accurate gauge—at least in your area—is the classified section of your local newspaper.

People who take out expensive classified ads tend to do their homework and know the current used-car prices. But keep in mind that many car sellers purposely overprice used vehicles by about 10 percent, in anticipation of the haggling they'll do with buyers.

So start your negotiation by offering about 15 percent less than the asking price. That way, you're still in the seller's ballpark, but there's room for negotiating.

By starting with that bid, you can go up 5 percent and still get the car for 10 percent less than the asking price. (So you'll save $800 on a $8,000 car.) But if you offer much less than that, the owner won't take you seriously—and he might stick stubbornly to his original asking price.

NEW CARS

Shopping for a new car is a hassle. But it's a learning experience. So don't hesitate to invest your time. The longer it takes, the more you learn. The difference between an impulse buy and a truly good deal can be hundreds—or thousands—of dollars.

Go to a number of dealers, and you'll find you'll be offered a number of deals. There are a lot of reasons for this—the amount of inventory on a dealer's lot, the occasional need for quick cash, the discounts available for volume selling. All these factors can work for you (and get you a better deal) or against you. It all depends on your ability to see through the "secrets" and negotiate with these professional negotiators. Here's how to play their game and get the most new car for the least amount of money.

Be a Johnny-Come-Lately

Timing plays a crucial role in buying a new car, and the "worse" your timing is, the more you can save. In other words, your best strategy is to shop late.

Arrive at a dealership late in the day—especially on a Saturday (which tends to be busy)—when salespeople may be exhausted and less likely to be in their best negotiating frame of mind.

Or go late in the month, when many dealers are closing their books and want good sales figures—or the individual salespeople are under tougher orders to meet their sales quotas or commissions.

Either way, being a Johnny-come-lately could save you thousands because salespeople are more hungry for a sale and less likely to haggle you to death. But shop only when you're fully energized. If you go to one dealer tired from a day of car shopping, your guard is down, and you'll fall victim to promises that may not be kept.

Shop near Christmastime

Some insiders say that the best time to buy a car is the last two weeks before Christmas, when many car salespeople are at their most desperate to make sales.

With everyone else thinking about gifts and the holidays, many car dealerships are virtually empty—yet salespeople still must move their inventory in order to meet their quotas and make their end-of-the-year goals in commissions.

At this time of year, they may be willing to take smaller profits to make a sale.

All things considered, you should be able to negotiate the best deal during the last two weeks of December and through early January. And avoid the "busy" times—such as the middle of spring or summer—when nice weather and travel plans send people to car lots in droves.

START YOUR CAR SEARCH
AT THE LIBRARY

Before you decide on a car, it pays to do a little research, and your local library is the best place to start.

For determining the value of an automobile, there's the *Auto Price Almanac* by Pace Publications as well as the *Automobile Red Book*. (If your library doesn't carry either, try a bookstore or newsstand.) These books will give you an idea of prices, but keep in mind that actual prices change monthly or more frequently.

Magazines such as *Car and Driver, Road and Track, Automobile* and *Motor Trend* describe (often in great detail) new cars available at the beginning of the model year. These descriptions are usually in the September or October issues, but test drivers and magazine writers perform road tests and comparisons throughout the year. At your public library, you can find issues dealing with the specific models you're interested in buying.

While these magazines give you some insight into the car's performance and "fun quotient," the most practical information comes from *Consumer Reports,* which tests a wide variety of automobiles each year. This publication also has a 900 number you can call to find out the value of used cars (so you don't get ripped off when buying or selling one). Check a recent magazine for the number.

Avoid Ripoffs by Avoiding Red Tag Sales

A "red tag sale" or another special promotion at a dealership should be a red flag to you. In some cases, dealers use these special promotions to make people think they're getting a better deal, so customers are less likely to negotiate wisely.

One example is the "no-dicker sale," where dealers claim that prices are so low they can't haggle with customers. Don't believe it. It could be just one of the tactics used to let you think you're getting a deal. In reality, you're probably paying more during these special promotions than at any other time.

Dismiss Dealer Costs

Another way dealers can snatch money from your wallet is by charging you a $100 or more "prep fee." Also, be on the lookout for the "dealer-added profit" (DAP), "locator cost" or "procurement cost."

The dealer will try to make it look as if these additional costs are automatic and unavoidable. On the contrary, they're entirely optional. You don't have to pay any of them. The cost of "preparing" your car, for instance, is already included in the manufacturer's sticker price. The dealer gets a substantial profit, so why pay him twice with the DAP? As far as "locating" a car for you from another dealer, that's his job—and his problem if his inventory lacks what you're looking for.

The bottom line: These fees are negotiable, and savvy buyers don't pay them.

Pass on Luxury Options
Save 30%

Options always inflate the price of a car substantially, but some do it more than others. While "luxury" options such as sunroofs, power seats and windows are nice, dealers have a profit margin of about 30 percent on these items.

Install Your Own AC
Save 33%

One option you can have installed outside the dealership is air-conditioning. Generally, you'll pay up to $1,300 for factory-installed air-conditioning. (In some foreign cars, the air-conditioning isn't even installed until the car reaches the dealership.)

But if you buy a car without air-conditioning and get it installed on your own, you'll pay about two-thirds of what you'd pay the dealer for exactly the same option. Don't worry about not getting "quality" air-conditioning; all the same parts are used.

Play the Waiting Game over Extras
Save $1,000

You'll notice that every new car has two stickers—one from the manufacturer and the other with additional costs from the dealer.

MAKE LOANS SHORT AND SWEET

The worst part about buying a car, of course, is having to pay for it. Since most people can't pay cash, that means you need some sort of loan.

New-car dealers will tell you that they're happy to arrange for a loan—but be sure to shop around for better interest rates. Call your bank or credit union. Or check into getting a home equity loan. (A home equity loan may have very good rates, and in addition, you can take a tax deduction on the interest. With a car loan, you can't deduct any interest.)

Also, consider the length of the loan: The faster you can pay off the loan, the less money you'll end up spending on your car. Generally, interest rates are higher for longer payment schedules. For new cars, a two-year loan might be 6.25 percent, while a three-year loan from the same lender might be 6.5 or 6.75 percent. (For used cars, the interest rate is usually the same, whether the loan is for two, three or four years.)

On a typical new-car loan, the difference between a short-term loan and a longer-term loan could be more than $2,000. Here's a cost comparison.

NEW-CAR LOAN FOR $15,000

LENGTH OF LOAN	RATE	MONTHLY PAYMENT ($)	TOTAL PAYMENT ($)
24 months	6.25%	666.50	15,996.00
36 months	6.75%	461.44	16,611.84
48 months	7%	359.19	17,241.12
60 months	7.5%	300.59	18,035.40

USED-CAR LOAN FOR $10,000

LENGTH OF LOAN	RATE	MONTHLY PAYMENT ($)	TOTAL PAYMENT ($)
24 months	9%	456.84	10,964.16
36 months	9%	317.99	11,447.64
48 months	9%	248.85	11,944.80

The dealer's sticker explains that you're paying for extras such as paint sealant, undercoating, glazing and fabric protectors.

Paint sealant, which can carry a price of several hundred dollars, is basically a coating of wax. (Since dealer warranties generally guarantee against corrosion for six to eight years, it hardly makes sense to pay hundreds of dollars for a wax job.) And fabric protection, which can cost $200 or more, can be accomplished easily if you buy a can of Scotch-gard at the local supermarket and spray it on the fabric.

All told, each of these dealer "services" is unnecessary and expensive—and the additional costs can add up to $1,000 or more. Consider what you're actually getting for your money before you say yes to these options.

And here's a strategy that might get you some of those options at no cost at all: After you make your best deal, tell the salesperson you don't want the extras. Of course, he'll explain that all the cars on the lot have them. Unless you need the car immediately, tell him you'll wait for another car to come in off the truck without these features—and save $1,000 or so. (Since these are dealer extras, he can't argue that the car comes from the factory that way.)

Otherwise, offer one-half of the asking rate and save yourself about $500.

Pass on the Extended Warranty

Another thing to avoid is the extended warranty. For about $500, you'll be told, you can extend the manufacturer's warranty for several years and have peace of mind for the life of the car.

Don't sign before you read the fine print. The kinds of problems that are covered in the extended warranty are very unlikely to occur. (That's why the dealer pushes the warranty—the profit margin is so high.) And the niggling things most likely to go wrong generally aren't covered in the warranty. You might be a lot better off putting the money you'd spend on an extended warranty in a savings account, so you can use it for *any* repairs.

Seal the Deal with Small Stuff

Once you get to the point where the deal seems as good as it's going to get, take the initiative to make it even better. You can usually get

COLOR YOURSELF RICHER

The color of your choice of car can mean more green for you when it comes time to sell it. Other things being equal, red and beige are the most popular colors, and cars that are these colors have the highest resale value. Medium and dark blues are also popular. Green cars are the hardest to unload, followed by white, yellow and metallic colors.

some low-cost freebies thrown in—such as floor mats. These extra "incentives" may not mean a lot to a salesperson but can save you $150 down the road. (Yes, after making hundreds of dollars in profit from you, some dealers will still try to charge you for floor mats.)

Look for Anniversary Editions

They're called by other names, but these special models occur only at a special time and for a special price.

For instance, one year Ford priced three five-speed models of its Escort—two-door, four-door and station wagon—at the same $10,899 and equipped them with identical options. This one-price-for-all strategy made the station wagon, which usually costs several thousand more, an especially attractive choice.

That same year, Buick offered its LeSabre 90th Anniversary Edition, which sold for $19,000 and was equipped with many of the same popular features as its usual $27,000 Limited model. So alert car buyers could essentially get those features for about $8,000 less than usual.

Of course, these anniversary editions are few and far between, but if you see one advertised, check it out. The savings are usually very significant.

LEASING

There are lots of reasons why leasing a car makes sense. Most obviously, of course, it requires little or no down payment. Also, your monthly payments are significantly lower, allowing you to get more

How to Get the Car You Can't Afford

If you have Cadillac tastes and a Yugo budget, leasing is probably the best way to get the car that you can't afford. Automobile manufacturers faced with spiraling costs have come up with innovative programs to bring their cars more in line with what people can spend.

Take this plan for a BMW 525I, which retails for more than $37,000. All figures are based on financing by BMW and do not include trade-ins or down payments, which could lower costs significantly. (Sales tax of 6 percent, federal luxury tax of 10 percent over $30,000 and a $79 license fee are figured into the purchasing option. The rates also include a 4.75 percent annual interest rate.)

24 Months

	BUY ($)	LEASE ($)	LEASE ADVANTAGE (+) OR COST (-)
Manufacturer's price	37,705.00	37,705.00	
Initial payment	3,111.80	2,997.63	+ 114.17
Monthly payment	1,649.95	797.13	+ 852.82
Total payments	39,598.80	19,131.12	+20,467.68
Total cost	42,710.60	22,128.75	+20,581.85
Residual value (estimated resale value after 24 months)	19,983.65		
Adjusted cost	22,726.95	22,128.75	+ 598.20

car than your budget could typically handle. And with leasing, you can always drive a shiny, late-model car.

But don't automatically assume that you'll always save money leasing a car. Since you're basically "renting" a car, when your lease ends, you walk away with nothing. (When you buy, you own the car once your loan is paid off.) And since you're renting, you must return the car in the same shape as you got it: You must pay for

36 Months

	BUY ($)	LEASE ($)	LEASE ADVANTAGE (+) OR COST (-)
Manufacturer's price	37,705.00	37,705.00	
Initial payment	3,111.80	2,764.27	+ 347.53
Monthly payment	1,125.82	680.77	+ 445.05
Total payments	40,529.52	24,507.72	+16,021.80
Total cost	43,641.32	27,271.99	+16,369.33
Residual value (estimated resale value after 36 months)	17,344.30		
Adjusted cost	26,297.02	27,271.99	- 974.97

48 Months

	BUY ($)	LEASE ($)	LEASE ADVANTAGE (+) OR COST (-)
Manufacturer's price	37,705.00	37,705.00	
Initial payment	3,111.80	2,658.69	+ 453.11
Monthly payment	864.05	634.19	+ 229.86
Total payments	41,474.40	30,441.12	+11,033.28
Total cost	44,586.20	33,099.81	+11,486.39
Residual value (estimated resale value after 48 months)	15,082.00		
Adjusted cost	29,504.20	$33,099.81	- 3,595.61

that dented fender or torn upholstery—no matter how minor the defect.

Some experts say that all told, the typical driver who leases a car spends about 15 percent more than by buying it. Why? Because of some of the "hidden" costs of leasing that aren't ballyhooed as readily as the low monthly payments. But if you decide to lease, here's how to do it for less than those other guys.

TO LEASE . . . OR NOT?

If you're the type who likes to have a new car every few years and views car payments as a part of life—like paying the mortgage or the electric bill—leasing could end up saving you big bucks on that monthly payment. Just remember the one drawback: When the lease is over, you walk away with nothing.

Here's a comparison of various leasing arrangements—24-month, 36-month and 48-month programs. The figures are from one popular nationwide leasing program, aimed at those who prefer shorter leasing terms. (You'll note that payments were actually lower on the 24-month lease than the 36-month lease.) To make an accurate comparison between buying and leasing arrangements, note that you need to estimate the residual value of the car you buy—that is, the trade-in or resale price. All figures in the following comparisons are exclusive of taxes, which vary from state to state.

24 MONTHS

	BUY ($)	LEASE ($)	LEASE ADVANTAGE (+) OR COST (-)
Manufacturer's suggested retail price	23,532.00	23,532.00	
Dealer price	20,270.00	20,270.00	
Rebate	1,000.00		
Buyer cost	19,270.00	20,270.00	- 1,000.00
Money down	866.00	926.38	- 60.38
Monthly payment	905.93	373.74	
Total payments	21,742.32	8,969.76	+12,772.56
Total money out	22,608.32	9,896.14	+12,712.18
Residual value (estimated resale value after 24 months)	12,942.60		
Total cost	9,665.72	9,896.14	- 230.42

36 Months

	BUY ($)	LEASE ($)	LEASE ADVANTAGE (+) OR COST (-)
Manufacturer's suggested retail price	23,532.00	23,532.00	
Dealer price	20,270.00	20,270.00	
Rebate	1,000.00		
Buyer cost	19,270.00	20,270.00	- 1,000.00
Money down	866.00	1,022.08	- 156.08
Monthly payment	636.87	415.67	+ 221.20
Total payments	22,927.32	14,964.12	+7,963.20
Total money out	23,793.32	15,986.20	+7,807.12
Residual value (estimated resale value after 36 months)	9,412.80		
Total cost	14,380.52	15,986.20	- 1,605.68

48 Months

	BUY ($)	LEASE ($)	LEASE ADVANTAGE (+) OR COST (-)
Manufacturer's suggested retail price	23,532.00	23,532.00	
Dealer price	20,270.00	20,270.00	
Rebate	1,000.00		
Buyer cost	19,270.00	20,270.00	- 1,000.00
Money down	866.00	862.95	+ 3.05
Monthly payment	504.16	333.90	+ 170.26
Total payments	24,199.68	16,027.20	+8,172.48
Total money out	25,065.68	16,890.15	+8,175.53
Residual value (estimated resale value after 48 months)	7,030.24		
Total cost	18,035.44	16,890.15	+1,145.29

Bargain before You Sign
Save 15%

Perhaps the biggest mistake most people make is to assume that just because you're renting, you can't get a better deal. The most common misconception about leasing is that the payments are carved in stone—based on the car's sticker price.

They're not. Virtually all domestic vehicle dealerships and many foreign car dealerships will discount the price of a car on a lease just as readily as they'll negotiate price on a purchase. But they won't volunteer to give you a break—of course. You have to make the first move.

For best results, don't just walk into a dealership and say that you want to lease a car. Instead, bargain down the price of the vehicle as though you would buy it, then say you want to finance it on a lease program. It's not unusual to save 15 percent on a lease agreement this way.

Go through a Leasing Agent
Save 10%

Another way to save money on a lease is to forget car dealerships altogether—and, instead, lease a car through an independent leasing company.

These are businesses that do nothing but lease automobiles, to individuals as well as to businesses. Typically, you'll find rates about 10 percent less than for the same car leased through a dealership. You'll find leasing companies listed in the Yellow Pages.

Buy Extra Miles Up Front

One of the reasons leasing tends to cost more than buying (despite lower monthly payments) is the mileage agreements that are part of the lease agreement. With a standard lease, you cannot drive more than 15,000 miles a year without paying extra—usually around 10 cents per mile. So if you happen to drive 25,000 miles a year (which isn't unusual), you'll owe an additional $1,000 per year.

There is a way around this: buying excess miles in advance, when you sign your lease agreement. It will still cost you extra, but it's usually a lot cheaper than paying for the extra miles when you turn in your car. If you negotiate well up front, you could save hundreds each year that you hold the lease.

Go for a Short Lease

Particularly enticing because of their low monthly payments are long-term leases, usually five years. But let's face it: If you want to lease, the odds are it's because you like driving a new car. And five years is a long time to drive the same rented vehicle.

Mention this to the dealer, and he'll probably say there's no problem breaking the lease; he'll just lease you another new vehicle when you're ready. What he might not mention (but the tiny print in your lease contract does) is the "prepayment penalty" for switching cars in mid-lease. These fees can range from as little as $100 to more than $2,500. (And there may be other charges as well, if the two leased cars have different prices.)

The best way to get around this is to keep your lease agreement short—to two or three years. In fact, occasionally your monthly payments are even less for a short-term lease than they would be for a longer one. Ford, for example, has run lease programs that encouraged consumers to trade in their cars every two years. On such a program, the payments on a Taurus LX leased for two years were lower than payments on other cars that were priced the same as the Taurus LX but that had longer leases.

SERVICE AND MAINTENANCE

Keeping your car well maintained is the best way to prolong its life. And the longer it lasts, the less often you have to spend thousands buying a replacement. While your car will no doubt have some problems, there are several things anyone can do regardless of mechanical skills to hold the real "money costers" to a minimum and keep cars running relatively trouble-free.

Buy Your Own Filters

You probably already know that you should have your oil filter changed every time you change the oil—ideally every 2,500 to 3,000 miles (or every three months, whichever comes first). What you may not know, however, is the importance of buying a quality filter.

If you get your car's oil changed at one of those drive-through "quick-change" shops, make sure a quality filter is used. If not, you should buy your own filter at an auto parts store and take it with you. Some shops install off-brand filters, which don't adequately filter oil and which expose the engine to harmful contamination. (Some service stations also use cheaper filters.) Besides, you're paying a premium price for an inferior product. You may pay a couple of bucks more for a factory filter or for a brand name such as Purolator, Hastings or Atlas, but it's money well spent.

Play Taps Monthly—With Your Air Filter

Same goes with air filters: Quality means better performance. But since quality air filters cost more than $50 each, you could extend the life of your air filter with a five-minute maintenance check.

Once a month, simply take your air filter and tap it against the ground to dislodge dirt. Then run a garden hose through it to clean it. This extends its life by almost three times, saving you replacement costs. (If you find the oil filter clogged with oil, however, hosing won't help.)

Get Tire Maintenance for Free

You need to get your tires rotated and aligned periodically (or whenever you notice the car veering to one side) in order to extend their life. Unfortunately, many people shrug off this charge—which is usually around $50—and just assume they have to pay it. In fact, when you buy tires, you can often get these services for free, simply by asking.

Some tire dealers may try to sell you a maintenance program, but don't buy it: There are plenty of dealers who will give customers free wheel alignments and/or tire rotations for the life of the tires. And don't assume that you'll have to pay a premium price for your tires for this service. Membership merchandise clubs such as Sam's Club sell tires for below-retail prices—and provide this service to their customers.

Cut Your Spending on

TRANSPORTATION

- Airlines
- Rental Cars
- Buses and Trains

SPAN THE GLOBE WHILE YOU SPARE YOUR WALLET

On the road. In the air. No matter your method of traveling, it all comes "out of pocket"—and those costs can be staggering.

The average Joe spends a whopping $5,200 a year simply getting around. Of course, that price includes the daily commute to work, those trips to the supermarket, the drives to Little League practice and all those other ventures that are part of our day-to-day grind. It also includes the trips we take to visit friends, attend conferences and go to Grandma's house for the holidays.

And then, of course, there's the annual family vacation—when we log some *real* miles to get away from it all. One thing we never seem to escape, however, is the cost.

Vacationers, for the most part, use their own cars to travel—one reason why vacations are getting shorter, both in time and distance. But a significant 10 percent of American households spend nearly $2,000 each year traveling by air. And even though train and bus travel have waxed and waned in popularity, there are many who rely on these forms of transportation. But no matter your way of traveling, here's how to do it for less.

AIRLINES

While those skies may be friendly, they're definitely not cheap. Airfares can be chock-full of hidden surcharges and other hush-hush costs that push your expenses higher than a soaring 747. But you can ride high without spending that way—and here's how.

Don't Prepay for Tickets
Save $35

Prepaying for a ticket actually costs more than purchasing your ticket at the airport. That's because when you order a prepaid ticket, a

---

WHERE YOUR MONEY GOES

- More people fly on Thanksgiving eve than any other day of the year.
- Americans spend about $350 billion a year traveling on business and pleasure. The 50 states spend about $350 million a year trying to tempt you to visit.
- More than $5 billion a year is spent by corporations offering "incentive travel" bonuses and awards to their employees. These awards can be anything from a weekend getaway to an overseas extravaganza. Salespeople who exceed their quotas are the most frequent recipients of incentive travel awards.

---

charge of at least $35 (sometimes it's higher) is automatically added to the fare.

Some airlines itemize these charges on the ticket; others simply add them on to the fare. And airlines don't like to advertise this practice, which is done to offset handling and administration fees. You may avoid this charge by offering to pick up the tickets yourself at the airport.

But if you must pay when you make your reservations, ask the clerk if the quoted price includes any prepay fees. He may suggest ways to waive the fee. If not, ask to speak to a supervisor.

Try for a Free Room

When an airline cancels your flight due to a mechanical problem (not a weather delay or a missed connection), you don't necessarily have to pick up the $80 or more it usually costs for a nearby hotel room. First ask that the airline pick up the hotel costs.

Many airlines make it a policy to provide free lodging when their flights are canceled or delayed due to a problem that's the fault of the airline. With others, it all depends on the circumstances and the manager who's on duty in the terminal. But it never hurts to ask. If you can get free lodging because of a flight cancellation, then you've saved yourself a hotel bill.

Fly Midweek
Save 10%

Doing your flying in the middle of week can save you 10 percent or more off the same flight on other days. Airfares tend to be cheapest on Tuesdays and Wednesdays (and most expensive on Mondays and Fridays). For the lowest rates, look for flights leaving or arriving during midday or late evening.

Family Emergency?
Ask for a Special Fare

If you're taking a trip because of a serious illness or death in the family, ask the airline for a bereavement fare. Airlines don't publicize this service—and some don't have it—but when you do get a "compassion discount," it can be up to 20 percent off regular fares.

You're in the best position for getting a compassion discount if you make a personal appeal directly to the airline rather than go through a travel agent.

Ask for a Super Saver
Save 50%

Most airlines offer Super Saver round-trip fares that are at least one-half of the price of full-coach fares. But a Super Saver fare has some restrictions: It's usually non-refundable, and reservations must be made at least two weeks in advance. In addition, most airlines insist that your stay include all or part of a weekend. (In other words, you must not return until after Saturday or Sunday.)

Buy Two Tickets
Save 50%

Strange as it sounds, it's sometimes cheaper to buy two airline tickets and throw one away. That's because the best Super Saver deals are given to passengers who stay at their destination over the weekend—but businesspeople and others who are traveling only during the workweek can still save money.

Let's say you are traveling from Philadelphia to Miami and want to leave Monday (July 5) and return that Friday (July 9). Delta would charge you $920 for that round-trip. But if you use the Super Saver flight and stay the whole weekend, that same trip costs only $238 round-trip, as long as you make your reservation two weeks in advance. So here's what you do.

You buy one $238 round-trip ticket for a flight that leaves Philadelphia on Monday (July 5) and returns the following Monday (July 12). Then you buy a second round-trip ticket for a flight that leaves Miami on Friday (July 9) and returns on the following Friday (July 16) for $238. Your total cost: $476. You board in Philadelphia with the outgoing ticket on Monday, July 5, then throw away the return ticket. Then you board in Miami on Friday, July 9, using the first half of the Miami-to-Philadelphia round-trip ticket. Your savings: $444!

It's best to make your two reservations separately, however, because airlines frown on this "scheme." According to some airline officials, tickets may be impounded, and passengers will have to purchase a full-price ticket for the continuation of the trip.

Get a Refund
Find a Friendly Agent

In order for you to get a Super Saver discount, most airlines say you can't get a refund if you change your travel plans. But often you can—as long as you have a cooperative travel agent.

When you buy your ticket through an agent, the reservation is made immediately. But the airline usually doesn't get paid for several days or even one week. During this time, a helpful agent can cancel the reservation and get your money back. (Of course, the agent isn't obligated to do this; Super Savers technically are non-refundable. But if you're a good customer, the agent may be willing to do you the favor.)

Reserve Well in Advance
Save 40%

Even without a Super Saver, the longer between the time you make your reservation and your flight time, the more you save. Generally, making your reservations two weeks in advance will save you 15 percent compared with making them one week in advance and up to 40 percent compared with making them the same week of your departure.

RENTAL CARS

If only renting a car were as easy as running through an airport. Unfortunately, all too often it's car rental companies that do the running—right over you—with hidden charges, broken promises and bait-and-switch tactics that can add to your spending. But here's how to avoid being taken for a ride the next time you rent a car.

Be a Company Man
Save 25%

The lowest rates for rental cars go to corporations, so if you can find a legitimate reason to identify yourself as a corporate customer, you can save 25 percent or more.

If you do work for a company that qualifies for these rates, great. Even if you're traveling on pleasure—and not business—you may still qualify for the corporate discount. Sometimes the rental car agent doesn't even ask to see company identification.

Ask about Weekend Specials

Many companies offer lower rates on weekends—anywhere from 10 to 25 percent less than weekday charges. So if you're checking in at the rental car agency any time from Thursday noon to Sunday night, ask for a weekend discount.

RENTAL UPGRADES ARE NO DEAL

If you're a frequent flyer, you have probably received free coupons for auto rental upgrades.

Don't get too excited, because most are barely worth the paper they're printed on. The cost of an upgrade is usually only $2 to $5—and there are so many restrictions on these "free" rental upgrades that they have almost no value.

Instead, shoot for the "free rental day" certificates as a frequent flyer bonus. These are worthwhile because they can save you the $50 or more it costs to rent a car for a day.

Take a Shuttle
Save 10%

Since in-terminal agencies are more convenient to airline travelers, they tend to get premium prices for their cars. But by going to an off-site agency, you can get similar cars for up to 10 percent less. There's really no added inconvenience: A shuttle can take you to these off-site agencies from the airport baggage claim area. Just look up the off-site company in the Yellow Pages.

Go Far from the Airport
Save 20%

Of course, if you really want to save on car rentals, you want agencies in other parts of town. Most car rental business occurs within a mile or two of the airport, but in larger cities, there are agencies all over town—and since their cars are less in demand, many have rates cheaper than those near the airport.

By traveling to an agency in center city, for instance, you may be able to trim at least 20 percent off your rates.

Fill Up the Tank
Save 50%

Always buy gas before you return your rental car. If the rental agency has to fill the tank and charge you for it, the price could be nearly twice what you'd pay at a neighborhood pump. (And try to avoid gas stations near the airport, because they're also expensive.)

Say No to Their Coverage
Save $100

Rental agencies say they're not in the business of selling insurance; if they were, they'd be under the control of the state insurance commissioner. But instead of selling you "insurance," they often sell collision damage waivers and loss damage waivers at high rates.

At up to $15 a day, these waivers earn untold millions for rental agencies each year, since the high deductible—$2,500 is not uncommon—is enough to scare many renters into buying them.

If you're a car owner, you probably don't need the coverage at all.

Your own automobile insurance may cover most of the costs of theft or damage to rental cars, and your credit card may cover the rest. As long as you are an insured driver and are paying with a credit card, you may be better off declining the rental agency's insurance coverage. It's worth checking your policies, because if you're renting a car for a week, you could save $100 or more—and still have the same protection.

But before you drive the car, walk around it and inspect it closely for scrapes and dents. Report any pre-existing damage, so you don't get charged for bodywork when you return the car.

Protect Yourself
Ask for a Detailed Statement

You should avoid paying for "extras" such as additional-driver fees and drop-off charges (which aren't always advertised but may be tacked on to your bill) and for other hidden costs. The best way to avoid such charges is to ask for a detailed statement and read it before paying. Rental agencies are supposed to inform you of all charges before giving you the car keys. So if you notice an extra charge you weren't informed about, you should let the agent know. You may be able to get out of paying for it.

Rent a Used Car
Save 66%

If you think style and comfort should take a backseat to frugality, investigate used-car rentals. In many cities, there are rental agencies under names such as Rent-a-Wreck, Rent-a-Heap, Rent-a-Lemon and Rent Rex-on-Wheels. These businesses are bona fide rental agencies—except they rent older cars at about one-third of the price of a typical car rental business. Look in the Yellow Pages under "Automobile Renting and Leasing."

Be sure to give the car a test drive, however, before you take it on a long trip. Used cars may be just as comfortable to drive, but they're more likely to have breakdowns. And you can't get a replacement vehicle as easily as you could if you rented from a leading company.

BUSES AND TRAINS

Once *the* modes of transportation for the budget-minded, buses and trains have lost points among those looking for a cheap way to hop from point A to point B.

True, buses and trains aren't the penny-pinching transportation they once were, but there are ways to ride for less than you may think.

Leave the Driving to Them
Save 85%

Besides being more convenient, letting someone else do the driving is sometimes actually cheaper, especially if you are traveling alone. For instance, the distance between New York City and Washington, D.C., is 237 miles. While that trip takes about $15 in gas for an average car, the real cost of using your own car is about $110, based on the American Automobile Association's estimate of 45 cents per mile (besides gas, that also includes wear and tear on your automobile). And that cost doesn't even include tolls. By comparison, covering the same distance by train costs about $64. And by plane, it's about $90.

But for real savings, try taking the bus. For example, one bus line charges only $18 for the same New York–to-Washington trip. So the cost is nearly 85 percent less than it would cost to drive yourself.

For trips that take longer than six hours, however, you'll be more comfortable taking the train—and prices are usually only slightly more than what it costs to drive. And for trips that require a day or more of driving, the plane is often your best bet for both cost and convenience—especially if you're traveling alone.

Take Advantage of Kids' Fares

While airlines usually charge full price to anyone who requires a seat, children can ride to any destination on a bus or train for half-price—as long as they're traveling with an adult. So keep that in mind when you're comparing travel prices for the whole family.

Ride in the Winter
Save 15%

Summer is the season for traveling, and as a result, train fares tend to be higher. Most train routes have a range of prices—fares that increase during peak traveling season and decrease during less traveled periods. In most cases, the slow season for traveling by train is the winter months (except around Christmas), when prices usually drop 15 percent or more.

For instance, one year a coast-to-coast round-trip cost $297 in the summer and $254 in the winter—a savings of nearly 15 percent. A New York–to-Chicago round-trip is 30 percent cheaper in the off-season (winter). Round-trip from New York City to Miami, on the other hand, is about 15 percent cheaper in the summer, since winter is the busy season.

Get Excursion Rates
Save 20%

Amtrak offers round-trip excursion rates between many cities, but there are certain restrictions. Traveling between Philadelphia and New York City, for instance, you can save over 20 percent on a ticket by paying a round-trip excursion fare rather than two one-way fares. But excursion tickets between Washington, D.C., and New York City are not valid from noon to 7:00 P.M. on Fridays. (In other areas, there may be similar restrictions—so check when you buy your ticket.) If you board the train during a restricted time, you'll be charged the extra fare.

Take the Three-Stop Special in Winter

Amtrak has a much-ballyhooed three-stop special that's a great deal for travelers any time of year. Once you have the ticket, you can use it any time during the next 45 days, making three prearranged stops along the way. But many people don't know the ticket is about 25 percent cheaper in the winter than in the summer.

Cut Your Spending on

VACATIONS

- Hotels and Motels
- Bed-and-Breakfast Inns
- Low-Budget Overnights
- Rentals and Long-Term Housing
- Theme Parks
- RVs and Camping
- Cruises

First-Class Getaways
You Can Afford

All you want is a little R and R. But what you find is that it takes a lot of $ and ¢.

Whether it's the Ritz or the pits, lodging doesn't come cheap. A single night's stay in a finer hotel can cost more than $300; even so-called budget motels are often $50 or more.

And if you've been to Walt Disney World or another theme park lately, you know there's nothing Mickey Mouse about the cost of admission: A family of four can spend more than $150 a day just to enter these vacation wonderlands—and that doesn't include parking, refreshments, souvenirs and other expenses.

But there's a way you can spend a week or two away from home without spending a fortune. If you know the "inns" and outs of cut-rate lodging, the secrets of getting into theme parks for less plus a few savvy ways to chat with desk clerks, you can cut hundreds off your vacation spending without missing out on a minute of fun.

Hotels and Motels

Probably the most important thing to know about hotels and motels is that despite those little signs on the back of the room's door, there really is no such thing as a "set" room rate.

Sure, you may be quoted a price—the rack rate, as it's called in the business. But you should never pay that price. Instead, you can (and should) beg and bargain your way to a lower rate—as much as one-half of what others spend.

Ask for a Lower Room Rate
Save 10%

How do you bargain down the rack rate? Often all it takes is asking. When the clerk quotes you a price, simply ask "Don't you have anything better?"

264

Yes, it's often that easy. Frequent business travelers routinely ask for discounts and usually get them. That's because the pricing system for the hotel/motel business seems to be set up like the one for the car-selling business: Salespeople try to get as much money as possible (the sticker price) but will sell the cars for less to those who ask.

So the next time you're quoted a price, asking for a discount can save you 10 percent or more.

Call from the Lobby Phone
Save 25%

If you arrive at a hotel without a reservation, your best leverage for rate negotiating isn't to walk up to the front desk. Usually, the clerk will simply quote you the highest amount the hotel charges for its rooms.

Instead, use the lobby phone. This way, the desk clerk doesn't know you're at the hotel and will probably feel the need to "sell" you on coming in. And of course, the best way to get you to come in is to give you a good price—which could be anywhere from 10 to 25 percent off the rack rate quoted to walk-ins without a reservation.

Also, by using the lobby phone, you can have a more private conversation with the desk clerk, who won't be as concerned about someone

---

DID THEY MENTION THE TAX?

If you notice that your hotel bill is higher than you expected, you're not alone. Most hotels seem to forget to mention the occupancy tax when quoting room rates.

This little "slip" can cost you big bucks, since the occupancy tax—sometimes called the bed tax or room tax—can add a good bit to your bill. In New York City and a number of other cities, the tax is 20 percent or higher. (Usually, however, the occupancy tax rate is between 10 and 14 percent.)

There's no getting around the tax, but when calling for room rates, ask if the quote includes the occupancy tax. It rarely does. So ask the total your room will cost, including tax.

overhearing the rate discussion. This works in your favor, since the hotel doesn't want everyone to hear about your rate discount.

Call Late at Night
Save 10%

While the debate continues on where to call to get the best rates—the hotel directly or its 800 number—when to call for rate information is a bit easier: as late as possible.

Phones aren't so busy late at night, and the reservation clerk is more likely to have the time to schmooze with you. In fact, simply calling at the right time is a good way to get quoted room rates of 10 percent or more below rack rates. If you're a night owl, use this to your advantage by negotiating. An operator who isn't rushed will be more willing to discuss rate breaks and special deals. So call after 10:00 P.M. if you can.

Ask for the Corporate Rate
Save 15%

Business travelers routinely get the best rates in hotels. So whenever you're traveling on business, make sure you ask the desk clerk for the corporate rate—which typically is 15 percent or more off regular prices.

Even if you're not on business, you may be able to reap these discounts without lying. Let's say you walk into the hotel with kids in tow. Simply ask the clerk if the hotel has any special rates for frequent hotel guests or corporate travelers. That implies that even though it's obvious you are now on vacation, you frequently travel for business and presumably stay at that particular hotel.

You'd be surprised how many hotels will give you a room discount, just to keep its "frequent" customers happy. Of course, realize that unless it's obvious that you're traveling on business, the hotel isn't obliged to grant you any favors, so politeness is the key to success here.

"Read" the Parking Lot
Save 20%

If you are a walk-in, drawn by a lit "Vacancy" sign on a stretch of highway, take an even closer look—all across the motel parking lot.

The fewer cars you see, the better position you're in to haggle the rate down, since an empty room brings in no revenue.

Simply asking for a discount is one way of getting it, but you'll probably get no more than 5 or 10 percent off the rack rate. *Better:* Ask to inspect the room after the rate is quoted. Then say the room is acceptable but overpriced. If it's the only motel along a lonely stretch of highway, you might not get very far, but if the road is lined with lit "Vacancy" signs, you should seek (and will probably get) at least 20 percent off.

Go on Weekends
Save 50%

If you need a quick getaway, plan it for the weekend—especially if you're traveling to New York City, Chicago or another big city.

Most downtown hotels cater to business travelers, and because of this, most have incredible deals for weekend stays. These packages, usually for the entire weekend, can get you rooms at finer hotels for as much as one-half off the usual rates. Some hotels advertise these weekend "escapes," while others don't, but most big-city downtown hotels have them.

Mention Your Memberships
Save 30%

Hotels and motels routinely give membership discounts to those belonging to auto clubs, veterans groups, frequent flyer programs, the American Association of Retired Persons and other groups. Even college students may get a rate break by producing a university identification card.

So after you negotiate your best rate, ask if there are any additional membership discounts. Typically, these price reductions will get you another 10 percent off, but some groups—such as senior citizens— may qualify for as much as 30 percent off.

Traveling Abroad?
Save with Your Credit Card

If you're vacationing overseas, pay for your lodging with a credit card whenever possible. Because of wholesale exchange rates, card

(continued on page 270)

A GUIDE TO BUDGET MOTELS

Besides being the salvation of weary interstate travelers, the budget motel chain is the bread and butter of the lodging business—with more than 700,000 rooms in the United States (not including independent motels). Here's a brief rundown of the primary offerings and prices for the major chains catering to vacationers. Phone numbers can be obtained from 800 directory assistance, for those interested in making reservations.

Best Western is the world's largest association of independently owned hotels and motels—with nearly 2,000 in North America and another 1,500 in 49 other countries. Each property has a coffee shop or provides a continental breakfast; most also have swimming pools. Rates average $54 per night, and there's usually no charge for children under age 12. The chain's Gold Crown Club International carries special services and awards for frequent guests.

Budgetel offers hotel-type services at motel prices, such as complimentary breakfast delivered to your room, free local phone calls and limited free incoming fax service, extra-long beds, 25-foot phone cords and remote control TV. Some of the 100 Budgetels have a guest laundry and a nearby restaurant. Nonsmoking rooms and "leisure suites" with additional sleep sofa and work area are also available. Rates average about $40.

Comfort Inns offer free lodging to children under age 18 (staying in their parents' room), a complimentary continental breakfast and nonsmoking rooms. Many have swimming pools, fitness facilities and restaurants or coffee shops on the premises. Rates average $49.

Days Inns offer rooms as low as $29 when reservations are made at least 29 days in advance (similar to airline Super Savers) but average $52. Children under age 12 can stay for free in their parents' room. They also get free meals when accompanied by an adult who is a registered guest at participating hotels. About 15 percent of the motels offer suite or efficiency accommodations. Some also offer free in-room movies, coin laundries and on-premises cocktail lounges. This chain boasts the largest senior citizen discount program—from 15 to 40 percent off usual rates.

Econo Lodge has about 766 motels. Many have swimming pools. Rates average $36 a night. Children under age 18 are allowed to stay free with parents. Cribs are also free, but roll-away beds cost about $5.

Fairfield Inns comprise Marriott's economy chain, with 125 motels in 34 states. Most have swimming pools, whirlpool spas and complimentary continental breakfast. Rates range from $29 to $50. (They're lower on weekends than on weeknights.)

Friendship Inns have 137 motels in 37 states and Canada. The motels have "limited service," which means there may be free coffee in the lobby, but that's about it. Some, however, do have swimming pools. All rooms cost less than $35.

Hampton Inns were the first to advertise an unconditional satisfaction guarantee—if a guest is not satisfied with accommodations or service, he doesn't have to pay. This chain offers complimentary continental breakfast in the lobby, free local phone calls and in-room movie channels. Almost all have swimming pools (some indoors), some have exercise rooms, and those near airports offer free van service. Rates average $49. Children under age 18 can stay free. Also, a third or fourth adult can stay in the room for no extra charge.

HoJo Inns, launched in 1990, quickly expanded to 165 locations in the next three years. Furnishings and amenities vary from inn to inn. Rates average $40 per night, with children ages 18 and under staying free in their parents' room. Most have swimming pools.

Hospitality International operates more than 350 properties under various names: Downtowner Motor Inns (limited-service economy motels), Passport Inns (limited-service motels), Scottish Inns (limited-service motels), Red Carpet Inns and Master Host Inns and Resorts. All are franchises appealing to budget watchers. Rooms are in the $20 to $60 range. Swimming pools, free in-room movies and free coffee (or continental breakfast) may be offered. Some charge for children over age 6; others allow youngsters as old as 16 to stay free in their parents' room. At some motels, cribs may be provided free. (At others, there may be a $6 charge.) Roll-aways are $5 to $10.

(continued)

A Guide to Budget Motels—Continued

La Quinta Inns comprise 215 southwestern-style properties in 29 states, with most around the Sunbelt. Guests get free continental breakfast in the lobby, same-day laundry and dry-cleaning services (for a charge), outdoor swimming pool, fax machine and free local phone calls. You can eat at an adjoining family restaurant. Some offer van service to nearby airports. Rates average $50, and children ages 18 and under stay free in their parents' room. Cribs are free; roll-aways are $5. The chain's Returns Club offers 1 free night after 11 nights.

At Motel 6, there are no coffee shops, meeting rooms, bathtubs or even pictures on the wall. But most of these motels will allow you to make local phone calls for free—and long-distance access may also be free. The motels have swimming pools and thick towels. Rates for this 750-motel chain average $31, and kids under age 18 stay free.

Red Roof Inns debuted in 1973 with $8.50 rooms carpeted in orange shag and the slogan "Sleep cheap." Now rooms in this 210-motel chain are decorated more tastefully, and the average room rate is about $38. Features are extra-long double beds (or kings), free morning coffee and weekday newspaper available in the lobby. The inns have free CNN and Showtime. Children ages

companies get better deals than individuals, and since these savings are passed on to card holders, you could knock 15 percent or more off your hotel bill.

Let Quikbook Do the Work
Save 40%

Quikbook is a hotel reservation service that will discount up to 40 percent off the usual corporate rates at many locations. The discounts usually apply to medium- and upper-range hotels in major American cities.

For vacationers, Quikbook is a way to get a deal that's even better than corporate rates. And you don't have to be employed by a specific company or on a business trip to be eligible. The Quikbook

18 and under sharing their parents' room stay free; cribs are also free; and roll-aways are $2.

Sleep Inns offer remote control color TV and oversize showers. A security system is set up so that you use your personal credit card for room entry. Rates average $35.

Super 8 Motels, with over 1,000 properties in 49 states, are the behemoth of the all-economy chains. Many offer waterbeds and meeting rooms; others have free continental breakfast, kitchenettes and swimming pools. Children under age 12 stay free. Rates start at $38.

Susse Chalet Motels, mostly in New England, provide free continental breakfast in the lobby and use of hair dryers and irons. Most have swimming pools and adjoining restaurants. Rooms average $48.

Travelodge was America's first motel chain (founded in 1946) and now includes 500 motels. All have nonsmoking rooms and complimentary in-room coffee and tea. Local phone calls are free; complimentary morning newspapers are provided in the lobby. Many have swimming pools; others also have a playground, game room, waterslide, workout room, sauna or coin laundry. Many have their own full-service restaurants and/or cocktail lounges. Rates average $49. Children ages 17 and under stay free.

reservation service handles over 100 hotels in cities such as Atlanta, Boston, Chicago, Denver, Detroit, Los Angeles, Miami, New Orleans, New York City, San Diego, San Francisco, Seattle and Washington, D.C. To get information from the Quikbook headquarters in New York City, call 800 directory assistance or 212 directory assistance and ask for the Quikbook number.

Use a Coupon
Save 50%

Entertainment Publications, which is based in Troy, Michigan, publishes discount coupon books designed specifically for travelers. These books, available in most areas, offer significant discounts on lodging, meals and entertainment.

How significant? Most coupons offer one-half off the rack rates for hotels and motels in 125 American cities. These coupon books can be purchased for between $25 and $45. For more information, contact Entertainment Publications by calling 1-800-477-3234 or writing to P.O. Box 1068, Trumbull, CT 06611.

Save $$ on Every Phone Call

Making telephone calls from a hotel room can be notoriously expensive—even when you're charging them to a credit card. But it doesn't have to be.

Some hotels charge as much as $1 for each credit card call, so making a lot of calls (as many business travelers do) can end up costing you a fortune. But there's a way to make several calls and be charged for only one.

Here's how: First get all your phone numbers ready. After you complete the first call, let the other party hang up, and then push the pound button (#) without hanging up the receiver. A recorded voice will then tell you that you can dial your next call. It's not necessary to enter your credit card number again.

Since you haven't hung up, you haven't been disconnected, and most switchboard equipment registers your string of calls as only one. (There's only one hitch: If no one answers at the other end, you must hang up before you can place another call.)

As for local phone calls, some hotels boast that these calls are free. But if free local service isn't available, using the lobby pay phone may be cheaper than calling from your room.

BED-AND-BREAKFAST INNS

Bed-and-breakfast inns (B&Bs) are usually full of history, charm and the kind of romance that could rival a Johnny Mathis songfest. Such attractiveness, common wisdom suggests, must come at a price. So you'd probably expect to pay a heck of a lot more at a B&B than for a motel room with two double beds, a bolted TV set and a Gideon Bible.

Not necessarily. With a little insight and luck, you can get a great deal on a great room at any of the thousands of B&Bs in the United States.

Make Pals with the Owner
Save 15%

Just as hotels and motels have a rack rate that can be negotiated down, so do B&Bs. In fact, it's often easier to get a price break at B&Bs, since they're privately owned—usually by the folks working at the front desk.

Try to negotiate a discount when you make reservations. Even walk-ins have a good chance of negotiating a better deal, provided the inn isn't full and it's not peak season. Remember, B&B owners take pride in the charm, appearance and history of their houses. A good conversation about the B&B and its features might get you the price break you're looking for. Insiders say you can get as much as 15 percent off.

Not Getting Both B's?
Save 10%

Some hotels and motels provide a continental breakfast, which consists of coffee and a muffin or a piece of toast. One of the benefits of staying at a B&B is that you usually get an authentic country breakfast—an all-you-can-eat extravaganza with eggs, breakfast meats and waffles, pancakes or French toast.

If your B&B doesn't include this hearty kind of breakfast, ask for a 10 percent discount. Innkeepers know that customers expect the big breakfast spread, but few guests are daring enough to make issue if they don't get it.

Many B&Bs also include afternoon tea (or wine) and après-ski refreshments to help take the edge off your appetite (and possibly save you some dinner money).

Check Out Urban Offerings
Save 30%

Think B&B, and you probably picture a sprawling farmhouse in Vermont. But would you think of New York City? Or Chicago?

The fact is, some of the best lodging deals in a big city are B&Bs. In New York City, for instance, the Bed and Breakfast on the Park (113 Prospect Park West, Brooklyn, NY 11215) offers rooms for anywhere from one-third to one-half off a typical midtown Manhattan hotel—with a lot more charm to boot.

ALL THE COMFORTS
OF (SOMEONE ELSE'S) HOME

There are a lot of great things about bed-and-breakfast inns: the charm. The meals. The insider's view of the area. But if your vacation includes the kids and dog, bed-and-breakfasts (B&Bs) can be anything but welcoming.

So here's another alternative, particularly if you're vacationing in New York City or another metropolitan area: a hosted house or apartment.

Under this arrangement, you move in with a family that happens to have plenty of room to spare. Everyone in your group or family gets a private bedroom. Your host makes your meal—usually breakfast but sometimes more. Rates may be the equivalent of what you'd pay for a B&B or hotel—or even less! (In addition, you can also find "unhosted" homes and apartments, where you get the run of the place when the owner or renter is away.)

This type of lodging has become especially popular in the Big Apple. Travelers gladly pay $50 to $70 for a bed and meals in a hosted house or apartment, cutting their overnight costs at least in half. For a family or group, you might pay up to $200 for several bedrooms in a house or an apartment—a considerable savings when you're traveling with a crowd.

For more information, call the chamber of commerce or a B&B booking service in the metro area you want to visit. Some tourist and travel agencies may also have a listing of hosts.

In New Orleans, many B&Bs consist of private cottages behind beautiful mansions, some with their own pools and other amenities—for about 40 percent less than the cost of a downtown hotel room. (To find out how to get these deals in the Big Easy, write to New Orleans Bed and Breakfast, P.O. Box 8163, New Orleans, LA 70182, which has access to 300 beautiful homes in the area.)

No matter where you're traveling, contact the visitors bureau or chamber of commerce, which should have listings of B&Bs in that city. You can also contact Hometours International (1170 Broadway, Suite 614, New York, NY 10001), a private service that handles B&Bs ranging from $55 to $200 in most major cities across the country.

LOW-BUDGET OVERNIGHTS

For those who are looking for some real savings, there's another class of lodging: low-cost "pit stops" of hostels, college dorms and the local YMCA.

The furnishings may be sparse, but the price is right—in many cases, $10 or less will get you a clean, comfortable bed, access to a shared bathroom and even a free meal in a communal kitchen. In some cases, you may even be able to use swimming pools and other recreational facilities.

This alternative lodging isn't just for traveling college students: All ages and incomes are welcome, including vacationing families. Here's a rundown of some of your choices.

Hostels: More Than a Cheap Bed

Hostels have long had a reputation for providing bare-bones accommodations at minimum cost, but that doesn't mean they're hovels. In fact, if you visit one of the 300 hostels in North America (or one of the 5,000 worldwide), you'll discover a truly unique place to hang your hat. Lighthouses, mansions, even train cars provide shelter for weary travelers and excited adventurers.

Hostels emphasize value—not frills. Costs range from $9 to $15 per night at most hostels (slightly more for families). Usually, you need to supply your own linens. Sleeping accommodations and bathroom facilities are shared with other hostelers. Sometimes you can get a meal or two at the hostel—breakfast, dinner or both. Hostels expect guests to perform at least one chore during their stay in order to keep the facility clean.

How do you find out about them? For access to any hostel, you need a membership, which costs (annually) $10 for those under age 18, $25 for those between 18 and 54 and $15 for those older. Write to American Youth Hostels, 733 15th Street NW, Washington, DC 20005.

College Dorms: All the Trimmings for Less

Many of the nation's colleges and universities open their dormitories in the summer to those looking for short-term shelter in that area. The 400 or so dorm facilities available around the country are particularly good for long family reunions and other group activities.

The dorms have homey features such as linens, washers and dryers, central air-conditioning and small kitchens on each floor.

Also, vacationers can use the school cafeteria and recreational facilities such as the pool, tennis courts and bowling lanes. Sometimes there's a nominal charge (about $5 per day) for using these facilities. And some schools provide mini educational courses for their "guests."

Dormitory charges can be as low as $10 a night per adult. For children, lodging is either free or under $5. Rates rarely go above $35 a night for double occupancy, and when they do, they usually include something special. (For instance, the University of California, Los Angeles, has sightseeing tours of movie studios and area beaches.)

To learn more about dorm vacations, send $12.95 plus $1.05 shipping and handling for *The U.S. and Worldwide Travel Accommodations Guide* from Campus Travel Service, P.O. Box 5486, Fullerton, CA 92635.

The Y: Location at a Discount

For budget lodging in many big cities, don't bypass the YMCA. The Y runs about 40 lodging centers in North America and another 50 in foreign countries. You'll get cheap, short-term housing in the heart of most metropolitan areas, and the charges are usually between $30 and $40 a night.

The money gets you a clean, spartan room—often with access to the Y's recreational facilities. Even more significant, however, is the location: usually smack in the middle of downtown. For more on rates and availability, write for the Y's international directory at the Y's Way International, 224 East 47th Street, New York, NY 10017.

Religious Retreats: Low-Cost Relaxation

With prices starting around $25 a night, the weekend religious retreat is growing in popularity—especially among those who are frugal and devout. Some retreats are held at religious centers such as convents or monasteries, but you can also attend at resorts and other vacation locations. Although centered around religious activities—prayer or discussion groups, for instance—more now include activities such as swimming, canoeing and other outdoor recreation. Some retreats are aimed specifically at singles, couples or families.

Fees usually include all meals and activities as well as lodging.

Some require participants to work. At Holy Transfiguration Monastery in Redwood Valley, California, for instance, "guests" work alongside the monks performing their daily chores.

Your religious denomination probably has a central board or committee that sends out information. You can also get some information by writing for the *U.S. and Worldwide Guide to Retreat Center Guest Houses,* available for $14.95 plus $1.55 shipping and handling from CTS Publications, P.O. Box 8355, Newport Beach, CA 92660. Also, most bookstores carry (or can order) *Catholic America: Self-Renewal Centers and Retreats* and the *Traveler's Guide to Healing Centers and Retreats in North America.*

For Seniors: A Learning Vacation for Less

Hostels have been associated with college kids for so long that many folks still refer to them as youth hostels. But many people well over age 60 are enjoying low-cost, easy-living hostel experiences. In fact, with a program called Elderhostel, anyone over 60 has special privileges in the hosteling world.

Elderhostel is a popular program that has more than 250,000 participants worldwide. It offers lodging, food and special educational programs to folks 60 years of age and older. (As long as you're over 60, you can take a companion who is over 50.)

Programs are held on college campuses, on ranches and in learning centers, state parks, 4-H camps and other sites offered by nonprofit educational institutions. Programs are held in 1,900 locations in the United States and 47 other countries. Each Elderhostel vacation in the United States goes about a week (six overnights). In foreign countries, a typical Elderhostel program lasts between two and four weeks.

An Elderhostel week in the United States costs about $295, which includes everything except transportation. For a catalog and more information, write to Elderhostel, 75 Federal Street, Boston, MA 02110.

RENTALS AND LONG-TERM HOUSING

An extended stay-over doesn't necessarily mean an expensive vacation. Whether you're staying for a couple of weeks or several months, there are plenty of budget options for long-term lodging in exotic or desirable locales.

In fact, with a little ingenuity, you can cut the costs of your travel lodging in half—or even more—while enjoying a truly remarkable vacation in a home away from home. Some rentals come complete with full kitchen, laundry facilities and even a maid to do the dirty work. Here are some ways to track down a vacation paradise for an amazingly good price.

Head to Mexico
Save $2,000

It costs anywhere from $500 to $1,500 per week to rent a vacation house in the United States, depending where it's located. Now imagine having a beachfront vacation home you can rent for a month or more that costs one-half of that amount or even less.

In Mexico, for as little as $250 a month you'll get a vacation house complete with maid service and all utilities included. Guadalajara leads the list of bargain locations. There, many U.S. retirees live in luxury for as little as $600 a month (including all expenses). Beachfront towns such as Tampico (on the east coast) and Manzanillo, Mazatlán and Puerto Vallarta (on the west coast) may be more expensive, but you'll still pay a mere fraction of what it would cost you to rent a vacation home stateside.

Travel agents who specialize in Mexican vacations can tell you about these homes. You can also get information through the 800 number of the American Association of Retired Persons.

Get a Free Vacation with a House Swap

Whether you live on a mountain retreat or Main Street USA, the odds are that you can swap your home with someone else's for a rent-free vacation.

Here's how it works: You pay an annual fee of around $60 to join a home swap club. While there are only a handful of swap clubs to choose from, some have as many as 16,000 homes around the world. For the price of the membership fee, you get a directory that lists other members and also describes their homes and vacation preferences. Then it's up to you to write to another member to arrange a swap. (The swap club does not participate in the actual arrangements between members.)

It takes anywhere from two to six months to arrange a swap—usually through letters, photos and phone calls—but it's time well spent.

How to Swap Homes

With home swapping, you can trade homes on a weekly, monthly or even yearly basis. You can ask for a security deposit or rental fee if your home is obviously more desirable than the trade home. And in some rare cases, you can even swap if you don't own your home (provided it's a sublease and okayed by your landlord).

But you can't do anything until you know where to begin. Here's a list of the leading home-swapping agencies operating in the United States and abroad.

- Intervac U.S., P.O. Box 590504, San Francisco, CA 94159. Cost: $62 a year ($55 for seniors). The directory, published annually, contains 8,000 listings in 36 countries.
- Loan-a-Home, 2 Park Lane 6E, Mount Vernon, NY 10552. Its directory includes only 400 listings, but all are long-term swaps or rentals—one month or longer. Cost: $45 per year for two directories and two supplements.
- Vacation Exchange Club, P.O. Box 650, Key West, FL 33041. Cost: $60 for an annual directory (including a listing of your home) plus monthly updates for homes of 16,000 members worldwide.

Since it's a simple trade-off, you get to stay in the other member's home for no charge.

You don't have to live in an exotic city or a prime vacation spot for your house to seem attractive. Many foreigners are happy to spend a week or two in Anywhere, USA. In fact, if the swap works out well, you may want to do the trade-off for more than one year.

There may be some drawbacks, however. On rare occasions, a swapper changes his mind after plans have been made with a trade family, leaving that other family in the lurch at vacation time. Also, sometimes there's a big difference in housekeeping styles. But most of those problems can be avoided if you negotiate well during the early stages of correspondence.

If the swap just doesn't seem right, you can always withdraw your offer after a letter or two.

Rent a Condo with Friends
Save 50%

The average one-bedroom condo at a beach or ski resort rents for an average of $650 a week, which may not seem like bargain vacation lodging. Actually, though, it might be one of the best luxury deals around—especially if you and your mate are vacationing with another couple.

For one thing, every condo has its own kitchen. That means you can prepare meals yourself—which is important if you're renting for longer than one week. But even if you choose to eat out at restaurants three or four times a week while on vacation, you can still save 20 to 60 percent of your meal budget by preparing your own breakfast and lunch.

And you get real savings by renting as a group. A one-bedroom condo is designed to sleep four—two in the bedroom and two on a sofa bed. If you get the condo for $650, that translates to less than $170 a person a week. (In a luxury hotel at a beach or ski resort, you could easily pay that amount for one night.)

FLOAT ON A BARGAIN—RENT A HOUSEBOAT

If you prefer water to asphalt, a houseboat could be an economical vacation. Depending on the boat's size and the season, renting a house-on-water costs between $80 and $200 a day. For about $175 a night, you get a houseboat that sleeps up to ten people and provides all the comforts of home, such as kitchen and bathroom facilities.

If you're a family that likes to vacation on the water, a houseboat is an adventurous vacation in an ideal location. You'll save hundreds a week, when you compare the price with staying in a hotel or renting a vacation home. The only drawback is availability, since it may be hard to find a houseboat in the exact area where you want to spend your shorefront vacation.

For more information on renting houseboats, contact the Houseboat Association of America, 4940 North Rhett Avenue, Charleston, SC 29405.

Condo Pricing?
Negotiate a Discount

Like hotels, rental condos have a standard rate that's usually the first price quoted by the listing agent. Depending on season and availability, you can usually get a discount of at least 10 percent off the quoted price.

But if you call around, ask friends and browse through newspaper ads, you'll discover that while many condos are represented by listing agents and real estate agents, others are not. Many owners who rent out condos originally purchased them as investment properties. If the owner handles the rental, he's already saving the commission that would be paid to a listing agent.

Owners know that they make money only by keeping their summer rentals occupied. So if the owner tells you there's a vacancy, the odds are he can't rent for that week. You're in a great position to offer 15 percent below the asking price.

You're most likely to find owner-controlled rentals by looking in the classified section of your local newspaper. Word of mouth is another great source. If you decide to work through real estate agents, ask for guides that are put out by agents in the area where you want to rent.

THEME PARKS

Ever wonder why they call them amusement parks? No doubt because the owners are quite amused over how much people will pay for a few hours of fun and adventure. These days, most major amusement parks charge over $30 per ticket for adults and nearly that much for children over age three. And that covers just admission. There are usually a lot more ways to spend money once you're inside.

Unfortunately, the general philosophy seems to be you have to pay to play. But there are a few ways to avoid being taken for a ride the next time you want to experience Space Mountain or the Ferris wheel.

Show Your Union Card
Save 20%

One advantage of being a union member is that you may be entitled to admission discounts at various theme parks. A union card or union-issued coupon can get you between a 5 and a 20 percent reduction on your admission to Walt Disney World (in Orlando, Florida), Disneyland (in Anaheim, California) and their movie studio attractions. Members of most unions and many credit unions can get Magic Kingdom Club cards, entitling them to discounts at all Disney parks as well as up to one-third off Disney hotels. Sea World and other smaller amusement parks offer similar discounts.

Sometimes simply banking at a credit union is enough to get you these discounts. So even if you don't belong to a union, you may still qualify for cheaper admission.

Gather a Group
Save 15%

Many theme parks offer cheaper admission to groups of 15 or more, so if you're traveling with a large group, always ask about group rates that might be available.

But even if you're not on a field trip with your social club, there is a way to reap these rewards. Simply gather a group of people together in the parking lot.

Explain to other vacationers that by entering the front gate together, you all pay less for your tickets. Then your group goes to the ticket counter marked "Group Sales," gets the group discount and distributes the tickets.

Of course, it's wise not to reveal that you've all just met; theme parks frown on this practice. But unless the theme park insists on advance purchases for group sales—which you can determine by calling before you leave on vacation—it is perfectly legal and can save you anywhere from 5 to 15 percent per ticket.

Note: Disney has no group sales program for any of its parks.

Brown-Bag Your Refreshments
Save $25

Inside a theme park, you usually pay a premium for food and drink. Instead of putting yourself at the mercy of in-park vendors, take along a backpack or fanny pack that has a few sandwiches, fruits and sodas or box juices. Packing your own food can save a family of four at least $25 in refreshment expenses for an average lunch and afternoon snack. (Plus you avoid all the hassles of waiting in line!) Another benefit is that your home-packed lunch will probably pack a lot more nutrition and less fat than the poor-quality hamburgers and hot dogs usually served at theme parks.

RVs AND CAMPING

You can save a lot by learning from the tortoise: Travel and live in the same space. Renting a recreational vehicle (RV) combines the cost of travel with the cost of living in a bargain vacation.

The reason is obvious: A multipurpose RV gets you where you're going while also providing sleeping, cooking and bathroom facilities. And your accommodation-on-wheels can take you to some of the most beautiful sites in the country.

Try a Motor Home
Save 50%

Buying an RV can be expensive: Prices range from $2,000 for a simple trailer to about $63,000 for a deluxe motor home. But renting an RV can be one-half of the price of a hotel room and a car.

It costs an average of $909 for a seven-night vacation for a family of four using the family car and staying in motels. By comparison, renting a self-contained motor home is about $450 a week. That's for an RV that sleeps four and has a kitchenette. (Often the RV has bathroom facilities as well.)

Weekly rentals cover a wide range, depending how much comfort you want. For $205 to $532, you get the most basic travel trailer, which provides only sleeping arrangements. Prices for a motor home accommodating seven people range from $550 to about $1,500. At the top end of the line, you get a monster motor home equipped with all sorts of conveniences, from VCRs to microwaves. You'll find that prices vary during different traveling seasons.

Renting an RV?
Check Your Insurance First

Most auto insurance policies cover any damage you may cause to a rental car, but that's not the case with RVs. So before refusing the collision damage waiver—which costs about $12 a day for RVs—check with your insurance agent.

Join an RV Club
Save 10%

Considering that most RVs get only five to ten miles per gallon, cross-country travel in a motor home can add up. Luckily, there's a

---

WHERE TO CAMP

Rates in the country's more than 16,000 public and private campgrounds range from less than $10 a night to about $18 for a site that has water, electric and sewage hookups for recreational vehicles (RVs). To get information on where to camp, call the Go Camping America hotline (1-800-47-SUNNY), which also offers coupons for a free night's lodging at over 800 campgrounds. You can also write to any of the following.

- National Association of RV Parks and Campgrounds, 8605 Westwood Center Drive, Vienna, VA 22182
- RV Park and CampResort Council, 1220 L Street NW, Washington, DC 20005
- *The National Park Camping Guide* (Booklet 024-005-01028-9) outlines the 440 developed campgrounds with 29,000 sites in America's national parks. It is available for $3.50 from the U.S. Government Printing Office, Superintendent of Documents, Washington, DC 20402.
- For information on 4,500 campgrounds on Forest Service property, contact the U.S. Department of Agriculture Forest Service, Office of Information, P.O. Box 96090, Washington, DC 20090. (You can make reservations by writing to the same address or by directly contacting the campgrounds.)
- The U.S. Army Corps of Engineers (USACE) has developed 53,000 campsites at national recreation areas near oceans, rivers and lakes. For a list of district offices that handle reservations at these locations, write USACE, Publications Depot, 2803 52nd Avenue, Hyattsville, MD 20781-1102.
- For information on where to rent RV vehicles, contact the Recreation Vehicle Rental Association at 3930 University Drive, Fairfax, VA 22030-2515.

way to recoup some of your other expenses, especially camping fees.

There are about a dozen RV clubs in the country. The largest is the Good Sam Recreational Vehicle Club, with 660,000 members. Many of the clubs offer their members special discount programs, which reduce camping fees. Discounts vary, but in most clubs members can usually save at least 10 percent by taking advantage of the discount program.

For a complete list of RV clubs and the discounts they might offer, write the Recreation Vehicle Industry Association, P.O. Box 2999, Reston, VA 22090-2999. Or look under "Recreational Vehicles" in the *Encyclopedia of Associations,* a reference book available at most public libraries. You may also qualify for discounts through auto clubs or the American Association of Retired Persons (if you're over age 55).

Camp for Less

For the greatest deals in a cost-saving vacation, skip the RV and just get a tent. Camping is leisure lodging at its absolute cheapest.

Provided you have your own camping equipment, you can usually get a campsite in God's country for less than $20 a night—complete with bathroom and shower facilities.

For even greater savings, choose state parks over national parks. Although costs vary from park to park, entrance and site fees tend to be 15 percent less in parks run by the state compared with those run by the federal government. What's more, state parks are usually less crowded.

CRUISES

Most people think of travel on the high seas as being high-priced, but it doesn't have to be. Granted, a sea cruise isn't the cheapest vacation you can take—even "bareboat-chartering" a sailboat for a few days can cost over $1,000—but there are ways to hoist anchor without throwing away your money.

Ignore the List Price
Save 50%

The cruise line business is a highly competitive one. Since the 1980s, a tidal wave of cruise ships has poured into the world's

TIPS ON TIPPING

Getting there may be half the fun, but being there can be downright confusing—especially if you don't know how much to tip. Here are some guidelines on how much you should give and to whom. So before you make travel plans, figure these gratuities into your budget.

TIPPING IN THE UNITED STATES

SERVICE	SUGGESTED TIP
Airport or train porter	$1.00 per bag
Bartender	15% of bill; $1.00 for light drinkers
Busboy	Gets tips from the waiter
Cab driver	15% of fare
Cabin attendant	$1.00 per errand
Chambermaid	$1.00–$1.25 per room per night
Cloakroom attendant	$ .50–$1.00 if there's no charge; no tip if there is a charge
Doorman	$1.00 for hailing a cab or carrying bags
Head waiter/waitress	5% of bill (for special attention)
Hotel porter	$1.00 per bag
Parking valet	$1.00–$2.00
Room service waiter/waitress	15% of bill
Shoe shiner	$ .50–$1.00
Strolling musician(s)	$1.00–$2.00 for single; $5.00 for group (if you've made a request)
Waiter/waitress	15% of bill is standard; 20% for excellent service
Washroom attendant	$ .50
Wine steward	15% of total wine bill

oceans—resulting in rampant discounting in order to attract business.

In fact, the price dropping has gotten so intense that some lines offer trips at one-half of the usual price. One year, for instance, Costa Cruises lines, listed for $1,300 in a company brochure, were being booked for $650. Of course, you shouldn't expect these deals from

Tipping Abroad

Argentina. A service charge is usually added to your bill, but because it's so small, tipping is expected for good service.

Australia. The norm is to tip only for special treatment. Otherwise, a thank-you is appropriate.

Belgium. Tipping is not expected, since a service charge of 16 percent is customary on most service bills.

Brazil. Low wages make service workers depend on tips—even though a 10 percent service charge is typically added to bills. For fast and efficient service, plan on tipping car rental agents, desk clerks and others not normally tipped in the United States.

Canada. The policies are similar to those in the United States, but be sure to tip in Canadian money, or you'll be paying a premium.

The Caribbean. Most hotels state their tipping policy in your room literature: No tipping is necessary at establishments with service charges. When you do tip, do so in U.S. money.

China. The People's Republic has a strict policy that forbids the acceptance of tips from foreigners. Despite this, more workers have come to expect tips—but instead of money, they prefer U.S. trinkets such as phone books, postcards, pens or, for excellent service, a bottle of wine.

Denmark and Finland. Tipping is rarely done.

France. Service charges are usually added, but a tip goes a long way in appreciation.

Germany. Despite a 12 to 15 percent service charge, a similar tip is expected for good service.

Greece. A 15 percent service charge is usually added to bills, but the money rarely reaches the service workers. So expect to tip workers at 15 percent. And don't forget the busboy. (This is one of the few countries where it is customary to always tip the busboy.)

(continued)

every cruise line, but you should expect some significant discount.

So ignore the "list" price and negotiate. Cruise lines are anxious for your business and are often willing to cut prices in order to get it. A good travel agent can inform you of the rock-bottom prices the cruise lines will take.

Tips on Tipping—Continued

Hong Kong. A 10 percent tip in cash is expected; good service commands more.

Ireland. Tips should be done conservatively because a large gratuity causes embarrassment.

Israel. Despite additional service charges, tipping is expected—especially from Americans.

Italy. Tip well when you get good service. (There's a standard service charge in restaurants and hotels, but more is expected if you want to show your appreciation.)

Japan. For the most part, tipping is not expected. The exception is Japanese inns (not to be confused with hotels), where a 1,000-yen tip at the beginning of your stay ensures good service.

In restaurants, you should tip infrequently and only for outstanding service. It's customary to wrap the money for a restaurant tip in paper or small envelopes sold exclusively for this purpose. If you add the tip to your credit card, don't be surprised if that amount is deleted.

Mexico. Tipping is very important, since many workers depend on foreign gratuities for their existence. But you should be prepared to see a lot of open palms. It's also advised to pay street urchins 50 pesos for "watching" your car against theft and vandalism.

Russia. "No tipping" is the stated rule, but guides, maids, cab drivers and others have come to expect tips. In restaurants, a tip in advance to the maître d' ensures priceless attention and service. But whenever you tip, do it in private.

Spain. Tip as you would in the United States. Despite service charges, the money rarely reaches the workers.

Switzerland. Tip minimally, because wages are good and service charges are added.

United Kingdom. Service charges are often added to bills, but it's not unheard of for a hotel waiter to say that his service isn't covered by the extra fees. It is. Still, additional tipping is encouraged. In pubs, don't tip the bartender with money; instead, buy him a drink.

Travel in Early Winter
Save 20%

Slow season means lower rates, so if you want to slash up to 20 percent off your cruising costs, try to book in the off-season. The usual off-season is late October through early December. But you might find similar savings in April and May, another time of the year when cruise bookings decrease.

Sign Up Early
Save 40%

It used to be that you could get the best fare by booking at the last minute—which, in the cruise business, means within six weeks of sailing. But then passengers who had booked earlier and paid more

---

DON'T FORGET THE HIDDEN COSTS

One of cruising's greatest allures is the all-inclusive nature of shipboard travel. Accommodations, meals, entertainment, sports facilities and a variety of other services are included in one price, making it a predictably priced vacation.

Well, at least in theory. There can be several hidden costs in taking a cruise that can add hundreds to your bottom line. Among them:

Parking. If you don't book an air-inclusive cruise, you must get to the ship. A taxi is your best bet, because if you drive yourself, port parking fees can be steep.

Island hopping. Once you're on board, shore excursions—sightseeing, flight-seeing and sports extras—are additional. You will also be assessed port taxes for islands the ship visits, which can add about $80 per person per week.

Tips. On most cruise lines, you are expected to tip service employees. Figure on $50 per passenger per week—which will be distributed to the cabin attendant, dining room staff and other crew members. Bartenders should be tipped on a per-service basis.

---

money began grumbling that late shoppers were getting better cabins for less money. So cruise lines responded with incentives to book early. In some cruise lines, you can save as much as 40 percent off regular prices by booking well in advance—up to 18 months before the trip.

Book a Whole Group

The more people you book on a single cruise, the more you save. Some cruise lines offer one free trip for every 15 bookings. If airfare is involved, you normally get that gratis as well. Fifteen bookings may seem like a large group, but you should be able to get that many recruits if you're involved with a club or social organization.

Cut Your Spending on

ENTERTAINMENT

- Cultural Events
- Movies
- Television and Video
- Sports and Recreation
- Low-Cost Alternatives

HAVE FUN FOR A SONG

The best things in life may be free, but the cost of entertaining ourselves can get very pricey.

Between ball games and sports equipment, movies and concerts, hobbies and even being couch potatoes in front of the TV, the typical American family spends about $1,500 a year on entertainment. That's nearly 15 times the annual amount that household gives to charities.

It's easy to see why: A night for two at the movies averages $13 even before the popcorn. Throw in a babysitter to mind the young 'uns and a post-flick nosh, and you're looking at a casual night out for $50. Take the family to a professional ball game, and between tickets, parking and refreshments, you could spend $100 or more for about three hours of entertainment.

Sure, fun doesn't always come cheap. But there are plenty of ways to keep yourself occupied while saving a few bucks.

CULTURAL EVENTS

Some forms of culture may be highbrow, but they don't have to be high-priced. You can see top-quality performances without paying top dollar—and we're not talking about your kid's school play. In fact, you can often get a healthy heap of culture for free.

Enjoy Music for Free—At Rehearsals

If you're a culture vulture who's financially grounded, there's a cheaper way to see your favorite concerts and theater and dance troupes in action: You can get low-cost or free admission to their rehearsals on afternoons or weekends.

In fact, money aside, these rehearsals are often better than the real McCoy, since you get to see what the conductor or director does behind the scenes—and to find out how professionals prepare for their

---

WHERE YOUR MONEY GOES

- Among singles, women spend about half as much on entertainment and leisure activities as men, who average more than $1,000 a year. The largest chunk of the total (for both sexes) goes to buy tickets for movies and sports events, while the rest goes for TVs, stereo equipment and accessories.
- The single largest entertainment expense among American families is for TV. The typical family spends an average of $350 a year on cable. About $50 a year is spent on video rentals.
- Pet ownership is America's top leisure expense. Families that own pets spend about $400 annually on pet food. About the same amount is spent on veterinary medical care and items such as flea collars.

---

performances. Also, after rehearsal, you're more likely to get the opportunity to meet the performers up close and personal and to ask them questions about their craft.

Call your local arts council or area theaters and concert halls to find out about "public" rehearsals. Most community performance groups welcome visitors to free rehearsals. If you want to hear a big-name orchestra or watch a leading theater troupe, you'll probably have to pay some admission—although rehearsals are usually low cost. The New York Philharmonic, for instance, sets aside 24 rehearsals each season where audiences are welcome: You can listen to the orchestra perform, often with music director Kurt Masur, for only $10.

For Museum Passes, Go to School

Even though they may be supported by grants and tax money, many museums are darn expensive. But what you may not know is that most museums distribute free passes to area schools and, sometimes, even to libraries.

These passes are usually intended to generate children's interest, but some museums have no restrictions on who uses them. Your best bet is to call the museum you want to visit to find out about any free-pass programs. Even if you don't have school-age children, you can call someone who belongs to the Parent-Teacher Association and find out what tickets are available. Then take along your favorite niece or nephew.

Tour Factories for a Free Look

Granted, a local bottling plant isn't the ballet, but who says popular culture has to be glamorous and artsy? Most factories give tours, and if you're a parent, it's probably one of the best ways to keep kids entertained for little or no cost.

Most factory tours are free, because the companies view them as good for public relations. Even if you do have to pay admission, the charge is modest. Most tours last under an hour—short enough that the kids won't get bored.

In addition, you usually get something besides a hefty dose of corporate know-how and local culture. Visit a candy factory, for instance, and everyone will leave with a chocolate bar. But before you visit any factory, call the company or the local tourist bureau to make sure the tours don't prohibit children. (Occasionally, kids aren't allowed on tours for safety reasons.)

Treat the Kids to a Free Farm Day

If you want your kids to breathe in the fresh country air and pat a placid cow, try a farm tour. From large dairies to small family-run operations, many farming communities open their split-rail gates one or two weekends a year to give the curious a glimpse of farm life. The tours are usually organized courtesy of the local Cooperative Extension Service or 4-H club. Visitors may get to feed chickens or pigs or do some other up-close-and-personal chore. There usually is no admission charge but plenty of fun—especially for kids.

Get Hot on Summer Concerts

Another freebie for singles, couples or families: summertime outdoor concerts. The usual setting is a park, the town square or a band shell. You take the blanket and cooler, and someone else pays for the music.

The featured performers may be local bands and orchestras or headline acts such as the Boston Pops. Scores of communities, large and small, offer series of weekend concerts, usually held on Friday nights or Sunday afternoons.

Some are scheduled every weekend throughout the summer; others involve weeklong musical tributes. For aficionados of bluegrass, for instance, there's the annual festival in Asheville, North Carolina. But if your tastes are more varied, you can hear everything from polka to jazz at weeklong events such as Musikfest in Bethlehem, Pennsylvania.

CHEAPER WAYS TO SEE PLAYS

Many people never attend live theater because of the expense. But there are usually ways around the really big ticket prices, if you know the ways to make your theatergoing cheaper.

Look for "rush" tickets. Usually, these are extra tickets sold about 30 minutes before the opening curtain—at about one-half of the price of other seats. Call the box office an hour or two beforehand to check on availability.

Go to previews. Before the play officially opens, preview tickets are often discounted. Some theatergoers enjoy seeing a work in progress. In many professional theaters, however, the play or musical is very close to finished by the time it opens for previews.

Pay as you can. During off-periods such as weekday shows, many theaters have a "pay as you can" policy where you make a donation for your admission—no questions asked.

Go for subscriptions. If you really like theater, a season-long subscription can save anywhere from 10 to 33 percent off ticket prices, compared with buying individual tickets for those shows. Plans vary: Some give you admission to just a couple of performances at certain times, while other subscriptions will get you entry to all shows. So check with your favorite theater group.

Seek out twofers. These coupons yield two tickets for the price of one at top Broadway shows. To get them for the big New York City shows, send a self-addressed, stamped envelope to Hit Show Club, 630 Ninth Avenue, New York, NY 10036. Twofers to New York City shows can also be obtained at the New York Convention and Visitors Bureau at 2 Columbus Circle in Manhattan.

Whatever the style, these programs—usually sponsored by a local arts council or the host park—are a great way to see quality acts for little or no money.

Save on Instruments
Balk at the List Price

If you'd rather play than watch, there's a way to buy musical instruments cheaper. Simply balk at the asking price.

Insiders say that most instruments are priced between 10 and 20 percent over the usual retail price because music store owners expect their customers to negotiate with them. Unfortunately, many buyers don't realize that a good negotiation will get them a lower price, so they wind up paying top dollar.

Whether you're shopping for a new violin, zither or flute, call around to find out what different stores charge for the same make and model of the same instrument. When you visit a store, tell the clerk that the price is higher than you expected, and ask if he's willing to come down. And make it clear that you can shop elsewhere if you don't get the price you want. Unless the place does a booming business, the odds are you can get the 10 to 20 percent price reduction you're after.

MOVIES

In Hollywood, the cost of making movies keeps going up, up, up. But at your local theater, there are plenty of opportunities to trim your moviegoing costs—sometimes by more than half.

According to *Variety*, a film trade publication, there are nearly 600 discount movie theaters across the country. Their bargain-basement admission prices are less than $3 and sometimes as little as $1. That's quite a savings, when you consider that many a movie ticket in America costs $6.50 or more. But even if there are no discount movie theaters in your area, you can still save at many first-run theaters.

Go on Tuesday Nights
Save 20%

Traditionally, the slowest night for movie theaters is Tuesday. In an effort to beef up business, several chains and scores of independent theaters now offer reduced rates on Tuesday nights. Ticket prices are usually slashed between 20 and 50 percent.

Most theaters advertise these specials, so they're not a trade secret. If your local theater has no special Tuesday rates, however, call and find out why. If there are enough inquiring calls—that is, customer demand—the theater might introduce these specials.

Show Your Age
Save 20%

Students and senior citizens may also be entitled to movie discounts—usually $1 or so off the price of regular admission.

Depending on ticket prices, that means you could get anywhere from 20 to 35 percent off. To get the discount, be prepared to show proper identification.

Catch the Earlier Show
Save 65%

The best way to cut your spending at the movies is by going before dinner instead of afterward. Most first-run theaters—particularly the

LOOK INTO ENTERTAINMENT BOOKS

Whether you're interested in movies, concerts, sporting events or a day at the racetrack, you can probably enjoy it for less with an Entertainment coupon book.

These coupon books—which are also good for dining out—offer reduced rates or two-for-one deals for scores of recreation and entertainment opportunities in your area. There are approximately 150 different versions of the book, each of them regionally organized. You simply use the coupons you want.

Usually sold through nonprofit associations such as Kiwanis or publicized through companies and tourist organizations, the books cost from $25 to $45, depending on the area. For more information, contact Entertainment Publications by calling 1-800-477-3234 or writing to P.O. Box 1068, Trumbull, CT 06611.

newer multiplex cinemas in malls and strip shopping centers—have discount shows before 6:00 P.M.

If you scan the paper for matinees and "twilight show" specials, you'll find that admission is between 30 and 65 percent off normal prices. Some theaters offer this discount to all early shows; others simply have one twilight showing near the dinner hour.

Look for Sneak Previews
Save 50%

Although double features are rarer than they were a generation ago, many theaters still have them. You can usually catch a double feature on the first Friday that a new picture is released. Since you pay admission for one film and can stay to see another, you get two movies for the price of one. Check the entertainment section of your local newspaper for ads that say "sneak preview" or "double feature."

TELEVISION AND VIDEO

Watching TV is the most popular form of entertainment in the United States. Unfortunately, even being a sofa slug doesn't come cheap anymore. If you're hooked up to cable, which now is in the majority of American homes, you've got a fixed monthly cost. Add in a few movie rentals and a video game or two for the kids, and we're spending some serious money.

All told, we spend about $15 billion a year on TV and videos— about $400 a year per household (and that doesn't include equipment purchases). But here's how to take some of the dollars out of your TV viewing and make your video costs more palatable.

Cut Your Video Costs
Go to the Library

At most public libraries, you can borrow videos the same way you borrow books—with a library card. Even if there's a charge, it's usually quite small—no more than a dollar or so. And the selections are getting better and better, since many libraries have set up specific budgets to buy movies. Also, a number of foundations are making contributions that help libraries expand their collections of art, entertainment and educational videos.

Parents will be pleased to learn that most of the library movies are rated G or PG. And most libraries are careful to screen out any videos that contain excessive violence or deal with adult themes. Another bonus: Many libraries allow you to borrow up to five movies at a time and to keep the movies for a week or more.

Buy Previously Viewed Videos
Save 70%

If you're the buying kind, forget about paying retail for hot new videos. Instead of shelling out the usual $15 to $30, ask video store personnel to reserve you a "previously viewed" copy. That means you'll get a video that has been rented out numerous times for about a month. The used video can cost as little as $5—and usually the price is no higher than $15.

WHERE TO GET TV TICKETS

You can get in free to see the taping of a popular TV show, but you might have to wait up to two months for tickets. No harm in planning ahead, however. If you're planning a trip to Los Angeles or New York City and would like to see the taping of your favorite show, why not give it a try? Here's where to write. (Make sure you mention the show you want to see!)

- NBC Tickets, 3000 West Alameda Avenue, Burbank, CA 91523
- CBS Tickets, 7800 Beverly Boulevard, Los Angeles, CA 90036
- ABC, Audiences Unlimited, 100 Universal City Plaza, Building 153, Universal City, CA 91608 (Be sure to include a self-addressed, stamped envelope.)
- Fox TV Center, Audiences Unlimited, 100 Universal City Plaza, Building 153, Universal City, CA 91608 (Include a self-addressed, stamped envelope.)

You can also get a calender of TV tapings (for up to one month in advance) by sending a self-addressed, stamped envelope to Los Angeles Convention and Visitors Bureau, 4151 Prospect Avenue, Hollywood, CA 90027.

Don't worry about getting second-rate goods: Videotapes are manufactured to last for about 300 viewings, so the quality will still be
good when you get the tape even if it's been rented daily for several
months.

Save on Video Games

If your child is like most kids, every new Mega Man or Kirby's
Dream Land video game that comes down the pike is the newest
"must-have" item. Unfortunately, after a few days, the attraction
fades, and you're $35 in the hole.

Luckily, more video stores now rent these video games. For $2 or
$3 you get a couple of days' rental of most Nintendo or Sega video
games at a fraction of the purchase price. Sure, you may want to buy
the games later on, but if your child tries them out first, you can find
out whether a game holds his interest before you buy it. And as with
video movies, some stores sell previously viewed video games for a
lot less than you'd pay to buy a new one.

SPORTS AND RECREATION

If you take all the households in America and average their
spending on sports and recreation equipment, it amounts to
slightly more than $100 a year per home. But when you consider that
there are about a quarter-billion folks living out there—and most
aren't regular exercisers—that's a heck of a lot of money. Now add the
billions more spent each year watching sports, taking swimming and
tennis lessons and pursuing related activities, and you've got enough
to perhaps even pay a few professional athletes.

But seriously, there are ways to enjoy your favorite sports and recreation activities for less—even though you can't usually negotiate the
price of sports equipment and tickets.

Learn Good Timing
Save 50%

Movie theaters aren't the only places that offer discounts during off-
hours. The same holds true at bowling alleys, skating rinks, swimming
pools and other havens of recreation. During off-peak times, some of
these facilities offer as much as one-half off normal admission rates.

Surprisingly, the hours of "open" admission for skating, bowling and swimming—when prices are lowest—are the times when kids like to go, such as weekend mornings or early evenings.

Every business, however, has a different "deal." To find out the best hours to go, call the facilities near you.

Reduce Your Swim-Time Dollars
Go after Dinner

Most communities or townships have municipal pools for their residents to enjoy. And while these pools charge a reasonable price compared with private swim clubs—families can usually get a summer-long membership for about $100—evening swims are even better for the penny-pinching aqua nut.

Most municipal pools offer area residents free admission (or drastically reduced rates) after 6:00 or 7:00 P.M., when the daytime crowd goes home. And since most of these pools close at 8:00 or 8:30 P.M., you have plenty of time for a refreshing dip after work. And besides getting a bargain, you probably will also get a less crowded pool, without the usual splashing and commotion that you find in most municipal swimming spots. That's good news for lap swimmers!

See the Up-and-Comers
Save 60%

Go to a baseball game, and you'll learn that enjoying our national pastime can be pretty expensive. It can cost a family of four nearly $80, even if no one drinks beer: That's four box seats costing $48, $5 for parking, $22 for hot dogs and sodas and $2 for a program. But instead of paying major-league money to see the majors, you can enjoy the same excitement by viewing your nearest minor-league team.

There are 167 minor-league baseball teams scattered across the United States, most of which serve as training grounds for tomorrow's superstars. For less than $25, a family of four can see a minor-league game with all the same trimmings, including refreshments and parking. Best of all, your family may enjoy the minor leagues even more than the majors.

Minor-league players don't get as much press as the "pros," but that may actually be a benefit. Unlike big leaguers who now have little contact with the fans, the up-and-comers are willing—if not delighted—to talk to fans, autograph baseballs and even give pointers to Little Leaguers.

Because minor-league stadiums are smaller and more intimate, many fans claim that there's more crowd loyalty and team spirit. Crowds average about 7,000 at triple A league games, where the play is closest to the majors. You can expect to see crowds of about 4,000 at double A games and about l,500 in the single A (rookie league) ballpark.

Most of these 167 teams, which are based in smaller cities, represent major-league franchises. The Toledo Mud Hens, for instance, prepare players for the Detroit Tigers, while the Reading Phillies are connected to the Philadelphia team. For a complete list of teams near your home, write to the National Association of Professional Baseball Leagues, P.O. Box A, St. Petersburg, FL 33731.

Buy Camping Gear from the Girl Scouts
Save 80%

Camping has long been popular among the cost-conscious: After all, it's lodging at its cheapest. But there's a way to buy tents, stoves and other camping equipment for a fraction of retail prices: Call the Girl Scout troops in your area.

When equipment gets old or a troop unit closes because of dwindling participation, the equipment is practically given away. If you contact your area's local council to see about buying surplus equipment, you can almost certainly cut your camping gear spending. Often Girl Scout gear is sold for about 80 percent off retail prices.

Low-Cost Alternatives

Whether your radius of entertainment is a few blocks or a few hundred miles, there are plenty of ways to help yourself and your family have a good time without digging too deeply into your pockets. Here are some ways to spend time having a good time without making big dents in your bank account.

Visit Historical Houses

How did Ernest Hemingway live? What inspired sculptor Daniel Chester French? What kind of decorating taste did Ben Franklin have? If you like to sneak a peek at how others lived, visiting a famous person's house or another historical site can be educational, entertaining and cheap.

Although admission cost is higher at some sites such as Hearst Castle, the San Simeon, California, home of the legendary newspaper magnate William Randolph Hearst, the majority of historical and famous homes are less than $4 per person.

George Washington's home in Mount Vernon, Virginia, draws more than one million visitors each year. Other popular historic sites for tourists include Monticello, Thomas Jefferson's estate in Charlottesville, Virginia; Mark Twain's residences in Hartford, Connecticut, and Hannibal, Missouri; and Ernest Hemingway's house in Key West, Florida.

The National Park Service runs 72 historical sites, including the Jimmy Carter National Historical Site in Plains, Georgia; the Martin Luther King, Jr., National Historical Site in Atlanta; and Teddy Roosevelt's estate in Sagamore Hill, Long Island. And the National Trust for Historic Preservation manages 18 sites, including Frank Lloyd Wright's home in Oak Park, Illinois, and Woodrow Wilson's home in Washington, D.C.

Phone numbers for both the National Park Service and the National Trust can be obtained from Washington, D.C., directory assistance (202 area code). Or contact your local tourism bureau for more information.

Night Court: A Priceless Show for Nothing

For a wacky blend of real-life drama and comedy, check out your judicial system in action—especially at night. If you visit the local courthouse, you'll see the scales of justice tilt wildly back and forth, get a better understanding of the legal system and witness a slice of life not normally seen by John Q. Public.

Most cities, large and small, have some version of night court. Some are just small-time traffic courts, while other courts handle hard-core criminal cases. But whatever the size of the crime, viewing the court comes free.

Granted, not every moment is action-packed, but the scenes of high judicial drama can be unforgettable. And most judges are happy to see law-abiding citizens in their courtrooms, as long as they are quiet and behave appropriately.

Literature for Less: Go to Book Readings

If you're a bookworm, check out the scheduled readings at your favorite bookstore. You may be surprised at how many authors are planning to visit and read from their works.

Readings of poetry and literature are usually free, and they're growing in popularity. You can also enjoy food if you go to one of the bookstore cafes that are springing up around the country. To suggest just a few: There's Elliott Bay Book Company in Seattle; Kramerbocks and Afterwords Cafe in Washington, D.C.; Book Friends Cafe in New York City; Malaprop's Book Store Cafe in Asheville, North Carolina; and Borders in Philadelphia.

But whether or not you get a croissant and capuccino with your literature, this is a great way to spend an evening being amused, entertained and enlightened without spending money.

Shop for Surprises at the Mall

There's more than shopping at your local shopping mall. From rock concerts to dog shows, from children's story time to autograph sessions with soap opera stars, America's shopping malls have it all.

The purpose of malls is to attract people, and this is done through a variety of programs. Some, for instance, have mall-walking pro-

---

GETTING MUSIC FOR A SONG

There's a wide gap in pricing for the same tape or CD, depending where you shop. Music stores in malls are the most expensive—roughly 40 percent higher than discount stores such as K Mart. And if you buy used CDs at stores that carry them, you can save about 55 percent. Here's a comparison for a new-release CD (we used Eric Clapton's Grammy-winning *Unplugged*).

PURCHASE	PRICE ($)
New CD from retail store	17.99
New CD from discount store	10.99
Used CD from used-record store	7.99

THE TRUTH ABOUT MUSIC CLUBS

The advertisements are simple enough: You get several free CDs or tapes in exchange for agreeing to buy a few at regular club prices over the next few years. So you add up the total cost of the club prices, and you figure it's still cheaper than buying retail—right?

Not exactly.

While music clubs such as Columbia House and BMG Music Service do offer some good deals, subscribers can get socked in shipping and handling costs. Here's what we found.

Columbia House is the nation's largest club, offering hundreds of rock, jazz, classical and other selections in magazine advertisements. The standard offer is eight free CDs in exchange for buying six more at regular club prices over the next three years. The base prices are competitive—usually $12.98 to $17.99 for a single CD. But with sales tax and shipping and handling charges, you may need to add as much as $4 or so to each selection, depending where you live. So keep this in mind when calculating your bottom line. And also remember that you need to pay sales tax and shipping and handling for your freebies.

BMG Music Service has a smaller inventory to choose from, but you get more for your money. Its standard offer, also frequently advertised in magazines, is four freebies in exchange for agreeing to buy one selection at either the regular club price or one-half of that amount. (The promotions switch every few months.) For single CDs, the regular club prices are in the $14.99 to $17.99 range. Again, you pay sales tax and shipping and handling for freebies.

The bottom line is that while these offers seem appealing, there's little savings compared with buying CDs on sale at your local record store.

There are various smaller music clubs and catalogs. A catalog is available for $2 from Music by Mail, P.O. Box 090424, Fort Hamilton Station, Brooklyn, NY 11209. The catalog lists 10,000 titles.

grams for seniors—a great way to get exercise in a lively, weather-sheltered environment. Others feature animal shows and other programs for kids. Or just for variety, you may be able to attend a wine and cheese tasting party at a nearby mall.

Call the administrative offices of your local mall—listed in the phone directory—for a schedule of upcoming events. All are free.

Learn about Great Deals at College

Most colleges and universities provide a wealth of entertainment opportunities for just a fraction of the cost of enjoying the same events elsewhere. Concerts, movies, ballet, lectures and other cultural events are usually open to the public. Prices range anywhere from 20 to 50 percent less than you'd pay for admission to a public concert hall or theater. In fact, admission may be free if you're a student or senior citizen.

The events are diverse. In the past, Duke University in Durham, North Carolina, has had lectures by Kurt Vonnegut, Jr., Congressman Richard Gephardt and political cartoonist Doug Marlette. The entertainment schedule also featured a concert by the rap group Public Enemy, performances of Shakespeare and Broadway plays and several first-run films—all within a few months.

Even the small universities may have a wealth of offerings. To learn what's on the program for a college or university in your area, call the school's public relations office or the office of student cultural affairs. Ask for a calendar of upcoming events.

Cut Your Spending on

INSURANCE

- Car Insurance
- Homeowners Insurance
- Life Insurance

Cut Your Costs without Hurting Your Coverage

The thing about insurance is that you're paying for something you hope you'll never use.

But that's not to say you don't need it. You do.

The trick to buying insurance—whether for your car, home or health—is to pay as little as possible and still fulfill all your needs. Of course, how much you spend often depends on the value of what you own—not to mention the needs of family members who depend on your policies for their health and security. And you want to make sure you have a safety net for those miserable times when the roof springs a leak, your kid gets in a fender bender or a neighbor slips and falls on your ice-covered driveway.

Fortunately, you can have all you need—plus a bit more—and still cut your spending on insurance, if you know where to trim costs. In fact, you can cut as much as one-half off your insurance spending—even more in some cases. And while saving money, you can actually improve your coverage on your car, home and life.

Car Insurance

You wear your seat belts. You never drink and drive. Maybe you even have a car with dual air bags. Even so, accidents happen—and we all pay for those accidents in the form of car insurance.

But another reason we pay so much is because agents don't always give us the whole picture. Many people buy everything an agent recommends without double-checking to make sure it's necessary. And incidentally, the more you pay, the higher the agent's commission.

So here are some things you ought to know about how to reduce your car insurance premiums without sacrificing quality coverage.

> ## WHERE YOUR MONEY GOES
>
> - Insurance agents typically earn between 10 and 15 percent commission on your policies. That means if you pay $850 a year for auto insurance, your agent may earn as much as $127 in commission. For a $350 homeowners policy, the agent's commission could amount to as much as $52.
> - Over the span of ten years, the typical American household will spend $8,900 on auto insurance. But that typical household will file just one claim—for an average of $600.

Mention Accessories to Cut Your Insurance

Have air bags in your car? Mention them to your agent. Have an anti-theft device? Mention that, too. Same goes for anti-lock brakes. In fact, mention all the safety features in your car.

Depending on your insurance company, these features can qualify you for discounts of 5 percent or more compared with rates for similar cars lacking these features. Most companies will give you a list of discount items. Discounts are also listed in periodic policy statements from the insurance company. If your agent doesn't mention these items, you should bring them up.

Brag about Your Driving Record
Save 10%

Assuming you never have a claim, chances are the only communication you have with your car insurance agent is an annual Christmas card. Too bad, because that silence may be costing you money.

Every six months that you go without getting a ticket or being in an accident is cause for a phone call. Let your insurance agent know that you still have a clean record—and you may find out you're eligible for a discount. Once a previous ticket is cleared from your record, which takes about three years, you may be entitled to a 10 percent discount.

Of course, don't expect this discount every six months, but your clean record should be mentioned.

ARE YOU GETTING ALL YOUR DISCOUNTS?

Special accessories, classes or even circumstances qualify you for discounts in car insurance that aren't always advertised. Here's a list of some of the discounts you may be entitled to and how much they can save you on different parts of your policy. (For instance, anti-theft devices can trim 5 to 50 percent off the comprehensive part of your insurance—not off your total policy.)

DISCOUNT	COVERAGE AFFECTED	SAVINGS
Defensive driving course	Most coverage	5%–10%
Multi-car	All coverage	10%–25%
Good driver (renewal)	All coverage	5%–10%
Automatic safety belts and air bags	Medical	10%–60%
Anti-theft devices	Comprehensive	5%–50%
Anti-lock brakes	Collision, medical, property liability	5%–10%
Student driver training	All coverage	10%
Good student	Most coverage	5%–25%
Student away at school	Most coverage	10%–40%

Stick to the Station Wagon
Save 20%

Cars make a statement—to your insurance company as well as to other drivers. A hot sports car or big, powerful "muscle car" (such as a Pontiac Trans Am or Firebird) doesn't exactly project the image of a safety-conscious family of four.

As a result, muscle cars have traditionally been more expensive to insure—as much as 20 percent higher in some cases. (Other reasons: They tend to be favorite targets of car thieves and seem to be more popular with younger drivers, who have the highest premiums.)

So if you're looking to lower insurance rates when you're buying a new car, stick to models that project a more sedate image—big family sedans and wagons. These cars tend to be favored by family types, who are seen by insurance companies as safer drivers.

Revalue Your Car's Worth
Save 40%

If you have an older car, it's time to review your insurance coverage. If you don't periodically update the information on your policy, you'll wind up paying for the same amount of coverage for a ten-year-old car as when the car was brand-new. But the car is worth a lot less. So you're paying more than you should.

Since an older car isn't worth as much as a new one, it never needs to be insured for the same amount (unless it's a vintage model that increases in value). Collision coverage is the single most expensive part of your auto insurance costs, accounting for as much as 40 percent of your premium. Yet in the very worst case, if your clunker is

---

RAISE YOUR COLLISION TO SAVE THOUSANDS

The single most expensive part of your car insurance is your collision coverage. But you can cut your total premium by about one-third (and reduce your collision payment as well)—and not hurt your coverage—by raising your deductible.

The typical deductible on collision is $250. But if you increase your deductible to $500, you'll reduce your collision premium. That means an accident that does less than $500 damage will not be covered by your insurance company—you have to foot the bill.

With today's automobiles, almost any damage done to your car in an accident will cost more than $500 to repair. That's why it's smart to increase your collision deductible to $500.

For instance: In one state, a $250 collision deductible on a one-year-old Mazda MPV resulted in a premium of approximately $370 a year. Raising the deductible to $500 reduced that annual premium to $210 a year—a savings of $160.

totaled, your insurer will pay only the market value of the car, which may be only a few hundred dollars—or even less than your collision premium.

That's why it's important for you to periodically re-evaluate your car's worth. If your annual collision coverage costs are 10 percent of the car's worth, or the car's resale value is less than $1,000 (you can determine both by reading for-sale ads in the classified section of your newspaper), talk to your agent about dropping that coverage.

Put Junior under Your Policy
Save 50%

The cost of car insurance for a teenager is outrageous—especially when that teen is covered under a policy that's separate from yours. And it's worst of all for teenage boys. Insurance companies routinely double the premium for a male under age 20 who has his own policy, compared with what a man only a few years older has to pay.

That's not to say that you should pay for your teen's car insurance. Simply cover him under the family policy and have him pay you the additional premium cost.

Drive Junior's Car
Save 10%

If your teen has his own car, make sure he lets you drive it from time to time. Otherwise, your teen is the principal driver of a specific car—and as a result, there will be higher rates for that vehicle. But if you drive that car as well, rates will be lower—anywhere from 10 to 25 percent lower in some cases.

Extol the Schooling
and Cut the Premium

Teenage drivers may qualify for any number of discount programs related to their education. Discounts are given to good students (those with a B average or higher), students who attend college away from home (and therefore don't drive regularly) and even those who take driver education classes in high school.

So be sure to mention any of these situations to your agent. The discounts vary from 5 to 40 percent on what it costs you to insure your young driver.

Pay the Whole Premium
Save $50

Most companies allow you to pay your premiums quarterly, twice a year or in one lump sum. And some companies allow monthly payments. But the more often you pay, the more money you pay, because extra dollars are tacked on as interest charges. By paying in one lump sum (if you can afford it), you can reduce your annual premiums by $50 or more.

Shop Around Every Year

Even if you think you're getting a good deal on insurance, it's well worth your time to double-check. Insurance companies don't advertise their rates. When you comparison-shop, you may be surprised to see rates vary by 30 to 60 percent from company to company—for the same coverage.

Besides, some companies try to direct their product (the insurance they sell) to a specific kind of buyer. If you're a buyer who doesn't fit the profile for that market, you're going to pay more than the people whom the company wants to buy its insurance. And sometimes independent agents don't sign up their clients with the lowest-cost company for the simple reason that it would reduce their commission.

To make sure you're getting the best deal possible, it's a good plan to call no fewer than five different insurance companies or agents. When we shopped around, we found that rates could vary by a few hundred dollars a year for basically the same policy.

Put All Your Policies in One Company
Save 15%

Many companies will knock as much as 15 percent off the premiums for combined homeowners and automobile insurance if you keep both policies with a single insurer. Apart from the savings you get, there's a convenience factor, because you'll be dealing with one agent and one company for all your insurance needs.

WHAT COVERAGE DO YOU NEED?

There are more than a dozen different types of coverage you can get on your automobile insurance, but you may not need all of them. By getting rid of excess coverage, you can trim more than one-third off your car insurance costs.

But how do you decide what you do need and what you don't need? The requirements for auto insurance coverage vary from state to state—and your first priority is to get all the coverage that's required. But once you've done that, here are some other factors to consider.

Go for the Maximum

Bodily injury liability. Most experts recommend that you get the highest level of insurance you can, usually $100,000/$300,000. (The first number represents the maximum coverage per person; the second number is per accident.) You save very little—and risk everything—by getting less.

Property damage liability. Again, carry the highest level of coverage. The difference in cost for the highest and lowest levels is about $63 a year, but it's worth the money in terms of protection of your financial security.

Reconsider

Collision. This coverage is actually optional under most state laws once your car is paid off. (But all lenders require it until your

Open the Umbrella
Save $100

To reduce your premium costs even more, many insurers that offer package discounts also permit you to add an "umbrella" liability policy to the package. With an umbrella policy, you're covered for any home or auto liability cost that exceeds the dollar limits on those two policies. You can then purchase the lowest required liability limits on your auto and home—at considerable savings—and buy the umbrella policy to cover the rest.

loan is paid off.) Because collision accounts for more than one-third of your total premium costs, raising your deductible, or dropping the coverage for an older car, is the best way to lower your spending for car insurance.

Comprehensive. Again, most states do not require comprehensive coverage, which protects against theft, vandalism and other types of damage. It is, however, required by all lenders. Think twice about raising the deductible, however, if your car is a likely target for thieves.

Uninsured motorist protection. This coverage pays the cost of your own injuries if you're hit by an uninsured driver who's at fault or by a hit-and-run driver—but it's probably not needed if you have good life, health and disability insurance. This kind of protection is no longer required by most states, but a premium of less than $20 a year can buy you maximum coverage of $100,000/$300,000.

Underinsured motorist protection. If an at-fault driver has too little insurance to cover your damages, this kind of protection makes up the difference. It's still mandatory in some states but costs only about $3. If it's not required by the state, you probably don't need it.

Medical payments. These are rarely required by states anymore. They may be unnecessary for you, depending on your personal health insurance policy.

Check with your agent before deciding whether to purchase this coverage.

Buying $1 million in liability coverage will cost you only about $200 a year. That could give you an average savings of close to $100 annually compared with getting your homeowners and automobile coverage from separate insurers.

Buy an Easy-to-Fix Car
Save $500

Some cars are easier to repair than others, and because of this, they are cheaper to insure. A Ford Escort, for instance, may be as much as

$500 a year less to insure than a Volvo. In part, that's because it's a popular seller, so body replacement parts are plentiful. But it's also because all repairs on luxury cars tend to be expensive.

So if you're in the market for a new car, ask your insurance agent for a list of the cars that are cheapest to repair and those that are most expensive. Find out the insurance rates for those cars, and compare before you buy.

Forget Credit Insurance
Save $50

You can shave $20 to $50 off your car payment by not taking credit insurance on your loan. This is insurance that covers your loan, so your lender is protected against bad risks.

The lender might try to "demand" credit insurance, but in most states it isn't required. (However, the lender can decide not to make the loan because of this, if you appear to be a bad risk.)

If you need to convince the lender that the loan is well protected, ask him to accept partial assignment of a term life policy.

Changing Your Lifestyle?
Save 15%

Any change in your lifestyle could reflect a change in driving habits or car use and should be mentioned to your insurance agent. For instance, if you've recently retired and stopped using your car for commuting, that could mean lower premiums. (Simply turning age 60 usually qualifies you for a 15 percent drop in your rates; with some companies, the senior citizen discount begins at age 55.)

Or if you've gotten a divorce and your spouse no longer drives your car, that could mean another discount. Carpooling regularly to work qualifies you to pay less money (since you're not using your car as often). And if you're using only one car in a two-car family for commuting, that should also make you eligible for a lower rate.

HOMEOWNERS INSURANCE

From termites to tornadoes, there are any number of disasters that can befall a home—and they can cause every conceivable form of water damage, conflagration and structural dismemberment.

Luckily, a good homeowners policy will cover them all.

But good doesn't have to mean expensive. You can get all the coverage you need—and pay less. Here's how.

Don't Cover Your Lot

You can cut anywhere from 20 percent to one-half off your homeowners insurance with no change in coverage—simply by not including your land in your policy.

Most homeowners policies include the land in the coverage, yet even if your home is totally destroyed, that won't change the value of the land. (In other words, the insurance company will still reimburse you for only the house, not the property.)

The typical lot is worth about 20 percent of the value of a home.

VIDEOTAPE YOUR POSSESSIONS FOR FEWER INSURANCE HASSLES

If your home has a fire, there's a good chance you could get burned when it comes time to collect for your losses—unless you can prove your case.

Forget about making an inventory list, as many agents once suggested. People routinely lie and make fraudulent claims, which is exactly why insurance rates keep increasing.

Instead, today's experts suggest you make a videotape inventory of your possessions—room by room. This way, any claim you make can be backed up by visual testimony. (Of course, don't keep the tape in your home; it's safer in a safety deposit box or in a friend's or relative's home.)

In making your tape, be sure to include all items—such as jewelry, clothing, tools and other "non-furnishings"—and don't be shy to point out (on film) special features or the value of certain items. Remember, this tape is the evidence you'll present to the insurance company to back up your claims in the event of a problem, such as burglary, fire or flood.

But even with a videotape, you should still keep receipts or other written proof of the value of items in your home.

Don't Smoke? You'll Save Twice

It's no surprise that smokers have higher life insurance premiums. But if no one in your family smokes, you may also qualify for lower rates when you take out homeowners insurance.

Discounts vary, depending on your coverage and the insurance company, but smokers have a greater risk of house fires.

But in some states, such as California, land is so expensive that it contributes as much as one-half of the home's total value. Check with local real estate organizations and associations to find out what your property is worth—or if you're buying a new house, ask the real estate agent.

Increase Your Deductible
Save 25%

As with auto insurance, the higher the deductible on your homeowners insurance, the lower your premium. A typical homeowner who increases his deductible from $100 to $500 can cut one-fourth off his total premium.

This makes good financial sense, since the way construction costs are today, the chances of you having a claim under $500 are slim. And if you have replacement coverage on contents and valuables, you will eliminate the deductible completely on those items.

Show You're Prepared
Save 20%

Many safety features that may currently be in your home qualify you for additional discounts on your homeowners policy—as long as you let your agent know about them.

For instance, having an in-house security alarm system qualifies most homeowners for a 5 percent discount, while a system that automatically dials emergency numbers can translate to a 10 percent price break. And having dead-bolt locks is good for an additional 2 percent off.

Some policies will even give discounts for having properly working smoke detectors. (With other policies it's mandatory.) Fire extinguishers and fire-resistant steel doors can cut another 2 percent or more.

LIFE INSURANCE

Life insurance is usually something we'd prefer not to think about. But once you figure out how to weigh one policy against another and choose the route that provides adequate peace of mind—as well as financial security—you can cut some corners and still know that your family will be secure, no matter what.

Buy at Work
Save 50%

If you're employed full-time, the best insurance deal around is probably right in your personnel office. Many companies offer life insurance as part of their benefits package, providing your heirs with twice your annual salary (or more) in the event of your death. But in addition, many companies also allow workers to buy supplemental insurance at reduced group rates.

Penny for penny, this supplemental insurance could be the best deal you'll find anywhere. So be sure to compare. Although plans

---

HOW MUCH INSURANCE DO YOU NEED?

You know you need life insurance. But how much?

It all depends on your circumstances. Do you have small children? (If so, you probably want more insurance.) Do you have investments that could keep your survivors comfortable? Is your home paid off (or close to it)?

Generally, many experts say that your survivors will probably be safe if you're covered for eight times your annual salary. That means if you make $50,000 a year before taxes, your life should be covered for a total of $400,000—including the insurance you receive at work as a job benefit. If you have two or more children under age 10, however, some suggest you aim for more than eight times your salary until they reach age 18.

vary from company to company, a 30-year-old nonsmoking man can typically buy about $50,000 of additional insurance for less than $50 a year—or about one-half of the price of a similar low-cost term policy. The same amount of coverage for a 50-year-old would cost about $120. And for women in each of these age brackets, the costs are even less.

Unfortunately, often these group rates aren't widely advertised in the benefits package, so if you're not aware of this program, talk to the benefits manager where you work.

Switch to Term
Save 80%

For most people, term insurance gives full protection without the costs that are associated with the cash buildup of whole life policies.

That's because a whole life policy acts as something of a bank account: Your premium payments build up into a cash reserve, and you can borrow against the reserve during your lifetime. (Of course, if you don't pay back your borrowings before your death, your survivors get that much less.) Whole life policies do earn some interest, but not nearly as much as you'd get by investing that money yourself.

Because of this borrowing privilege, whole life premiums can be very expensive—anywhere from $15 to $35 per $1,000 of coverage.

MAKE THE MOST OF YOUR POLICY

Term life insurance is often your best financial bet, but only if you get the right type of term policy. With some policies, the rates may go up at certain intervals, and you may get charged a whole lot more for re-entering the program.

When you buy term insurance, be sure to ask your agent about all the variables. Make sure the policy will automatically be renewable—for as long as you need it—and find out what charges there are. Some policies can't be renewed after 10 or 15 years, which is why they're so cheap. If your policy isn't automatically renewable, you can get socked for a significant increase after you reach a certain age.

With term life insurance, you're only paying for insurance protection and not building up any cash reserves you can borrow against. But your heirs will be covered by the insurance payouts in the event of your death.

The big advantage is that term life insurance premiums are drastically lower, as little as $3 (or less) per $1,000 in coverage. So if you have a whole life policy, talk to your agent or financial advisor about switching to term—and investing the difference in other financial opportunities.

Don't Pay Commissions
Save 20%

If you don't like the idea of term insurance and want a cash value policy, there are still ways to do it for less. One way is with a "no-load" policy.

These policies are sold without agents, so there's no commission. You immediately accumulate cash value the first year—unlike traditional whole life policies, in which the agent gets your entire first year's cash buildup as his commission.

And because there's no commission, you also get a better deal. No-load policies tend to be about 20 percent cheaper than other cash value policies.

Since no-load policies are sold without agents, you'll have to learn about them directly through the insurance company. So write or call your insurance carrier for information about its no-load policies.

Cover Two People under One Plan
Save 35%

You can cut your premiums by about 35 percent if both you and your spouse get a new type of policy called first-to-die insurance. With this life insurance, two (or more) people are covered under one policy. It pays off when the first insured person dies.

A single first-to-die policy is more expensive than a single term policy but about one-third of the cost of covering two people under two separate policies.

Cut Your Spending on

CHILDREN'S EXPENSES

- Baby Stuff
- Child Care
- Toys

HALVE THE COSTS OF RAISING YOUR HALF-PINTS

If you have kids, you know they cost. But since you're a parent, you probably haven't had the time to sit down with pencil and paper to determine exactly how much they cost.

Between Nikes and Nintendo, McDonald's and movies, the typical American family with two kids spends almost $15,000 a year on children's expenses—and even though that price includes food, it doesn't include the mortgage, the payments for the mini-van and other so-called adult expenses. Add it all together, and you'll spend an average of $218,260 per child from the time Junior leaves the maternity ward to the time he leaves for college. (And then, of course, you get to spend some *real* money.)

Since it's too late to nip those parenting instincts and settle for a less costly gerbil, you'll be pleased to know that there are still plenty of ways to cut your child-raising expenses by as much as thousands each year—no matter how old your children.

BABY STUFF

Of course, you really get socked in those first two years. Only moments after Baby gets that monumental swat on the tush, you also get hit hard—with expenses for diapers, baby strollers, cribs and other paraphernalia for your new bundle of joy. But here's how to put a lid on some of those costs.

Hire a Diaper Service
Save 50%

Although 85 percent of households use disposable diapers, using cloth diapers on your baby's bottom is better for your bottom line.

WHERE YOUR MONEY GOES

- Children under age 12 receive about $9 billion a year in income through allowances and part-time jobs; but indirectly, they account for the purchase of 15 times that amount in consumer goods.
- Households with children under age 18 spend about 27 percent more than households that have no children. Households with children spend 45 percent more on housing than childless households, 40 percent more on clothing, 35 percent more on entertainment and 32 percent more on food. In homes without children, the adults spend more on alcoholic beverages and health care (because many of the "childless" households are elderly people).
- Nearly $14 billion is spent every year on toys. In addition, families spend about $10 billion annually renting or buying video games. School supplies cost about $2 billion each year.

Most diaper services charge about $15 a week to do the dirty work—washing and delivering the 80 to 100 cloth diapers needed for newborns. But that weekly cost decreases as the child gets older and uses fewer diapers.

By comparison, it costs between $25 and $35 a week to buy disposable diapers, and as a child gets older and needs larger sizes, you get fewer diapers per box. (So you actually pay more on a per-diaper basis.)

What's more, diaper services usually throw in a complimentary diaper pail and other accessories, so you don't need to spend money to store the soiled diapers; with the plastic diapers, you pay for trash bags.

Buy Store-Brand Disposables
Save 40%

Even though disposables are more expensive, many parents can't be weaned from them. If you decide to go with disposable diapers because of their convenience, go with the store brand, and you'll save big! These store brands—sold under the names of drugstore, supermarket or toy store chains—are about 40 percent less expensive than brand-name diapers.

Generally, you'll pay about 14 cents per diaper for the store brands, compared with nearly 24 cents per diaper for the top brand names. That amounts to saving anywhere from $30 to $35 a month by buying your diapers at Toys R Us, Phar-Mor, Eckerd Drug, Thrift Drug, Pathmark, Publix or other such stores.

It may take a little comparison shopping to find the best brand to fit your baby, but rest assured that today's generics have been improved. They don't leak any more than brand-name diapers. And most generics are just as absorbent. In fact, studies show that most off-brands tend to be as effective as the more expensive name brands.

Clip Coupons
Save 10%

Nearly every Sunday, the newspaper has coupons for $1 or more off the purchase of diapers. Simply clipping and redeeming these coupons can save you anywhere from $50 to $70 per child a year if you use disposable diapers—more if you get friends and family members to help you clip.

Besides scanning the newspaper, ask your pediatrician for addresses of drug companies that may supply you with free samples of over-the-counter medicines. Some companies may put your home on their mailing lists to receive coupons for various products.

Get a Car Seat from the Cops
Save $100

In every state, it's mandatory that your child be secured in a car seat whenever riding in an automobile. (Your child's pediatrician can tell you what your state's age and weight regulations are.) Because of this, your state highway patrol—as well as some police or sheriff's departments—may offer use of child safety car seats to motorists.

Although some of these programs are targeted for low-income families, many law enforcement departments have no income requirements, so anyone can "lease" a child's car seat. In many cases, it's free for the asking—although supplies may be limited. But even if there's a slight charge, it's usually in the $5 range. That means you'll save the $60 to $100 it takes to buy a car seat. Just call your local hospital or state health department to see if these programs are available to you.

Buy Used Furniture
Save 40%

The best way to cut your spending on baby accessories such as cribs, high chairs, playpens and strollers, of course, is to get them as presents. If you can't, however, there's no need to run to Toys R Us waving your wallet. Since these items are used for only a year or two, you can get great deals buying them used.

Generally, these used articles of furniture are anywhere from 25 to 40 percent cheaper than the new and can be found in mint condition. Furniture that shows its age but is still fully functional can cost 70 percent less than new items. Many baby-furniture shops sell used items, but you'll do even better at garage sales or consignment shops. Also, always scan supermarket or church bulletin boards, where people often advertise these wares.

Stretch Your Savings
Get Next Year's Clothing

Clothing is one of the most popular gifts for the newborn—and one of the most foolish. Why? Because newborns hardly need a stitch. It's the older child who really needs clothing.

Think about it. Infants have little occasion for wearing anything but a T-shirt and diaper, since they don't go out much. And when they do wear one of their special outfits, the baby clothes usually don't fit right. (Baby clothes are notoriously undersize, no doubt to make parents feel as though their child is larger than the norm.) Even so, most gift givers give for the moment—and not for the long run. By the time the child's a toddler, you've got a closet full of worthless outfits.

So if you want clothes for your baby, ask gift givers for clothing that will fit next year. When your baby arrives, ask for clothes to fit a 12- to 18-month-old. When your baby celebrates his first birthday, you want duds for a two-year-old. That way, he'll have the right clothes to wear when they're needed.

CHILD CARE

Perhaps the most troubling part of being a parent, if not the most expensive, is trying to find good child care at a reasonable price. The typical day care center charges $100 a week for full-time care (from about 7:30 A.M. to 5:30 P.M.)—and that may not include diapers, meals and other expenses. Even your night on the town can be expensive if you have to recruit a babysitter who charges anywhere from $3 to $5 an hour per child. But here's how to cut some of your costs without sacrificing quality care.

Supply Your Own Meals
Save $60

Many day care centers include breakfasts and hot lunches in their weekly rates. If so, you have no choice but to pay. If you have an option, however, don't pay meals-included rates. You should be able to get nearly a $3-per-day discount if you supply the meals for your own child. That adds up to a savings of $60 a month if your child attends day care full-time.

Is Your Child Potty-Trained?
Save 10%

Kids under age two need more supervision and care than older kids—especially if they're still in diapers. Once a child reaches school age, the primary role of a day care center is more supervisory than caregiving. So why pay for the diaper-changing and spoon-feeding services if your child is already potty-trained and feeding himself?

If your day care center doesn't have a floating rate scale—where charges decrease as a child matures—shoot for a 10 percent discount for any child older than age four and 15 percent for those over age six. Often all you have to do is ask.

Enroll All the Kids
Save 30%

The more children you take to the day care center, the less you should pay on a per-child basis. Some day care centers offer slight discounts for each additional sibling (no matter the age). Ideally, you should get 25 to 30 percent off for each additional child. Day care centers know that older siblings are somewhat easier to look after, since the older kids tend to help supervise their young brothers and sisters.

Get Unlicensed Day Care
Save 20%

Depending on your annual income, up to 30 percent of your day care costs can be deducted from your federal income tax. You need only know the name, location and identification number of your child's day care center. If you are paying a friend or a neighbor to care for your child, you need to know that person's Social Security number. Of course, you can receive a tax deduction only if the caregiver is claiming child care services as income.

If not, you should pay 20 percent below market rates to caregivers who help you out on an informal basis. And you don't need to feel guilty about it, either. Most people who offer child care services are happy to have the extra money—and they're not likely to quibble if you explain that you're losing a significant tax deduction because they lack the right license.

Trade Work for Day Care
Save 10%

Another way to cut your day care bill is to work off some of your expenses. Many day care centers allow parents to put in a few hours a week reading, playing and otherwise supervising the children. If you put in two to five hours a week, you can knock anywhere from 10 to 15 percent off your weekly bill.

Best of all, this expense cutting is time well spent: You have an opportunity to bond with your children and their playmates, to see how your kids interact with others and to get an up-close-and-very-personal view of the service provided by your hired caregivers.

Let Uncle Sam Help
Save 10%

Depending on your income, you may qualify for any of the scores of government programs that offer working parents financial assistance for day care. (There are plenty of nongovernment programs as well—many of them sponsored by local church groups and other organizations.)

To learn about these programs, which can save you 10 percent or more off your bill, go to any public library and ask for the book *Free Money for Day Care* by Laurie Blum. This publication lists numerous foundations, government organizations and corporations that offer help.

Split a Babysitter
Save 50%

The cheapest route in babysitting is to simply barter services: You watch your friends' kids one night (or day) so that they can go out, and they watch your brood another so that you can enjoy some free time.

But what if you both want to spend an evening on the town? Unless either of you has infant children, why not have a babysitter watch all the kids and split the cost? You'll cut your expenses in half. And the babysitter won't suffer, because it's usually easier to watch several children: They entertain each other (whereas the babysitter must do the entertaining with only one tyke). Sharing babysitters is especially effective with children over age five, who can play nicely without constant parental supervision.

Barter for Babysitting

If your teenage neighbor has something you need—babysitter potential—start thinking of how you can barter your skills for babysitting time. That teenager may need free driving lessons or help with homework. An even hour-for-hour swap of skills can be more valuable to babysitters (and their parents) than an hourly wage, and it can save you a lot of money.

Toys

Any parent who has ever watched his child hard at play with a new toy knows at least one way to cut toy spending—forget the toy and just buy the cardboard box.

Studies show the average preschooler receives between 10 and 12

Christmas gifts when he asked for only 3. So one way to cut your spending is to divide the number of toys you feel like buying by 4. Here are some other ways to save money on every toy you buy.

Go to a Police Auction
Save 50%

Ever wonder what happens with stolen bicycles that are recovered by the police? If they're not claimed by their owners within 30 days, they join the other two-wheelers lining the police storage room, which also include dozens of abandoned bikes and those used in the commission of a crime.

Most police agencies hold annual or twice-yearly auctions to sell off these bicycles. (The money usually goes to a police fund.) The bikes go to the highest bidder. This is a great opportunity to buy a bicycle for one-half of its retail worth—or even less.

Some police agencies advertise these auctions in the local newspaper, but many others don't. You can call your local police department or state highway patrol and ask the head of the property room when the next auction is being held.

WHICH BIKE IS BEST?

If you have gone shopping for a child's bicycle lately, you may have found yourself spinning your wheels. Prices can range from $100 to $1,200—and unless you're a bike connoisseur, you probably can't even tell the difference in construction. So it's not always easy to make the most of your money. But here are some guidelines.

Children under age eight should get the cheapest bikes you can buy. They outgrow their bikes quickly—almost yearly—and they don't need features such as extra gears and a superlight frame, which add to the price. You're best off buying used at a flea market or garage sale.

But for kids ages eight and over, spend the extra money and get a sturdy, quality bike. Older children tend to be rougher on bicycles and will use them for several years.

TURNING TRASH TO TOYS

Your children can enjoy hours of fun while you save hours cleaning up trash—simply by transforming leftover wood, cans and other materials into playthings. Among the projects you can make in less than one hour:

Beads. Let your kids paint pieces of stale macaroni and then string them onto a necklace. For variety, they can use several types of macaroni.

Blocks. The easiest method is to take leftover wood scraps (two-by-fours are ideal) and cut and sand them into usable sizes. To make large, lightweight blocks, cut the bottom third off an empty half-gallon milk container, tape a piece of cardboard over the open end, and cover the whole thing with contact paper. For smaller children, place tiny bells inside the milk container blocks.

Bowling. Paint empty juice cans or plastic bottles. Get a small ball and let the kids try to knock down the cans or bottles.

Cornstarch clay. For homemade clay that rivals the store-bought varieties, mix ½ cup of cornstarch, 1 cup of baking soda and ½ cup plus 2 tablespoons of water in a pot. Stir constantly over medium-high heat until it comes to a boil and is the consistency of mashed potatoes. Dump onto a plate, cover with a paper towel, and allow to cool. Knead on a surface dusted with

Rummage through Rummage Sales
Save 80%

Yard sales, garage sales and other secondhand opportunities are a toy shopper's paradise. Toys are among the most frequently displayed items at these rummage sales. And the prices are unbeatable—up to 80 percent off the original price. Best of all, while you rarely find exactly what you're looking for, you'll likely find something both you and your kids never expected—and that translates to extended play appeal. Just be sure that all the parts are included, since missing pieces may explain why it's being sold.

Cleaning is usually the easy part: Just place plastic toys in the dish-

cornstarch until smooth. If the mixture is too sticky, add a little more cornstarch. The kids can then mold it like any other kind of clay. Then let it air-dry. Cornstarch clay can be painted with food coloring when it's dry.

Sidewalk chalk. For children ages five and up, it's easy to make chalk for just a few pennies. Wash and dry six eggshells. With a smooth rock, grind the eggshells on a smooth concrete surface until they turn into a powder. Put the powder into a dish, throwing away any big pieces of shell. In a second dish mix one teaspoon of flour with one teaspoon of very hot tap water. Add one tablespoon of the eggshell powder, mix and mash until it sticks together, then form and press it firmly into a stick shape. Roll the stick tightly in a strip of paper towel and allow to dry until rock-hard (about three days). This chalk works very well on sidewalks—but not on chalkboards. It's easy to erase: Just scuff it off with your shoe.

The savings, as you can see, are substantial.

TOY	HOMEMADE VERSION ($)	STORE-BOUGHT VERSION ($)	SAVINGS ($)
Blocks	2.99	10.00	7.01
Bowling	0	15.99	15.99
Clay	1.28	6.20	4.92
Sidewalk chalk	0–.10	3.95	3.85

washer on a normal cycle. Most stuffed animals can be cleaned in a washing machine. And here's an easy way to clean items that have down filling or other materials not suited for a washer: Place the item in a large plastic bag with a generous amount of cornmeal or baking powder. Shake the bag well, then take out the item and brush it.

Metal toys can be cleaned with a damp rag, then dried.

Buy after the New Year
Save 50%

The after-Christmas sales offer savings of 50 percent off regular prices, but there's no need to rush out on December 26 for these bargains. Toys remain on sale until mid-January in most stores and as long as February in others. Consider buying some of your kids' toys in January for gift giving the following Christmas. This works best for classic toys—tricycles, game boards and so on—rather than faddish fun stuff such as Rollerblades.

Take Out a Toy on Time

Public libraries, as you may have noticed, now lend much more than books: Although videotapes and records are more readily displayed, more than 400 public libraries around the country lend out toys to anyone with a card, usually for the same time period as books. Just call your local library—or ask at the desk—to find out whether these items are available for public use.

You can also find free toy libraries affiliated with public schools, hospitals and special needs organizations as well as independent organizations that charge their patrons a modest membership fee. To locate a toy library near you, send a self-addressed, stamped envelope to the USA Toy Library Association, 2530 Crawford Avenue, Suite 111, Evanston, IL 60201.

For Cheap Books, Check the Library

Most public libraries hold annual sales offering quality paperback and hardcover books—for children and adults—for as little as 25 cents each. In fact, some libraries have bookstores offering these bargains year-round. These sales aren't always widely advertised, however, so call your library to find out about them. It's a great way to buy bargain books for your children.

Check Out a Used-Toy Store
Save 40%

Before you pay retail, check out a used-toy store such as Toy Traders, which has several stores in the Maryland area. These toy-trading stores (which go by various names in different states) are beginning to sprout up across the country and may offer quality used toys at savings of 40 percent or more. To find one near you, check the Yellow Pages under "Toys."

Buy at Membership Merchandise Clubs
Save 25%

Membership merchandise clubs such as Sam's Club, BJ's Warehouse Club and the Price Club offer great bargains in some items and are competitively priced in others. For toys, figure you'll save about 25 percent off regular prices—although selections may be limited.

Investigate Off-Brands
Save 20%

Several manufacturers make the same or a very similar toy. You can find near-duplicates of the name-brand toys made by Playskool, Fisher-Price, Tyco and other big-name companies in toy stores as well as in supermarkets, drugstores and discount stores such as K Mart and Jamesway—usually for 10 to 20 percent less. The quality may not be quite as good as the name-brand item, so you should inspect for sharp edges and loose parts. But often the cheaper toys will be just as durable as the more expensive name-brand equivalents.

Cut Your Spending on

COLLEGE COSTS

- Improving Your Need
- Choosing a School
- Gifts and Grants
- Low-Interest Loans
- Savings for Everyone

SMART MOVES TO PAY THE WAY

The American Dream of sending the kids to college has become an impossible dream for many. By the early 1990s, the cost of getting a four-year college degree averaged nearly $60,000—and at some premiere schools, it was twice that much. And that price was exclusive of "extras" such as recreation and transportation costs. It didn't even include books.

Don't expect college costs to get any cheaper. By the time today's newborns are ready for college, some experts predict, the costs will be nearly four times higher.

But getting a sheepskin doesn't have to mean financial slaughter. While higher education is usually high-priced, it can be cheaper than you may think—as long as you know how to make the most of the many opportunities to reduce college costs.

Each year, more than $31 billion in financial aid is given out to nearly one-half of America's college students. Usually, it's awarded on the basis of need, not necessarily for academic achievement.

How can you get some of this money?

The best way to reduce your contributions to your child's education is by making yourself appear as needy as possible. Financial aid packages are often determined based on what the "givers" calculate as the family's contribution, the amount of money parents are expected to contribute based on their income and any assets such as stocks, bonds and savings accounts. The lower this family contribution, the theory goes, the more money your child will likely get in financial aid.

That's not to say you have to quit your job, give away all your money and live in a cardboard box in order to get help with Junior's tuition and living expenses. With smart planning and savvy comparison shopping, you may be able to cut as much as one-half off the cost of a college education for your child.

338

IMPROVING YOUR NEED

The first myth of financial aid is to think that it automatically goes to the best students. Sure, you have to be a good student—with a solid B average—in order to be considered seriously for "free" aid such as scholarships and grants. But more often than not, average students from middle-class families can also get aid—if their parents know how to please the financial aid officers, who decide who gets these grants, scholarships and low-interest loans.

That sometimes means "rearranging" assets—legally—to make a student appear more deserving (or needier) to financial aid officers. Here's how the parents do it.

Make Investments in Your Own Name

Perhaps the biggest mistake many parents make years before their child enters college is to start a savings account in Junior's name.

Granted, there may be some short-term tax benefits for keeping the money in your child's name—and you should talk to your tax advisor about the advantages of having an account under the Uniform Gift to Minors Act (see "Your Saving Strategy" on page 340). But as college time approaches, you should consider transferring most of it to your name.

Reason: The formula used for determining financial aid requires that the child contribute up to 35 percent of his savings. Parents, on the other

YOUR SAVING STRATEGY

Where you invest your money in preparation for your child's college costs depends on several factors: your income, your investment style and your children's ages when you begin saving.

Many financial experts recommend mutual funds invested in the stock market as your best saving strategy, but more conservative investors might consider other options, such as U.S. savings bonds.

There are various options, and your accountant or financial advisor is the best person to consult for your specific needs and situation. But here are some investments to consider, all which are available at your local bank.

Series EE bonds are one of the better investments for long-range savings purposes, especially if they've been purchased since January 1, 1990. The interest accumulated on these bonds will be partially free from federal taxes, provided the bonds are used to finance a child's education and your family's adjusted gross income is less than $96,200.

The Uniform Gift to Minors Act is an account that allows you to accumulate funds for college in the child's name (and thus under a child's lower tax liability). Under this program, each parent may contribute up to $10,000 per year for each child. A custodian is responsible for managing the funds until the child turns 18, at which time the person may do with the money as he pleases. (If you're going to receive financial aid, however, it may be more advantageous to have the money under your own name—so be sure to discuss this with a tax expert or your financial advisor.)

Zero-coupon Treasury bonds are often used as a way of paying for college. These bonds are bought at deep discounts: They don't pay interest at intervals but rather pay the full face value amount at maturity. That future value is determined ahead of time, along with the date of maturity, so parents know exactly how much money they will receive when tuition time rolls around. Treasury bonds are safest, since they cannot be "called" before they reach maturity. Be aware, however, that tax must be paid yearly on the "phantom" interest earned.

hand, are expected to ante up no more than 5.6 percent of their savings as part of the family contribution. That means a college fund with $10,000 under your child's name may require a contribution of $3,500; the same money in your name requires you to provide only $560.

Buy a New Car

Buying a new car or making another expensive purchase just before you're about to send a kid off to college may seem like the last thing any responsible money manager would do. Actually, it may be one of the best ways to help yourself qualify for more financial aid.

Let's say the car you want to buy costs $20,000. By paying for it in cash from your savings accounts, you reduce your reported assets, making you look $20,000 poorer. And that could qualify you for an additional $1,000 in aid.

Of course, this doesn't mean you need to buy a new car in order to send your kid to college. But any large purchase you make—and pay for with cash—helps reduce your assets, making your available family contribution appear smaller. Just be sure to do it a year or two before you fill out the financial aid forms, since the financial aid officers examine your previous year's income. Besides, these "last-minute" purchases may look suspicious to financial aid officers.

Borrow against Your Home

Don't have the cash for your new car? Then take out a home equity loan. By borrowing against your home, you reduce the equity you have in your home, which also reduces your "on-paper" assets. What's more, you'll save in another way: The interest on home equity loans tends to be lower than the interest on car loans, so you'll pay less for the money you borrow.

But you can also reduce your assets and possibly get more aid by doing the opposite—build your equity by using savings to pay down your home mortgage.

Lowball Your Home's Value—
But Only Slightly

Most financial aid forms ask what you paid for your house and its current market value. While you should always underestimate rather than overestimate its worth (remember, the purpose is to look poorer), don't go overboard in your lowballing.

Financial aid officers expect your home to have risen in value by a certain amount, based on a national or regional housing index. If you grossly underestimate this rise, you'll hurt your chances of getting aid, since everything you say will be questioned. Instead, you should report that your house just matches, or is slightly below, the national housing index.

Invest in Your Retirement

In applying for aid, you'll have to disclose your bank accounts, mutual funds, real estate, stocks and bonds (as well as your home equity and other assets). But you usually don't have to reveal money you saved in retirement plans such as 401(k)'s and individual retirement accounts.

So consider the possibility of taking some money from stocks, bonds or another asset and investing it in a tax-deferred annuity or retirement account. You should check with your financial advisor before making this move, but it could be advantageous. For instance, by

---

SHOULD YOUR CHILD BE INDEPENDENT?

It's a parent's delight to have a college-bound child with the chutzpah and drive to put himself through school by working part-time as a babysitter or fast-food employee. But while you may categorize your hardworking kid as independent, don't expect financial aid officers to share the same opinion.

While universities like to see their future students working hard to help pay their way through school, having your child declared independent is a complicated process. To be eligible for many types of financial aid, an independent student must truly earn that title. For instance, the student must have a separate address and be able to prove it by showing canceled checks for rent. A student who simply helps pay for college isn't considered independent as far as the financial aid office is concerned.

How Much Aid Will You Get?

Most financial aid officers determine a student's need by deducting the family's possible contribution from the cost of attendance (tuition plus room and board). Of course, simply saying that you have only a certain amount to contribute isn't enough: When applying for financial aid, be prepared to show several years' worth of federal income tax forms and other proof of your income.

Then most financial aid officers determine a figure that's somewhere between 65 and 100 percent of the amount that the student needs to make up the difference. That figure will be the amount of your offered financial aid package. This package usually consists of "gift" aid (which doesn't have to be paid back) as well as "self-help" aid, which usually comes in the form of loans. Of course, the better the student did in high school—both academically as well as in extracurricular activities—the more likely that he will receive more gift aid.

---

reinvesting $15,000 from stocks or savings in a 401(k), you not only protect your money from federal taxes but also may be able to qualify for an additional $800 or more in aid—while making yourself more comfortable for your old age.

Keep in mind, however, that this is no guarantee you'll get extra aid. Some universities have stipulations on these "hidden" assets—especially state universities. And making this transfer puts your cash out of reach, albeit in a productive fund. So before making a transfer you may later regret, get financial aid forms from the schools your child will likely apply to a few years beforehand.

Choosing a School

Where your child attends college plays a dramatic role in how much financial aid you may receive. Private universities, for instance, are more likely than public schools to consider home equity when evaluating a financial aid package, which means long-term homeowners may have a much tougher time getting aid from a private school. On the other hand, since private schools tend to charge higher tuition, they're usually more generous in offering grants and loans.

Of course, your child shouldn't choose a college simply because of its financial aid package. There are other more important factors to consider, such as the school's reputation and the strength of its academic program. But here are some factors to consider when looking for ways to lower college costs.

Cash In on a Top-Quarter Standing

All things considered, students who are in the top 25 percent of the applicant pool get the best financial aid packages—whether applying to Harvard or to the local community college.

So no matter where your child is applying, he's more likely to get more aid if he's a shining star. From a financial standpoint (although not necessarily an academic one), it's better to be a big fish in a small pond than vice versa.

Use the "Pay Now, Learn Later" Plan

If college is a decade or more away but you already assume that Junior will attend the local state university, take note: Several states—including Alabama, Alaska, Florida, Pennsylvania, Ohio and Wyoming—have prepaid tuition programs that allow you to pay for your child's education in advance at today's rates.

Here's how it works: Any time after your child is born, you can enroll him at a specific state university. A monthly payment is determined based on your income and today's admission costs for a four-year degree. If you're enrolling a newborn, for instance, that cost might be $50 a month; for a preteen, $200 a month.

When your child is ready to attend college, the tuition has already been paid. The savings are substantial, since you're paying the tuition rates that are in effect at the time you enroll your child. In fact, enrollment costs are expected to rise so much that, even according to conservative estimates, you can save anywhere from $30,000 to $60,000 in the long run with this type of program.

One advantage to this program is that it's a good hedge against the rising costs of college tuition, which at some schools have been twice the rate of inflation. Besides, there's no risk involved—as there would be if you invested this money in the stock market—and no tax considerations.

Of course, there are some drawbacks: Your child must meet all the admission requirements (otherwise, you get back your payments, but the school keeps earned interest). Also, he has to go to that school. And should he flunk out at any time, you forfeit the money. So you'll want to get all the details before you enroll in such a program.

But it's a good way to save for college, especially if your state has a well-respected university system. For more information on prepaid tuition plans, contact the school directly.

Protect Your Bottom Line
Ask for an Itemized Bill

Just because a school has low tuition doesn't necessarily mean it costs less to attend. One way many universities keep their advertised tuition rates low is to tack on as much as $2,000 for "extras" such as orientation, student activities, health services and even graduation. Yet these charges aren't apparent until you get the bill.

There's no way of getting out of these charges, but you can know what you're paying for. Ask for an itemized account of the total costs for a year at that school (not just the tuition and room and board rates). This way, when you're shopping around for the cost of a college education, you can make your decision based on your total "bottom line" costs rather than just tuition alone.

Negotiate with the Financial Aid Office

You can negotiate for a better aid package with the financial aid office—but only if the college really wants your child. And that depends on your child and his achievements: Good grades and SAT scores, of course, lead the list.

But don't underestimate the influence of involvement in extracurricular activities such as sports, clubs, theater and music. Your child's ethnic background and geographic origin may also help determine whether he gets funding.

When you're negotiating, you should also mention financial aid offers from other schools. Colleges compete for students—whether they're academically talented, involved in activities or simply diverse.

Get Teachers' Endorsements

There's power in numbers. So keep in mind that any negotiation with the financial aid office carries more weight if your student has strong endorsements from teachers, school counselors and coaches.

Don't stop at one letter of recommendation. The more you have, the better. And don't forget "character" endorsements from bosses (if your child holds a part-time job), church leaders and others in the community.

GIFTS AND GRANTS

There are basically two categories of financial aid: the kind that is free, such as grants and scholarships, and the kind that you have to pay back in money or through work. Obviously, you want the freebies.

If you're looking for a free ride through college, the best direction to turn is toward Washington, D.C. The federal government is the largest contributor of scholarships and grants. State governments come in second place, although corporations and private foundations are also good providers. And of course, many universities offer scholarship money to deserving students.

The best place to find out about all these scholarship and grant opportunities is at the high school guidance counselor's office or by writing the financial aid office of a university for a list of its offerings.

Improve Your Chances
Apply Earlier Than Advised

No matter where you're applying, don't wait too long: The early bird usually gets the money.

Conventional wisdom suggests that you should get the forms by November of the child's senior year and have them completed and returned by mid-February. But the earlier, the better—so try to get the forms filled out and returned by early January, just after the Christmas break.

While there's no guarantee that you'll secure more money by applying early, there's a tendency among financial aid offices to be more generous in the beginning of the awarding process, when there are more funds available.

Seek a Pell

The largest and most significant gift program by the federal government is the $5.5 billion offered each year in Pell Grants. These gifts go to about 3½ million students a year.

To be eligible for a Pell Grant, the family income can be no more than $42,000 (this figure can change). But other factors are taken into consideration, such as divorce and other "hardships." Pells offer a maximum of $3,700 a year per student, based on how much income your family has and how much you can contribute toward college.

Even if you don't meet the financial criteria, you should apply anyway, since some colleges won't even consider you for financial aid unless you've first been turned down for a Pell Grant. In fact, there have been many cases of students getting turned down for Pells who were eventually awarded even more money in other grants. You can get an application for a Pell at any high school guidance office.

Fund Some Learning with an SEOG

Another reason to apply for a Pell Grant is that it can lead to another government grant. The Supplemental Education Opportunity Grant (SEOG) is awarded in increments of $100 to $4,000 per year. Priority is given to those who receive Pell Grants.

With SEOGs, it's especially important that you apply early— months before the deadline. Applications are available at guidance offices.

Check Employer Plans

Many businesses have scholarship programs for the children of employees. These scholarships vary in amount and criteria from company to company, but usually they're in the neighborhood of $500 or more a year, given only to children of employees.

These are a great opportunity to get some money for college, since there's usually not a lot of competition. If your company has 1,000 employees, for example, the odds are that only a few dozen students are eligible. Compare that with other scholarships, which could have tens or even hundreds of thousands of students applying.

How Much to Save?

The obvious answer is: The more, the better. Since there is no guarantee that you'll get any financial aid, here's a rough guideline of how much you'll have to put away each month to accumulate funds by the time your child goes to college. (This assumes the child has no outside gifts or loans.) Total savings are indicated by the dollar amount at the top of each column. Figures are based on a fixed 8 percent interest rate, compounded monthly.

AGE OF CHILD NOW	TOTAL SAVINGS ($)					
	40,000	50,000	75,000	100,000	125,000	150,000
1	92.64	115.80	173.69	231.59	289.49	347.39
2	103.30	129.13	193.69	258.26	322.82	387.39
3	115.59	144.49	216.74	288.98	361.23	433.48
4	129.86	162.33	243.49	324.65	405.81	486.98
5	146.56	183.20	274.81	366.41	458.01	549.61
6	166.31	207.89	311.84	415.79	519.73	623.68
7	189.95	237.44	356.16	474.88	593.60	712.32
8	218.64	273.30	409.96	546.61	683.26	819.91
9	254.08	317.60	476.40	635.20	794.01	952.81
10	298.80	373.50	560.25	747.00	933.75	1,120.50
11	356.78	445.98	668.97	891.95	1,114.94	1,337.93
12	434.66	543.33	814.99	1,020.73	1,358.32	1,629.99
13	544.39	680.49	1,020.73	1,360.97	1,701.22	2,041.46
14	709.85	887.31	1,330.97	1,774.63	2,218.28	2,861.94
15	986.79	1,233.48	1,850.23	2,466.97	3,083.71	3,700.45

Get a New Job
Save 50%

One of the most common benefits to employees of universities is free or discounted tuition for themselves and their dependents. While this strategy obviously isn't for everyone, if you manage to secure a job at a local university—be it as a professor, an administrative assistant or a security officer—there's a very good chance that your child will be able to attend for free or at a significantly reduced rate. Even if tuition is slashed in half, you can still save several thousands of dollars a year.

LOW-INTEREST LOANS

Rare is the student who gets a financial aid package with no pay-backs. In other words, even if a student snags some grants and scholarships, he has to foot at least part of the bill. But instead of using all your hard-earned savings, you and Junior should check out some of these lower-cost alternatives.

Leave College Debt-Free
Work and Take Classes

One of the best ways to get the money you need up front without the hassles of a long-term repayment plan is through the College Work Study Program. This federal program is administered through the school's financial aid office and is open to students with unmet financial need, regardless of income bracket.

Basically, the school finds the student a job, usually on campus. He is paid at least minimum wage (and sometimes higher) and must work a certain number of hours until he's paid off the borrowed figure. Then the job commitment is over.

For instance, if a student borrows $3,000 under the work study program and gets a job paying $5 an hour, he must work 600 hours. At 20 hours a week (or 4 hours a day), he'd work for 30 weeks and then owe nothing.

While these jobs are designed to not interfere with classes, they don't always jibe with the school schedule. Some work study students must work through summers and other vacations. (Often the jobs are in the school's administrative offices, which may remain open.)

Make sure you apply early for work study, since it's an extremely popular program—especially with middle-class students who don't qualify for low-income grants and loans but don't have enough money to pay tuition outright.

Ask about a Perkins Loan

The cheapest college loans available are Perkins Loans, which charge 5 percent a year. They're also the hardest to get. They're awarded by the school (with federal money), usually on the basis of need, to lower-income students.

Even if you're in a higher income group, however, you should ask about Perkins Loans if you're a divorced or single parent trying to put your child through college. The loan is worth investigating because the income of the noncustodial parent may not be considered in the family contribution, even if child support is being paid.

With a Perkins, students can get up to $3,000 a year. No interest has to be paid during school and for nine months after graduation. Students then have up to ten years to repay at 5 percent interest.

Shop Around for a Stafford Loan

The most common loan is the Stafford Student Loan (named after Robert Stafford, a retired senator from Vermont). The interest on these loans is 3.1 percent more than the bond equivalent of a 91-day T-bill, which translates to anywhere from 6.5 to 8.5 percent, depending on the T-bill rate when you apply. There is a 9 percent cap.

Freshmen can borrow up to $2,625 a year; sophomores can get $3,500 a year; juniors and seniors can get $5,500 a year. The government pays the interest while the student attends college and for six months after graduation. Students then have up to ten years to repay.

Unlike Perkins Loans, Staffords are issued through banks, savings and loans and other lending institutions—so shop around. Some banks charge as much as a 3 percent "origination fee" and also tack on other charges that could add more than $500 to your annual costs. Look for other banks that don't charge such fees.

SAVINGS FOR EVERYONE

If you have a nice house and a good job, you probably consider yourself lucky—until you apply for financial aid. At that point, you realize you have enough money—at least on paper—to make some underpaid financial aid officer laugh in your face when you sing the blues about the high cost of college.

Sound familiar? It ought to. Many parents believe that their income level and style of living disqualify them for financial assistance. Often it does: A household making over $50,000 a year may find it difficult to get financial aid if investments aren't reinvested to lower the available family contribution. Those making over $70,000 may find it impossible to get that aid—even if they are paying a high mortgage or have other debts.

If you find yourself in this boat, you can still cut your college spending. Here's how.

Go on the Family Plan
Save 50%

If you have two or more college-age children, some colleges and universities will slash tuition if both siblings attend the same school. These discounts vary from school to school, but you can slash up to one-half of the tuition costs for one or even both students on this family plan.

Granted, not all universities are this generous. But expect discounts in the range of 20 percent off when you send a second child to the same school. And if there are more, you can anticipate a flat fee discount—usually between $500 and $800 per year—for all attending family members. Some schools even offer a free ride to a third sibling.

Check the Alumnus Angle
Save 20%

A variation of the family plan is to have Junior attend the same school where a parent is an alumnus. Although the tuition breaks aren't so generous, some schools will slash the costs as much as 20 percent to students who are the children of alumni.

Having your child attend the same school you did is no guarantee of lower college costs, but it certainly doesn't hurt, especially if you've been an active alum. Some universities particularly like to see the children of alumni attending and may be more willing to offer money to those who usually wouldn't qualify.

Like the multi-child discounts, this program is rarely automatic. You'll have to remind the school's financial aid officer of your alumni status and then request a discount—if your alma mater offers it.

Earn Early Credits

Your child can get an early jump on college—and begin saving money before college—by taking advanced placement courses under the College Level Entrance Program (CLEP).

In most schools, academically talented students can start taking these college-level courses as early as eleventh grade. With CLEP, they earn credits that are recognized at more than 1,000 colleges and universities across the country. For each course passed, a student is allowed to skip a course when he's enrolled in college. A student who's been through CLEP can save as much as $300 per credit—or anywhere from $900 to $1,500 per course.

By taking two advanced placement classes per year, students can earn up to 16 credits by the time they reach college—an entire semester's worth—and pocket over $4,000 they might have spent in tuition.

Spend Two Years at Community College
Save 40%

One of the most often practiced ways of trimming college costs is also one of the most effective: Have your child spend the first two years at a community college.

Assuming that the student's credits can be transferred (which is usually the case), enrolling in a public community college for the first two years can slash up to 40 percent—in tuition alone—off the cost of getting a four-year degree. In real dollars, that can amount to anywhere from $15,000 to $35,000, depending on the school where the education is completed.

There are other savings as well. Since community colleges are just that—colleges for the community—most don't have the room and board expenses that a student incurs at most four-year universities. (Most community-college students live at home with their parents.) And since these colleges are commuter schools, there's generally more concentration on studying and less of the party atmosphere that prevails at many live-away universities (which should sit well with tuition-paying parents).

Best of all, a community college gives students who aren't sure that college life is for them an opportunity to test the waters without making a large financial investment. Although community colleges usually don't offer as diverse a curriculum as four-year schools, most offer a solid education in the introductory courses—which is exactly what students take during their first two years anywhere.

In fact, there's only one possible drawback. If some credits from a community college aren't transferable, the student may have to spend an extra semester at the university.

Encourage Hard Studying
Save 10%

Any student who goes to a community college can improve the odds of getting a scholarship later on.

In a community college, the "average" student may have an opportunity to really shine. And the student who gets top grades is more likely to get an academic scholarship once he transfers to a university.

Of course, no student is likely to get a free ride for the last two years simply because he's made dean's list in community college. But a hard-working student from a community college who's earned good grades (especially while holding a part-time or full-time job) often improves his chances of getting financial help. He's a good candidate for a one-time grant or a partial scholarship that could trim 10 percent or more off the cost of tuition when he's finishing up at a four-year school.

Get Junior to Join ROTC
Save $1,200

Junior's idea of fun may not be marching around and saluting, but joining the Reserve Officers' Training Corps (ROTC) program is a good way of having him help pay for college. The first two years earn "recruits" no money, but students can earn $100 a month—or $1,200 a year—in their junior and senior years. After graduating, they are placed in ROTC reserves for an additional two years, which requires a minimal time commitment.

There are also separate ROTC scholarships, which offer as much as $8,000 a year—but they're awarded on the basis of academic achievement to students interested in making the military their career.

Go Public
Save 50%

Generally speaking, a student (or parent) who doesn't qualify for grants, scholarships and other financial aid will spend up to twice as much for an education at a quality private school compared with a comparable state college or university.

There may be less ivy and college "ambience" at State U., but finances aside, most experts agree that it's better to attend a top-notch public school than a second-rate private institution. Besides, since public universities are supported with tax money, they are less likely than private universities to have significant tuition hikes.

Cut Your Spending on

LUXURY ITEMS

- Fine Tableware
- Diamonds and Jewelry
- Antiques and Collectibles
- Fine Art
- Grand Pianos
- Fur Coats

SECRETS TO OWNING THE FINER THINGS IN LIFE

The odds are slim that you'll find a Picasso amid the $5 velvet Elvis paintings sold on street corners. And rare is the lucky soul who happens onto some Baccarat crystal at his neighbor's rummage sale.

But even if you can't count on "lucky finds," you can buy the finer things in life for less. And we're not talking about fancy cars, killer stereos and other high-ticket items that start depreciating the moment they leave the showroom. We're talking about *real* luxury goods: Sterling silver. China. Fine jewelry. Antiques. Fine artwork. Grand pianos.

Best of all, if you know where to look, you can buy these finer things for less than what others pay—sometimes even at one-half of the price. Here's how.

FINE TABLEWARE

Best-quality silver and china can last a lifetime, but that doesn't mean they should cost a life's savings. When you see something you like in a department store or china shop, don't assume the price on the label is the price you have to pay. You can buy top-quality china, crystal, silver and giftware at rock-bottom prices—but you have to know where to find the bargains.

Outlets and mail-order discounters offer the best-known brands at a fraction of the usual price. And even if you buy retail, you can still get first-rate savings without settling for second-best quality. It's all knowing how—and when.

Check into Outlets
Save 70%

Although few and far between, tableware factory outlets offer discounts ranging from 40 to 70 percent off retail prices. And since a

356

WHERE YOUR MONEY GOES

- Nearly $700 billion is spent on luxury items every year in the United States.
- The way people spend their "extra dollars" (discretionary spending) doesn't seem to be adversely affected by hard economic times. On average, we spend about $4,300 per year on nonessentials such as jewelry, art and other luxury items.
- The typical American spends nearly $1,000 per year buying gifts. Those between the ages of 45 and 54 are the most generous, spending nearly $1,600 a year. The most frequently purchased gift items are articles of clothing.

---

true outlet gets its merchandise directly from the manufacturer that supplies the goods, an outlet may have better inventory in that brand than many retail stores.

Outlets are probably the best bet for those who know exactly what they want—particularly when buying entire sets. Most purchases are cash-and-carry, since outlets usually don't ship merchandise. Savings abound. But when you're visiting an outlet, be careful that you're not buying seconds or discontinued patterns. Usually, the seconds and discontinueds are well marked, but it doesn't hurt to double-check with an experienced salesperson or manager before you make a purchase.

Most tableware outlets are located in "outlet cities" such as Reading and Lancaster, Pennsylvania; Orlando, Florida; and Barstow, California. But the highest concentration of tableware outlets is in and near the town of Lawrenceville in central New Jersey.

Look into Look-Alikes
Save 50%

When you buy Waterford crystal, you're getting great quality. But you're paying for a name. Luckily, there are a few companies that specialize in look-alike merchandise—quality goods that are comparable to the prestige name brands. The look-alikes are sold at a fraction of the cost because they don't carry the high-priced name.

(continued on page 360)

ORDER BY PHONE—AND SAVE UP TO 65%

If you know what you want in fine tableware, but you want it for less, there are more than a dozen leading mail-order houses that price their goods at 65 percent or more below retail. Even at the deepest discount, the product quality is just the same, and the selection, just as good. In fact, if you're not sure of the pattern or style you want, your first step should be to contact a mail-order house and have a catalog sent to you.

While mail-order stores usually ship in-stock orders within 48 hours, special orders may take anywhere from four to eight weeks (about the same as retail stores). Some even offer over-the-phone tabletop design consultation and computerized bridal registries. Among the leading mail-order houses:

- Albert S. Smyth Company, Timonium, Maryland; 1-800-638-3333. Major brands of china, crystal, silver and giftware, including Noritake, Wedgwood, Royal Doulton, Spode, Waterford, Villeroy & Boch and Oneida, at 20 to 60 percent below retail.
- Barron's, Novi, Michigan; 1-800-538-6340. More than 1,500 patterns and all major manufacturers of china, crystal, silver and accessories, including Lenox, Yamazaki, Wedgwood, Orrefors, Reed & Barton and Gorham, at 20 to 65 percent off.
- China Cabinet, Tenafly, New Jersey; 1-800-545-5353. Fine china, crystal, silver and giftware from Royal Copenhagen, Hutschenreuther, Rosenthal, Kosta Boda, Orrefors, Reed & Barton, Towle and others. Regularly 25 to 50 percent below retail, but will match any price that can be verified.
- Corsons Glasshouse, Hingham, Massachusetts; 1-800-533-0084. China, crystal, glassware, sterling and gifts from Lenox, Waterford, Lalique, Noritake and more at 20 to 50 percent off retail.
- Eastside Gifts and Dinnerware, New York, New York; 1-800-443-8711. Carries most major brands of china, crystal, silver and giftware, including Wedgwood, Royal Doulton, Mikasa,

Baccarat, Lalique, Limoges, Orrefors and Kirk Stieff, at 30 to 65 percent off retail.

- Geary's, Beverly Hills, California; 1-800-243-2797. China, crystal, silver and silver plate from companies such as Tiffany, Bernardaud, Villeroy & Boch, Royal Worcester, Wedgwood, Christofle and Gorham regularly priced at 25 to 50 percent off retail, but will match any competitive price. Special sales in January and July offer lower prices.
- Michael C. Fina, New York, New York; 1-800-288-3462. Carries tableware from most major manufacturers of china, crystal and silver, including Lenox, Wedgwood, Reed & Barton and Mikasa, at 20 to 50 percent off retail.
- Michael Round Fine China and Crystal, Lorton, Virginia; 1-800-752-6622. China, crystal and silver from companies such as Lenox, Gorham, Towle, Spode, Noritake, Royal Worcester, Christian Dior and Cartier at up to 60 percent off. Promises to match or beat any other "legitimate dealer."
- Midas China and Silver, Chantilly, Virginia; 1-800-368-3153. Offers tableware from most major manufacturers of sterling and stainless flatware, crystal, china and giftware, including Wedgwood, Lenox, Rosenthal, Villeroy & Boch and Waterford, at 20 to 60 percent off.
- Nat Schwartz and Company, Bayonne, New Jersey; 1-800-526-1440. China, crystal and silver, including Lenox, Minton, Royal Doulton, Waterford, Haviland, Limoges, Wallace, Reed & Barton and Lunt, at 25 to 50 percent off.
- Ross-Simons, Cranston, Rhode Island; 1-800-556-7376. Carries most major manufacturers, including Lenox, Wedgwood, Spode, Gorham, Noritake, Haviland, Royal Copenhagan, Atlantic, Schott, International and Lunt, at 40 to 50 percent off retail.
- Thurber's, Warwick, Rhode Island; 1-800-848-7237. China, silver and crystal by Royal Doulton, Minton, Wedgwood, Gorham, Lenox, Villeroy & Boch and Fitz & Floyd at 20 to 50 percent off retail.

For instance, the Irish Crystal Company, of Thousand Oaks, California, imports hand-blown, hand-cut and hand-polished lead crystal stemware, hollowware and giftware that is similar to fine Waterford crystal. But because it does no advertising, Irish Crystal sells this merchandise at about one-half of the price of Waterford.

Since many department stores sell these types of goods, the best way to find out about the companies is to visit the glassware department of a local fine department store and ask for the names of look-alike manufacturers. (That will also give you a chance to compare the appearance of the crystal.) When you've picked a maker or importer, call the company directly and ask for a catalog. Most phone numbers can be obtained from 800 directory assistance, and the manufacturers will ship goods anywhere.

Buy at Special Sales
Save 50%

It's convenient to buy tableware in department stores—but if you do, look for sales, when prices are significantly better. If you live in Chicago, check out Marshall Field's during its popular Field Day sales in the spring and fall. As with other merchandise, tableware is discounted up to 50 percent off its usual prices. And if you're in the New York City area, look for the Barney's New York special warehouse sale in mid-August: You'll find high-end tabletop goods, accessories and giftware from designers such as Fornasetti, Mary Rose Young and George Jensen—all at 30 to 50 percent off.

Shop at the Right Time
Save 20%

If you don't live in those cities, you can still save buying retail—if you buy at the right time of year. Generally, prices tend to be discounted the most during the months of May and November.

Although individual patterns may be discounted throughout the year (usually so the store can unload unpopular inventory), you'll typically find across-the-board discounts of about 20 percent or more during these two months, when competition is stiffest. In May, shoppers are buying gifts for the summer bridal season. In November, tableware goes on sale to lure buyers for Christmas and Hanukkah.

Ask for Free Financing
Save 25%

Between the china, silver and glassware, an entire tableware set can easily cost $3,000 or more. If you go for the whole shabang, ask the store for free financing.

Reason: Although most stores charge between 15 and 20 percent interest for credit accounts, you could actually be paying 25 percent or more in real interest dollars if you put the balance on a credit card and spread your payments over several years.

While you probably won't get free financing for small purchases, most stores will give you a special interest-free account (at least for six months) for purchases over $1,000. Unless you can pay the full amount on the spot, be sure to ask for the free financing—and be prepared to shop elsewhere if you can't get it. Paying interest can add as much as 25 percent to the final purchase price.

DIAMONDS AND JEWELRY

Retail jewelers typically mark up their goods anywhere from 50 to 150 percent—and sometimes as much as 400 percent—over the wholesale price. But by knowing a few tricks of their trade, you can buy gold and gems for a fraction of what others pay.

Tell Exactly
What You Want

When buying retail, one way to get a jeweler to reduce his markup is to tell him exactly what you are looking for: a round-cut, one-carat stone with a specific rating. (A book on gems or a gemologist can give you information on how diamonds are rated.)

By being that specific, you benefit in two ways: The jeweler knows that you're a serious customer who has obviously done some research (and knows what's a good deal for that item) and that he can probably make a quick sale provided he can get you the item at a good price. In the jewelry business, the name of the game is to move merchandise quickly. For a quick sale, many jewelers are willing to cut their profit to as little as 10 percent—saving you 40 percent or more compared with what others might pay.

ARE YOU PAYING 25 PERCENT FOR YOUR 15 PERCENT CHARGE CARD?

Credit cards may be convenient, but they're even more costly than you might imagine—at least for large purchases.

The following schedule shows what happens if you use a credit card with an interest rate of 15 percent to make a $3,000 purchase and then pay off the bill at $100 a month. If there were no interest, you would pay off the full amount in 30 months. Adding on the interest, you'll take 39 months to pay for the purchase. And the total interest amounts to $782, or 26 percent of the actual purchase price.

Of course, your figures will vary depending on the actual interest on your card—and also on how quickly you pay off the bill. But if you're like many folks who put large purchases on a charge account and then pay a set amount each month, you could be paying a lot more than the stated interest.

NUMBER OF MONTHS	MONTH	BALANCE ($)	INTEREST ($)	PAYMENT ($)	NEW BALANCE ($)
First Year					
1	January	3,000.00			
2	February	3,000.00	37.50	100.00	2,937.50
3	March	2,937.50	36.72	100.00	2,874.22
4	April	2,874.22	35.93	100.00	2,810.15
5	May	2,810.15	35.13	100.00	2,745.28
6	June	2,745.28	34.32	100.00	2,679.60
7	July	2,679.60	33.49	100.00	2,613.09
8	August	2,613.09	32.66	100.00	2,545.75
9	September	2,545.75	31.82	100.00	2,477.57
10	October	2,477.57	30.97	100.00	2,408.54
11	November	2,408.54	30.11	100.00	2,338.65
12	December	2,338.65	29.23	100.00	2,267.88

NUMBER OF MONTHS	MONTH	BALANCE ($)	INTEREST ($)	PAYMENT ($)	NEW BALANCE ($)
Second Year					
13	January	2,267.88	28.35	100.00	2,196.23
14	February	2,196.23	27.45	100.00	2,123.68
15	March	2,123.68	26.55	100.00	2,050.23
16	April	2,050.23	25.63	100.00	1,975.86
17	May	1,975.86	24.70	100.00	1,900.56
18	June	1,900.56	23.76	100.00	1,824.32
19	July	1,824.32	22.80	100.00	1,747.12
20	August	1,747.12	21.84	100.00	1,668.96
21	September	1,668.96	20.86	100.00	1,589.82
22	October	1,589.82	19.87	100.00	1,509.69
23	November	1,509.69	18.87	100.00	1,428.56
24	December	1,428.56	17.86	100.00	1,346.42
Third Year					
25	January	1,346.42	16.83	100.00	1,263.25
26	February	1,263.25	15.79	100.00	1,179.04
27	March	1,179.04	14.74	100.00	1,093.78
28	April	1,093.78	13.67	100.00	1,007.45
29	May	1,007.45	12.59	100.00	920.04
30	June	920.04	11.50	100.00	831.54
31	July	831.54	10.39	100.00	741.93
32	August	741.93	9.27	100.00	651.20
33	September	651.20	8.14	100.00	559.34
34	October	559.34	6.99	100.00	466.33
35	November	466.33	5.83	100.00	372.16
36	December	372.16	4.65	100.00	276.81
Fourth Year					
37	January	276.81	3.46	100.00	180.27
38	February	180.27	2.25	100.00	82.52
39	March	82.52		82.52	0.00
Total Interest			782.52		
Total Payments				3,782.52	

Play Off the Competition
for a Better Deal

If you live where the economy is suffering and competition among jewelers is keen, just shopping around and comparing prices may be enough to get you a great deal on jewelry.

After you've made a good deal with one jeweler, tell another. *Example:* "I can get a one-carat stone with a GVSI rating for X amount from your competition. Can you do better?" (GVSI is an indication of color, *G*, and clarity, *VSI*.)

Usually, you can, since most area jewelers get their gems from the same wholesalers. Faced with the prospect of losing the sale or lowering the profit, most jewelers would prefer to take less money for a sure sale.

Try a Discount House
Save 50%

Although few and far between, diamond and jewelry discount houses can offer you quality gems and rings at one-third to over one-half off retail. They get their jewelry at lower wholesale prices because they buy in volume. Discount houses also have less overhead because they're located in out-of-the-way places and they have little or no advertising. All these cost-cutting measures result in savings that the discount house can pass along to you.

Retailers poo-poo these discount houses because some have been charged with selling secondhand merchandise. To be on the safe side, whenever you're buying precious gems, insist on a statement of replacement—an appraisal letter from a certified gemologist. Or make sure you get a written guarantee that the company will refund your money if a subsequent appraisal contradicts the salesperson's description.

Although many jewelers call themselves discounters, it's unlikely you'll find a true one in a mall or another "prime" real estate location. (*Remember:* They can't discount heavily if they have to pay high rent.) A good place to start is by looking in your local Yellow Pages. Look for a discounter who is located outside a mall or business center. And if there's more than one in your area, shop around and compare prices on comparable jewelry.

GOLDEN TIPS FOR BUYING DIAMONDS

Diamonds may be a girl's best friend, but to make sure you get the best deal when buying these precious stones, keep these tips in mind.

- Don't assume that you're necessarily getting a better buy on one diamond that has a lower price than another of the same carat weight. It's the three C's that determine the quality of a diamond—its cut, color and clarity. The cut determines the stone's light-reflecting properties (and hence, the other two) and can influence the stone's value by as much as 30 percent.
- Bigger isn't always better with diamonds. A smaller diamond of high quality will appreciate more in value than a larger stone of lesser quality.
- Insist on a certificate from a certified gemologist-appraiser that documents a diamond's quality. That and your jeweler's word are your only protections against misrepresentations.
- To make sure your diamond's setting is worthy, look for a label or stamp that confirms it is 18-karat or 14-karat gold. Jewelry without this marking has probably been electroplated, a technique that gives the illusion of real gold but has no real value.

Sacrifice Service for Price
Save 20%

If you want a certain piece of jewelry and aren't particularly worried about its pedigree, you can usually buy it for less at membership merchandise clubs such as the Price Club, Sam's Club and Costco. Many of these stores carry diamonds and jewelry—usually for about 20 percent below regular retail prices.

Understand, however, that you may be sacrificing a certain amount of service for price. Since membership merchandise clubs, unlike specialty stores, deal in a wide range of goods besides jewelry, the clerks may not know very much about the jewelry they're selling.

Check Out Wholesalers

Technically, a wholesaler cannot sell to the public. (Beware of those who do, since they may not "back up" their goods with authentic documents and money back guarantees.)

However, many legitimate wholesalers can help you make the most of your money. Simply have the wholesaler show you a stone, and then ask him to give you the name of a retail jeweler who's willing to sell it to you at a low price. True, the wholesaler is probably getting a cut from his retailer buddy, but keep in mind that "friends" usually give each other the best merchandise at the best price.

Slice the Price on Custom Jewelry

You're always going to pay more for a custom-designed, handmade piece of jewelry. But you can cut up to one-fourth off the price of handmade jewelry if you buy the stone or gem yourself—and then have the artist make the piece. For a diamond engagement ring, for instance, the diamond alone represents about 90 percent of the ring's value. So make your own deal on the diamond, and then take it to the artisan or jeweler for a custom-designed band and setting.

And don't assume that custom jewelry makers get a better deal than you can. Since they don't buy gems in volume, they pay a premium price to wholesalers (which is why so many charge you top dollar for their wares). But by buying the gem elsewhere, you could easily knock 25 percent or more off the total cost of certain items.

Buy Reconditioned
Save 50%

A well-made watch will last forever. And a quality watch that has been cleaned and reconditioned by an expert jeweler is as good as new again.

So instead of buying a top-quality watch that's brand-new, you're ahead if you find a watchmaker who repairs and reconditions quality timepieces. For instance, you can save anywhere from 30 to 50 percent by buying a three-year-old Rolex that's been completely reconditioned—and you can usually get a two-year warranty to boot. Generally, the older the reconditioned watch, the more you'll save.

Many local watchmakers can recondition quality watches, but

companies such as Gray and Sons in Coconut Grove, Florida, specialize in this service. Other brands known for their never-ending quality besides Rolex include Vacheron Constantin, Patek Philippe and Audemars Piguet.

Deal with the Manager or Owner
Save 10%

Whenever you're seriously shopping for jewelry, ask that the store manager or owner wait on you—especially if you're shopping in a "chain" jewelry store with more than one location.

That's because no matter where you shop, you should always bargain when buying watches and jewelry. Some experts suggest you initially offer 15 percent less than the asking price (but prepare to settle for 10 percent). But more important than what you offer may be whom you offer it to.

In these chain stores, prices are usually mandated by the "home office"—and clerks aren't in a good position to negotiate. But managers or store owners do have the authority to lower the price—and often will for certain customers.

What makes you that customer? Often it's simply paying with cash. With cash-paying customers, the manager or owner doesn't have to worry whether a check will clear—and he doesn't have to pay a service fee to a credit card company. (Usually, this fee is 3 percent of the price.) A cash sale is a sure thing, and many managers would rather move the merchandise for a lower price than haggle over a few dollars. By-the-hour clerks don't worry about inventory (only their commissions) and won't be as willing to bargain with you.

ANTIQUES AND COLLECTIBLES

There's gold in old. Whether it's furniture or jewelry, music boxes or bric-a-brac, buying antiques and collectibles can be a very profitable pastime. It's not unusual for many pieces to appreciate 10 to 15 percent annually.

Of course, the first rule of antique collecting is to know what you're looking for. It takes years of study to master the art of spotting a worthy item. But while it may take you a while to learn all the ins and outs of collectible collecting, here are some general principles on spending less.

Visit Pawn Shops
Save 30%

Don't write off pawn shops as a potential gold mine for antiques and collectibles. Pawn shops used to have a reputation for fencing stolen goods, but no more. Today's pawn shop businesses are heavily regulated, and reputable dealers won't handle any merchandise that they suspect might be stolen.

In fact, pawn shops are a favorite haunt of Main Street antique dealers, jewelers and diamond wholesalers—and with good reason. Some merchandise is as low as 30 percent below wholesale.

That's because a pawnbroker's main business is making loans. As a result, the broker wants as much capital available as possible. Most pawnbrokers will negotiate with you if you make any reasonable offer. Rather than get top dollar, they just want to move merchandise out the door.

Cut the Price by Finding "Hidden" Faults

One of the best ways to negotiate a discount on an antique is to point out all its flaws—even those that don't exist. Examine the item several times with a careful eye, mentioning to the dealer everything that's wrong with it. If you see a difference in wood between the top and legs, or the knobs don't fit the piece, or there's cracked glass, mention it. All these flaws raise the question of the item's authenticity.

IS IT A REAL ANTIQUE?

Most folks describe anything old as an antique. In reality, the accepted definition of a true antique is that the item is 100 or more years old. Anything newer is considered a "collectible" or a "vintage" piece.

When it comes to value, however, age isn't the only factor that's important. Some collectibles and vintage pieces can be more valuable than true antiques; it all depends on the particular item and its popularity.

"Are those knobs original? They don't look like they are."

"Is this all the original wood? This looks like it's not."

Even if the dealer disagrees with your points, stand firm and offer less than the asking price. Insiders tell us that dealers are more likely to grant discounts to "troublemakers" than to those who fawn over an item—especially when the fault finders have loud voices.

Protect Your Money
Know Your Dealer

If you know little about antiques, then know something about your dealer. Although many are honest businesspeople, the industry has plenty of charlatans who sell items that are not what they're presented to be.

Before handing over any money, call your state's watchdog group to see if there have been any complaints about that dealer. (By calling the information desk of your state capitol, you'll be able to get the number of the watchdog group.)

Focus on Antique "Supermarkets"
Save 15%

The size of antique stores can work to your advantage. Many antique dealers are experts—but not on everything. In a larger store with several hundred period pieces in a wide range of categories, the chances are that some (if not much) of the inventory will be underpriced.

Although antiques and collectibles aren't exactly a "volume" business, you can save about 15 percent on items purchased in large antique supermarkets, compared with what you'd pay for similar items purchased in specialty stores. (A specialty store concentrates on a specific type of antique, such as nineteenth-century porcelains or Queen Anne furniture.)

One such supermarket is the Antique Outlet in Englewood, New Jersey, which bills itself as an "antiques discount center." While the merchandise includes some replica items as well as antiques, you can find something from every era in the 7,000-square-foot showroom. A wide selection of American and European furniture, art, lamps, jewelry, crystal and sterling is featured. Nearly everything is marked less than you'd pay in specialty shops.

Discuss the Meaning of Value
Save 10%

Whether you're shopping for antiques at a large discounter or a smaller specialty store, you'll be likely to hear a lot about how valuable an antique is. This, of course, is to justify the asking price (which can be very high).

First of all, realize that much of this talk about "value" is merely a way for dealers to gauge your knowledge (or rather, lack of knowledge) of antiques. Many dealers realize that their expertise and knowledge aren't shared by the masses, and they use this to their advantage by charging (and usually getting) top dollar for their merchandise.

That's not to say you need to be an expert in antiques in order to get a good deal; but you do need to be skeptical. The price on the item is not what the dealer actually expects to get. Never agree to pay the asking price without making a counteroffer of at least 15 percent less. Chances are the dealer will dicker with you, but you can probably settle on a price that's 10 percent less.

If the dealer tries to explain the value of the item in order to justify its high asking price, remind him that it's still unsold . . . so there's obviously a discrepancy between his and the customer's perceived value of the item. Most dealers will take your meaning and make a sale for less money.

Hit the Road
Save 30%

Generally, the farther inland you travel from the coastal metropolitan areas, the better the deals. That's why so many antique dealers from New York City and other East Coast cities are doing their shopping in the Midwest, where prices are as much as one-third lower than on either coast.

That doesn't mean you have to go to Chicago or Des Moines for a good deal. More "antique malls" are opening on the outskirts of large antique meccas such as the Big Apple—with anywhere from 10 to 100 dealers under one roof and literally thousands of items on display. Granted, these malls can be overwhelming, but prices tend to be between 10 and 30 percent off those found at specialty shops. Usually, you'll do better price-wise if you frequent malls off the beaten track; the farther away from the city, the better.

Frequent Ritzy Resale Shops
Save 60%

Certain consignment shops can be a gold mine for the luxury goods consumer. While most merely provide a way for people to get rid of their discarded (but still decent) merchandise, a growing number handle goods such as crystal, sterling silver, antiques and home furnishings at 60 percent or more off retail.

Where do you find these stores? First of all, be sure to check out the best neighborhoods in your area, since the merchandise usually comes from the homes of the wealthiest residents. However, a handful of resale shops now specialize in luxury goods.

For instance, Uniquities is a consignment shop located in a well-heeled Los Angeles neighborhood that sells antiques and collectibles for about 10 percent of their "retail" value. Across town in affluent Pasadena, a consignment shop benefiting the Huntington Memorial Hospital has 12,000 square feet of merchandise—offering liquidation prices on antiques as well as oriental rugs, pianos and other luxury goods.

Granted, these stores may be hard to find in other cities, but if you're searching for secondhand luxury items (as well as other top-quality goods at bargain prices), you'll probably find them only in the best neighborhoods.

Come Early, Buy Late
Save 25%

Don't expect too much success at garage sales and flea markets, but if you happen to come across a vintage piece worth buying—and you are willing to play a "waiting game"—you might get a very good price.

The rule of thumb is to visit flea markets and garage sales just as they open in order to get first crack at the best merchandise. If you see something you like, make your "best offer," which could be as much as 25 percent below the asking price. If the seller doesn't accept your offer, tell him you can't go any higher—but you'll stop by later to see whether the piece has been sold.

If the seller gets a better offer during the day, you might lose the piece. But if your offer is reasonable—and you keep coming by to see whether he's changed his mind—your chances get better and better as the day goes on. Most dealers would much rather move their merchandise than pack it up again. If yours is the best offer, and you're still around at the end of the day, you might get what you want for the price you offered in the first place.

Become an Estate Sale Junkie

One way to educate yourself in the value of collectibles—and pick up a few bargains in the process—is by frequenting estate sales.

In estate sales, you often buy the goods in "lots," so you get more than you pay for. Often along with the cast-offs there are some useful items—particularly tools and the like. But for antique collectors, estate sales are a great place to meet dealers, who often do a lot of their buying there.

To find estate sales in your area, read "freebie" newspapers (such as the *Merchandiser*) that are filled with classified ads. Also, check the listings under "Estate Sales" in your local newspaper's classified ads.

Local auctioneers who run the estate sales have mailing lists of potential buyers. Ask to be put on the list, and you'll get regular notices of upcoming auctions.

FINE ART

If you're among those museum walkers who say there's no real difference between the work of a famous abstract artist and the scribbles of a toddler, maybe you should be reminded of the thousands of dollars some artists get for their squiggles (while all your kid's "masterpiece" gets is a place on the refrigerator door).

No doubt about it: Art doesn't come cheap. A single painting or etching from a young "unknown" can sell for several hundred dol-

---

INVESTING IN ART

If you're planning to invest in art, look at what's being sold to museums. An emerging artist who has recently sold a work to a major museum is a good investment bet, since acceptance in the museum functions as a stamp of approval.

"Purchased" artists are also viewed as the newest wunderkinds. So as soon as their work is snapped up by a museum, all their other pieces tend to increase in value.

lars; some fetch tens of thousands. But whether you collect art for home decoration or consider it an investment, you can always find ways to get better deals.

Say You'll Spread the Word
Save 10%

You usually pay top dollar when buying art from an established gallery. But some dealers offer a 10 percent discount to good customers—people who they think will continue to buy from them or who will send other buyers their way.

So when shopping at a gallery, don't be shy: Let the dealer know that you're the kind of customer who talks about art—and that you'll recommend the gallery to your friends. The "retail" art business is largely through word of mouth, and your promise of spreading the word is well worth the cost (to the dealer) of a modest price reduction.

Shop 'til You Find a Discounter
Save 70%

In major art centers such as New York City, you're more likely to find "discount" art galleries, where hundreds of original works of art are available for up to 70 percent off retail gallery prices.

Art Insights, a gallery in Manhattan, is one such discounter. But remember: Just because a gallery calls itself a discounter doesn't mean it really offers lower prices. Some might discount individual works, but a true discounter offers across-the-board bargains on most of its inventory. To get a true idea of a good deal, it's usually necessary to comparison-shop at many galleries.

Deal Directly with the Artist

Art can be an excellent investment, but like stocks, baseball cards or any other investment, the purpose is to buy low and sell high. Unfortunately, when it comes to art, many people feel strange about negotiating for a better deal.

Don't. Many artists appreciate selling any of their pieces, since sales are often few and far between. You can negotiate a lower offer than the asking price, but keep in mind that you're not bargaining for a flea market item.

Here's an approach that may get you a price break: "I really love your work and want to enjoy it in my home. But the price is a little higher than I planned to spend. Would you consider an offer of . . . ?"

Every artist likes to have his work appreciated and enjoyed—and a number of famous artists were practically supported by appreciative buyers who came back repeatedly to purchase their art. So you have a good chance of getting it at the price you want, particularly if you look like you might be a potential patron of the arts.

Ask for the Artist's Input

Many people feel more comfortable talking turkey with gallery personnel than dealing with the artist directly. After all, gallery personnel should consider any offer and not be insulted. They're just acting as agents for the artist.

But what if you're making an offer much lower than the asking price? You can ask gallery personnel to get the artist's reply to your offer. Even though the gallery carries his work, it's still the artist who decides whether he'll sell it.

Some artists won't deal with customers and insist that the gallery act as their "agent." But if the gallery asks for your phone number or agrees to consult the artist, that probably means your offer is the best received to date—and the odds are good that there will be a counteroffer or that you'll get the artwork for the price you want.

Check Out Student Shows

Forget about getting a discount on the work of any "hot" artist. Once an artist reaches a certain status, there are no bargains for his work.

But keep an eye on art students—who are the greats of the future. Student shows are held at art schools and universities as well as at galleries. And if you know what you like when you see it, you can get excellent work for hundreds or thousands less than the work of established artists. For a new collector, or just for someone who appreciates art, insiders tell us that student art shows are where the real deals are.

Join the Dealers

If you simply don't have the time to visit numerous galleries, there is an easier way for you to get the knowledge you need to stretch your art-buying dollars: Visit dealer art shows.

Every winter in New York City, for instance, dozens of art dealers exhibit at the Armory Art Show. Anyone can attend, and it's a good opportunity to compare prices on the art shown by different dealers and to possibly negotiate some purchases.

For information on art shows in your area, write to the Art Dealers Association of America, 575 Madison Avenue, New York, NY 10022. The phone number can be obtained from New York City directory assistance (212 area code).

Rent, Don't Buy

If you are not a collector but need to collect art—to decorate your home or office, for instance—consider renting instead of buying. Some museums rent art to businesses and individuals for a nominal fee—from $6 to $45 a month for art that has a purchase price of $100 to $10,000.

Many of these works are done by emerging local artists, who don't yet have national reputations. But you can find a wide variety of works from established artists as well. (No Picassos or Rembrandts, of course, but there are hundreds of pieces from which to choose.) After renting, if you decide you like a piece and want to buy it, you can usually apply the rental fee to your purchase price.

Museums with established rental programs include the Albright-Knox Art Gallery in Buffalo, New York; the San Francisco Museum of Modern Art; and the Los Angeles County Museum of Art. (But there are dozens of others that also have rental programs.) It's best to call local galleries or museums to find out what's available in your area.

GRAND PIANOS

There's a good reason why these pianos are called grand. It takes several grand to own one.

But you can pay a lot less for a grand or baby grand if you buy from a dealer who's willing to bargain. The average retail markup on any piano is 100 percent, which means you pay twice as much as the dealer paid for it wholesale. And that means the dealer will make money even if you pay 20 or 25 percent less than the retail price. So here's how you can own the Cadillac of keyboards for a lot less.

Dicker for a Discount
Save 20%

Price reductions of 10 to 20 percent are not uncommon when buying any piano. In fact, pianos are specifically priced with that "discount" in mind. (Unfortunately, many buyers aren't aware that dealers don't really expect them to pay the sticker price.)

With grand pianos, there's room for even more of a discount. Grands are specialized instruments—even baby grands require a lot of room and money, so pianos are not exactly moved on a volume basis. And since a dealer has the potential to make $5,000 or more in commission from the sale of one, there's plenty of room to negotiate for a lower price.

A good place to start is 25 percent or more below the sticker price. You may not get it, but even settling on 20 percent can save you several thousand dollars.

Rent to Own
Save $2,000

Some stores will offer interest-free financing on a piano—as an inducement to buy. Look for one of those stores before you even think of doing business. If you have to pay the typical 15 to 20 percent interest on a store charge account, you could add $2,000 or more to the cost of a grand piano.

If you can't afford to pay cash, or you just don't want to make the initial investment, try a short-term rent-to-own program. While the payments are slightly more than an outright purchase, it still costs less than financing. Unlike electronics, for which rent-to-own programs can cost you three times as much as buying the item with cash, a piano can usually be owned for little or no interest.

Buy Used
Save 50%

Used grand pianos cost significantly less money than new ones—in some cases, half as much. And since basic piano design hasn't changed in the past 100 years, there are no real improvements that would make an old piano obsolete.

You can also save thousands by buying factory seconds, dealer demos or those obtained through other special circumstances. Ask any reputable piano dealer about these deals.

But whenever you buy one of these bargains, it's advised that you have the unit inspected by a piano technician. Grand pianos that need repairs or reconditioning can raise the total cost of purchase considerably.

FUR COATS

The ultimate in luxury garments doesn't have to be purchased at the ultimate price. Ever since animal rights activists have likened the wearing of fur to critter genocide, the price of fur coats has dropped dramatically. But if you've fixed your sights on fur, there are ways to save a bundle on your next pelt.

Buy in Warm Weather
Save 50%

The best time to buy furs is when no one is thinking about them—and that's usually in the spring or the dog days of summer. Since the slowest time of the year for furriers occurs in late July through August, you can get quality merchandise for up to one-half of the regular price—and up to 70 percent off when you buy last year's merchandise.

Recut a Coat
Save 75%

If you already have a fur but have grown tired of it, you can use the pelts for a new coat. By restyling, as it's called in the business, you can get a completely new design. The old coat is cleaned, then recut and remodeled. All you pay for is the labor, which is about 25 percent of a coat's cost. So you save up to 75 percent of the cost of a comparable new fur.

Negotiate a Deal
Save 20%

It's a buyer's market for furs, so don't be afraid to negotiate a discount on the sticker price. Insiders say that furs are priced to sell from 10 to 20 percent lower than expected—which means a good ne-gotiator can knock up to 20 percent off the asking price.

When looking at furs, don't be afraid to mention competitors' prices. But remember: Only those who ask for a discount get it.

Buy in the Big Apple
Save 30%

If you're heading to New York City, check out Seventh Avenue, around 28th or 29th Street. This area is a fur lover's paradise, with store after store of furriers offering near-wholesale prices. You'll save at least one-third off regular retail prices, and most of these shops are open on Sunday.

Mail Your Fur Home

Once you select a fur, you can save even more by mailing your pelt home. New York City has a high sales tax, which can add nearly $400 to the price of a $4,500 coat. To get around this, visitors and tourists can buy their furs in the Big Apple and have them mailed to their home address (provided it's out of state). Just be sure to adequately insure your garment.

Cut Your Spending on

SPECIAL SALES

- Government Auctions
- Flea Markets

FIND SOME BIG BARGAINS IN UNLIKELY PLACES

The secrets to some of the best deals around are right at your fingertips—literally. Sure, you might have to squint at that small print way in the back of the classified section, but each week your local newspaper reports the little-known bargains that await you.

From government auctions to estate sales to flea markets, there are plenty of special sales where you can buy new and used items for significantly less than retail—sometimes pennies on the dollar.

GOVERNMENT AUCTIONS

Nobody passes along a bargain more often than your Uncle Sam. Whether it's property taken from lawbreakers or wrong-address packages that end up somewhere in the postal service, the federal government has plenty of goods to sell. When government agencies auction off their big lost-and-found collection, the citizens of the United States get first grabs. And if you're on the buying end of this transaction, you may be able to get a great deal. Just make sure you take cash or a certified, cashier's or traveler's check to any government auction that you attend. Credit cards aren't honored.

There are scores of government sales each year. The goods for sale include everything from old office furniture to the latest in luxury automobiles. And you can usually buy them for a lot less than their appraised worth.

While deals abound—you usually pay pennies on the dollar—the key to getting these deals is knowing about them. So here's what you need to know to make the most of your green with the least amount of government red tape.

Pick Up a Bargain at the GSA

The General Services Administration (GSA) is the federal government's "housekeeper," with duties that include buying, selling and managing government possessions. Because the GSA is the central clearinghouse for practically everything the federal government owns, it's one of the largest sources of government surplus.

Though many of the wares being sold are old office supplies, there's more in the warehouse than that. GSA sales may include everything from microscopes to jewelry. Often cars, trucks and

---

BUYING BY THE LOT

Many federal auctions consist of selling items in lots— many items that come as part of a package deal. Since everything is sold "as is," some items may be in good, workable condition while others are not. But it's not all junk. The government often replaces inventory on a fixed, prearranged schedule, which means items get sold off that are in perfectly good condition just because there's money budgeted to replace them.

To give you an idea of some of the prices on merchandise, here are some of the lots and the winning bids from one General Service Administration auction we checked out.

- A lot consisting of a King kitchen stove, four gas burners, seven stainless steel sinks, seven Rangemaster gas stoves and four metal kitchen cabinets with double doors; $278
- A lot containing six electric printing calculators, six adding machines, 15 electric typewriters, a fax copy machine and a Xerox copy machine; $301
- A lot with 17 bookcases, ten filing cabinets, three weighing scales, three desks, two vacuum cleaners, one gym set, a stereo, a worktable, a cabinet, a water dispenser and a doctor's examining table; $261

In addition to items like these, you can also get official gifts and awards from foreign countries. These are handled in separate sales, with the items listed in the *Federal Register*. For more information on this program, write the U.S. Department of State's Office of Protocol, 2201 C Street NW, Room 1238, Washington, DC 20520.

other vehicles are also for sale. While some of these goods are in excellent condition, others are suitable only for scrap.

GSA sales are handled in any of four ways.

Sealed bid. You receive a sales catalog from your regional GSA office, listing the property and where it's located (which could be in several places in several states). You then fill out a bid sheet for items you want and return it to the regional office. Bids are opened on a specified date, and contracts are awarded to the highest bidder. Winners are notified by mail and given a deadline to pay for and remove the items.

Auction. You go to a particular location, where items are displayed and auctioned to the highest bidder—either individually or in lots, which are groupings of items (sometimes similar items, sometimes just an assortment) that are sold all at once. You can find out about these auctions by contacting your regional office.

Spot bid. This is similar to an auction, but instead of voicing your bid, you write it up and send it in.

Fixed price. You arrive at a sale site, where prices are posted on the property and listed in a sale catalog. Items are sold on a first-come basis.

For information about sales in your area, ask the GSA to place your name on a mailing list and request a Surplus Personal Property Category Selection Sheet. This form allows you to specify the types of property and geographical areas that match your interests. Contact the regional office closest to your home.

- National Capitol Region: Washington, D.C., nearby Maryland and Virginia; (703) 557-7785
- Region 1: Connecticut, Maine, Massachusetts, New Hampshire, Rhode Island and Vermont; (617) 565-7326
- Region 2: New Jersey, New York, Puerto Rico and the Virgin Islands; (212) 264-2035
- Region 3: Maryland and Virginia (except metropolitan D.C. area), plus Delaware, Pennsylvania and West Virginia; (215) 656-3400
- Region 4: Alabama, Florida, Georgia, Kentucky, Mississippi, North Carolina, South Carolina and Tennessee; (404) 331-3058
- Region 5: Illinois, Indiana, Michigan, Minnesota, Ohio and Wisconsin; (312) 353-6061
- Region 6: Iowa, Kansas, Missouri and Nebraska; (913) 236-2500
- Region 7: Arkansas, Louisiana, New Mexico, Oklahoma and Texas; (817) 334-2352

- Region 8: Colorado, Montana, North Dakota, South Dakota, Utah and Wyoming; (303) 236-7702
- Region 9: Arizona, California, Commonwealth of the Northern Mariana Islands, Guam, Hawaii and Nevada; (415) 744-5120
- Region 10: Alaska, Idaho, Oregon and Washington; (206) 931-7566

Pick Up a Bonus from the U.S. Marshal

Any item used in the commission of a felony or purchased as a result of an illegal act can be seized under federal law. That means that federal officials have the right to confiscate the boat used to transport drugs and to foreclose on the house owned by the drug dealer if authorities believe these possessions were purchased with illicit profits.

Because of this policy, the U.S. Marshals Service gets the best that the underworld has to offer. This branch of the Justice Department seizes property primarily through three investigative agencies—the Federal Bureau of Investigation, the Immigration and Naturalization Service and the jackpot provider of confiscated goods, the Drug Enforcement Administration.

You won't find kitchen appliances or desks in this inventory. Instead, there are luxury cars, yachts, airplanes, art collections, real estate and other highly desirable goods. Most of the merchandise is in excellent shape and of superior quality (what else were you expecting from drug dealers . . . Yugos?).

Once the property is seized, the U.S. Marshals Service sells the goods, usually at a local public auction for cash or a certified check. That means you can get property seized in local crimes, such as drug busts. The agency doesn't have a national or regional mailing list to notify citizens of these sales, but you can track them yourself if you look for classified advertisements in local newspapers. The office of the agency that seizes the property always places notices in these papers and sometimes in national publications such as *USA Today* as well.

For further information, write to the U.S. Marshals Service, U.S. Department of Justice, 600 Army-Navy Drive, Arlington, VA 22202-4210.

Become a Customer of Customs

The U.S. Customs Service has two duties: to seize and destroy illegal contraband, and to collect revenue from duties and fees on imports. When tourists and importers can't pay the duty on items they have purchased abroad, they must leave them behind at the customs office. Before long, there's a hefty supply of goods at the customs office, including foreign wines, oriental rugs, leather goods, silks, furniture, cars and collectibles.

To a lesser extent, customs agents apprehend people engaged in fraudulent practices that circumvent customs laws. Customs agents can also seize this property, which is then sold off. And the U.S. Customs Service has the right to seize the real estate of those who engage in fraudulent practices.

Approximately 180 sales are held each year. Some are public auctions held at local auction houses, while others are open bid sales, in which bidders write their offers on a publicly posted bid form.

Public auctions are held about once a month in two cities— Yuma, Arizona, and Chula Vista, California. Regular sales are held periodically (according to the volume of seized property) in Los Angeles; Miami; Jersey City, New Jersey; Nogales, Arizona; and three Texas cities—El Paso, Edinburg and Laredo. These sales are usually advertised in the classified section of newspapers in those cities.

You can also subscribe to periodic news bulletins on seized property to find out when it will be available for sale. It costs $50 to buy the bulletins for national sales and $25 each for the eastern or western region. For these bulletins, write to EG&G Dynatrend, U.S. Customs Support Division, Attention: Subscriptions, 2300 Clarendon Boulevard, Suite 705, Arlington, VA 22201.

Take Your Pick at the Post Office

Although selection is more limited, you'll probably find your best bargains at regional postal service auctions, which are held regularly in five different cities around the country.

What's for sale? All the packages that the post office can't deliver because the addresses are incorrect, labels are torn or writing is illegible. After sitting for months in the Undeliverable Mails Branch, unclaimed parcels are sold by auction to the highest bidder.

When insured parcels are damaged in transit, the postal service pays the insurance claim and retains the packages. These items are labeled "damaged goods" and are sold "as is."

To find out the date of the next sale, call or write the Superintendent of Claims, care of the U.S. Post Office, at the nearest address where auctions are held.

- J. A. Farley Building, 380 West 33rd Street, New York, NY 10199-9543
- 2970 Market Street, Room 531A, Philadelphia, PA 19104-9886
- 443 East Fillmore Avenue, St. Paul, MN 55107-1206
- 730 Great Southwest Parkway SW, P.O. Box 44161, Atlanta, GA 30336-9590
- P.O. Box 7837, San Francisco, CA 94120-7837

As with other government auctions, you must pay for your purchases with cash or by cashier's, certified or traveler's check. Customers are responsible for supplying containers and transportation for purchases. And the goods must be removed from the premises by 4:00 P.M. on the day of the sale.

Shop for Bargains at the IRS

Known tax dodgers are given several notices to cough up what they owe Uncle Sam. If they don't arrange payment, the Internal Revenue Service (IRS) files a tax lien and seizes the property—which can include the house and everything in it (depending how much is owed).

The IRS then advertises its intention to sell the property in the classified section of the newspaper serving the area of the seizure. Notices are also placed in local post offices and other government buildings. (You should call your local IRS office, however, to find out about sales in your area.)

At an IRS sale, you never know what will be up for grabs. Expect to find everything and anything—homes, cars, airplanes, boats, TV sets, furniture and kitchen equipment, even law books. Prices defy all reason: One buyer purchased a $50 tea set for less than $3, a closet full of women's clothing appraised at $200 for $15 and an $800 Queen Anne desk for $175 in one sale.

The auction procedure is fairly standard. A minimum bid is placed on each item, and goods are sold to the highest bidder.

Put In Your Bid
with the Department of Defense

One of the largest inventories up for grabs is offered by the Department of Defense at periodic sales. While you shouldn't expect a good deal on SCUD missiles or late-model tanks, you can find thousands of other items—from clothing and office equipment to jeeps and motor-cycles. Anyone over age 18 and not a federal employee (or a member of a federal employee's household) is eligible to buy at these sales, as long as you have a way of removing your purchase: Uncle Sam doesn't deliver.

For complete information, contact the National Sales Office, Defense Reutilization and Marketing Office, 2163 Airways Boulevard, Building 210, Memphis, TN 38114-5211. You'll be sent a sales catalog describing the property, sale location, property location and inspection and upcoming sale dates. You can also get on the mailing list for scheduled Department of Defense sales by writing the Superintendent of Documents, Government Printing Office, Washington, DC 20402.

Buy Cheap from Salvage Sales

Moving companies, department stores and motels and restaurants that are going out of business also periodically hold salvage sales that can offer terrific bargains. And don't forget about the lost-and-found departments of local schools and colleges as well as police departments—which usually hold annual or semiannual sales where recovered bicycles and other property are sold at bargain-basement prices.

With the exception of police sales, most of these sales are held on an as-needed basis and aren't widely advertised, so it's up to you to call for information.

FLEA MARKETS

There are literally thousands of flea markets in the United States, but only a handful are truly exceptional. For interesting inventory and bigger bargains, here are the flea markets that insiders call the most unusual. They're scattered around the country—but of course, true flea market aficionados will travel anywhere for a bargain. And you'll probably want to drop in if you're near one of these markets on vacation.

Wherever you go, the rules remain the same: Travel lightly, wear comfortable shoes, and take a roomy shopping bag. And take cash—most dealers frown on checks and credit cards. Other useful carry-alongs include a notepad, tape measure and flashlight.

East

- Annex Antiques Fair and Flea Market, New York City. About 400 dealers meet every weekend along Sixth Avenue between 24th and 27th Streets in Manhattan. Don't expect bargains, since it's popular with top dealers (and gawkers). But a great place to browse. Admission: $1.
- Intermediate School 44 Flea Market, New York City. With over 300 booths from all over the world, this flea market definitely has an international flavor. Here you'll find everything from African-made fabrics to pottery from Peru. Proceeds support parents' associations. Corner of 77th Street and Columbus Avenue. Sunday, 10:00 A.M. to 5:30 P.M.
- Outdoor Antique Show, Brimfield, Massachusetts. Billed as "the country's largest sale without walls," this flea market features some 3,000 dealers, who have set up shop along a one-mile span of Route 20. The shows are Thursday through Saturday in May, July and September.
- Renninger's Antique Markets, Kutztown and Adamstown, Pennsylvania. Top antique dealers consider these among the nation's best for furniture and collectibles. The Renninger family runs two markets all year—Kutztown hosts 250 antique dealers on Saturday, while 30 miles away, Adamstown opens every Sunday with about 375 dealers.

Midwest

- Ann Arbor Antiques Market, Ann Arbor, Michigan. Dealers guarantee the authenticity of their wares. Washtenaw Farm Council Grounds, 5055 Ann Arbor Saline Road, Exit 175 off Interstate 94. Third Sunday of every month, April through October, 6:00 A.M. to 4:00 P.M.
- Kane County Fleamarket, St. Charles, Illinois. Don't let the late Saturday starting time fool you: Large numbers of buyers are willing to pay extra to gain early Saturday morning access, where the best deals are. Kane County Fairgrounds, Randall Road, between Route 64 and Route 38. First weekend every month, except New Year's Day and Easter. Admission: $3. Saturday, 1:00 P.M. to 5:00 P.M.; Sunday, 7:00 A.M. to 4:00 P.M.
- Shipshewana Flea Market, Shipshewana, Indiana. Thousands of treasures are displayed beneath tents and sheds in this center of

Amish and Mennonite culture. Some 1,200 vendors sell crafts and quilts. Off State Road 5, May through October, Tuesday and Wednesday. Antique auctions held Wednesday all year long.

- Springfield Antiques Show and Fleamarket, Springfield, Ohio. The specialty is country antiques. You'll see a lot of professional dealers doing their thing. Shows are held the third weekend of every month, except July, at the Clark County Fairgrounds. Friday, 5:00 P.M. to 8:00 P.M.; Saturday, 8:00 A.M. to 5:00 P.M.; Sunday, 9:00 A.M. to 4:00 P.M.

South

- The French Market Farmers Flea Market, New Orleans. You'll be amazed at the prices and the variety of "finds" in this large open-air market. Eel-skin purses, luggage and silver jewelry can often be found at below-wholesale prices. If you get hungry, stop at the adjoining farmers' market. The flea market is open every day, 9:00 A.M. to 6:00 P.M.
- Lakewood Fairgrounds Antique Market, Atlanta. Because most of the show is indoors, you'll see more delicate merchandise, such as porcelain, glass, old books, valuable paintings, fixtures and furniture. Lakewood Freeway, east off Interstate 75 and Interstate 85. Second weekend of every month. Friday, 9:00 A.M. to 6:00 P.M.; Saturday, 9:00 A.M. to 6:00 P.M.; Sunday, 10:00 A.M. to 5:00 P.M.
- Metrolina Expo Antiques and Collectibles Market, Charlotte, North Carolina. The largest shows are held in April and November. For sneak previews, early birds are admitted Wednesday for a $50 fee. The market is located at exit 16A off Interstate 77. First full weekend of every month. Thursday, Friday and Saturday, 8:00 A.M. to 5:00 P.M.; Sunday, 9:00 A.M. to 5:00 P.M.
- Scott Antique Market, Atlanta Exposition Center, Atlanta. An art lovers' paradise, with some 1,200 dealers selling lots of folk art and southern primitives. Held the second weekend of very month.
- Scottsboro Market, Scottsboro, Alabama. This market is a direct descendant of the cattle sales that were held at the same spot. There's lots of local color and primitive furniture. Between Highway 72 and Highway 79. The first Monday of every month and each preceding Sunday.

West, Southwest and Hawaii

- First Monday Trade Days, Canton, Texas. Started in 1875, this is the Big Daddy of flea markets, with nearly 3,000 dealers on 100-plus acres. More than 90,000 folks convene for four days of shopping starting on the Friday before the first Monday of every month. So popular, motel rooms are all sold out in a 30-mile radius when the Trade Days are on.
- Maui Swap Meet, Maui, Hawaii. A tourist's delight, with the best buys you'll find on the island: jewelry, seashells, crafts, tropical clothes. Kahului Fairgrounds in Maui, Highway 35 off Puunene Avenue. Open Saturday, 7:00 A.M. to 1:00 P.M.
- Pike Place Market, Seattle. With so many great stores and stalls to choose from, you won't know where to shop first. Opened in 1907, Pike Place Market now sells everything from fish to fashion. (The staff of the "Northern Exposure" TV show shops for vintage clothing in Grandma's Attic.) Corner of First Avenue and Pine Street. Monday through Saturday, 9:00 A.M. to 6:00 P.M.; Sunday, 11:00 A.M. to 5:00 P.M.
- Rose Bowl Flea Market, Pasadena, California. Some 1,500 dealers, with special emphasis on antiques. Even if you don't find what you're looking for, you'll likely see some Hollywood celebs. Second Sunday of every month. Admission: $5.
- Trader's Village, Grand Prairie, Texas. On 106 acres, over 1,600 dealers set up shop to sell wares ranging from birds for $7.98 to bedroom sets for $799. If you can't make up your mind, there's even a psychic to consult with. Trader's Village also has amusement rides and food. Admission is free; parking is $2. Open Saturday and Sunday, 8:00 A.M. to dusk.

Index

Note: **Boldface** references indicate illustrations. <u>Underscored</u> references indicate boxed text.